IDEOLOGY, CULTURE, AND TRANSLATION

Society of Biblical Literature

Semeia Studies

Gerald O. West, General Editor

Editorial Board:
Fiona Black
Gay L. Byron
Jione Havea
Avaren E. Ipsen
Jennifer L. Koosed
Jeremy Punt
Ken Stone
Yak-Hwee Tan
Caroline Vander Stichele

Number 69

IDEOLOGY, CULTURE, AND TRANSLATION

IDEOLOGY, CULTURE, AND TRANSLATION

Edited by
Scott S. Elliott
and
Roland Boer

Society of Biblical Literature
Atlanta

IDEOLOGY, CULTURE, AND TRANSLATION

Copyright © 2012 by the Society of Biblical Literature

All rights reserved. No part of this work may be reproduced or transmitted in any form or by any means, electronic or mechanical, including photocopying and recording, or by means of any information storage or retrieval system, except as may be expressly permitted by the 1976 Copyright Act or in writing from the publisher. Requests for permission should be addressed in writing to the Rights and Permissions Office, Society of Biblical Literature, 825 Houston Mill Road, Atlanta, GA 30329 USA.

Library of Congress Cataloging-in-Publication Data

Ideology, culture, and translation / edited by Scott S. Elliott and Roland Boer.
    p. cm. — (Society of Biblical Literature. Semeia studies ; no. 69)
    ISBN 978-1-58983-705-8 (paper binding : alk. paper) — ISBN 978-1-58983-706-5 (electronic format)
    1. Bible—Translating—History and criticism. I. Elliott, Scott S. II. Boer, Roland, 1961–. III. Series: Semeia studies ; no. 69.
    BS449.I34 2012
    220.5—dc23
                                                                 2012041818

Printed on acid-free, recycled paper conforming to
ANSI/NISO Z39.48-1992 (R1997) and ISO 9706:1994
standards for paper permanence.

Contents

Abbreviations vii

Introduction
Scott S. Elliott and Roland Boer 1

Part 1: Exploring the Intersection of Translation Studies and Critical Theory in Biblical Studies

The Dynamic Equivalence Caper
Roland Boer 13

Translating from This Place: Social Location and Translation
K. Jason Coker 25

Translation and Narrative: Transfiguring Jesus
Scott S. Elliott 39

Postcolonialism, Translation, and Colonial Mimicry
Raj Nadella 49

The Translator's Dilemma: A Response to Boer, Coker, Elliott, and Nadella
George Aichele 59

Part 2: Sites in Translation

Augustine's Bible
Virginia Burrus 69

"His Love Has Been Our Banner on Our Road": Identity Politics and the Revised Version
Alan H. Cadwallader 83

Seeing Is Believing: Children's Bibles as Negotiated Translation
Jaqueline S. du Toit 101

The Earliest Greenlandic Bible: A Study of the Ur-Text from 1725
    Flemming A. J. Nielsen 113

Configuring the Language to Convert the People: Translating the
    Bible in Greenland
    Christina Petterson 139

"A Gift for the Jewish People": Einspruch's *Der Bris Khadoshe*
    as Missionary Translation and Yiddish Literature
    Naomi Seidman 151

Masculinidad en la traducción de la Biblia en Latinoamérica
    Esteban Voth 169

Is There Justice in Translation?
    Matt Waggoner 187

Language, Power, and the "T-Word"
    John Eipper 201

Works Consulted 207
Contributors 227

Abbreviations

CCSL	Corpus Christianorum: Series latina. Turnhout: Brepols, 1953–.
CSEL	Corpus scriptorum ecclestiacorum latinorum
KJV	King James Version
LSJ	H. G. Liddell, R. Scott, and H. S. Jones, *A Greek-English Lexicon*. 9th ed. with revised supplement. Oxford: Clarendon, 1996
NA[27]	*Novum Testamentum Graece*. Edited by Eberhard and Erwin Nestle, Barbara and Curt Aland, et al. 27th ed. Stuttgart: Deutsche Bibelgesellschaft, 1993.
NIV	New International Version
NRSV	New Revised Standard Version
RV	Revised Version
UBS[4]	*The Greek New Testament*. Edited by Barbara Aland et al. 4th ed. Stuttgart: United Bible Societies, 1993.

Thanks

The editors would like to say a special word of thanks to Ms. Sarah Selden for her exceptional editorial assistance throughout the production of this volume.

Introduction

Scott S. Elliott and Roland Boer

Translation: we all do it, but we spasmodically think about how and why we do it. As scholars who work with ancient texts, translation is our bread and butter, our daily task. Without it, we would not be who we are. In the act of translation, we create the texts that create us—a recurring theme in the essays that make up this volume. Yet we reflect on that act far less often than we should. The purpose of this volume is to offer a series of reflections on that *process* of translation. Drawn together from a number of years of the Ideology, Culture, and Translation group of the Society of Biblical Literature (SBL), the chapters collected here offer various perspectives of what it means to translate. The group itself has met since 2005, at the Philadelphia annual meeting. Initially, the chair was Scott Elliott, one of the editors for this volume, but after Elliott's tenure, the task was taken up by Christina Petterson, who has been the incumbent since 2010. Over the years, we have explored a rich range of themes relating to translation, such as ethics, postmodernism, critical theory, narratology, psychoanalysis, gender, masculinity, constructions of the law, Jewish-Christian difference, professional intercultures, children's Bibles, popular consumption, the foreignization and domestication in politics, literature and film, along with specific histories and practices from Peru to Greenland.

In light of these themes, it should be clear that by "translation" we mean not merely the collection of tasks involved in moving from one language to another, with its many overlaps, poor fittings, closing down of meanings, and the generation of new ones. For translation is a "carrying across"—*translatus, transfero*—a transfer that means we leave something of ourselves behind as we make the border crossing, yet find a new dimension of ourselves on the other side. Hence, just as we create the texts that create us, we ourselves are translated in the processes of translating texts.

Translation—interpretation: the two are inseparable, and they take place within the complex webs of ideology and culture.

So that readers may gain an overview of the volume and thereby dip in wherever their appetites may be whetted, we follow convention and offer a synopsis of the book's chapters. The first section of five contributions is drawn from the session held in Boston (2008), entitled "Exploring the Intersection of Translation Studies and Critical Theory in Biblical Studies." It includes works by Roland Boer, K. Jason Coker, Scott S. Elliott, and Raj Nadella, before closing with the response from George Aichele.

Roland Boer's "The Dynamic Equivalence Caper" opens the volume, presenting a concise criticism of what remains the dominant theory of biblical translation—dynamic equivalence. Championed by the long-lived Eugene Nida (who died in August 2011 at the age of 96) and the Summer Institute of Linguistics, dynamic equivalence focuses on the message— and, its champions might say, effect (whether actual or desired)—rather than the medium and has been put forward as a radical break with the tension between free or literal translation. After a brief outline, Boer mounts four criticisms: first, dynamic equivalence is by no means new, for it is a reworked version of the old approach known as paraphrase. Further, dynamic equivalence operates with an instrumental understanding of language, which becomes the tool of meaning. Third, despite its apparent evangelical provenance, dynamic equivalence is theologically suspect, for it follows a gnostic incarnational model, with the message moving from body to body. Finally, the parallels of dynamic equivalence with commodity relations under capitalism suggest that it is the ideal (and therefore problematic) type of translation for our own era.

K. Jason Coker follows with "Translating from This Place: Social Location and Translation," arguing that Bible translation has always been and continues to be a text-centered endeavor. For Coker, the primary issues in Bible translation revolve around what the original author/editor wrote and how best to convey/translate that in a modern context. The primary focus of debate has been theories of translation based on dynamic equivalence and literal translation. However, as recent scholarship has shown in hermeneutics, a simple shift of emphasis from text to translator can radically challenge the foundations of the discipline. And so Coker argues that by decentering the text, by focusing more attention on the social location of the translator, and by emphasizing translation as a place of intersection between text and translator, we may explore new possibilities for Bible translation.

From here, Scott Elliott tackles the significance of narratology[1] for translation studies (and vice versa) in "Translation and Narrative: Transfiguring Jesus." Both approaches, argues Elliott, have experienced similar changes in scope and application as a result of engagements with critical theory (changes that, as it turns out, are reflected in the more recent work of Bal, beginning with the revised edition of her classic *Narratology*, published in 1997). Both have come to be seen as ubiquitous, multifunctional, integral to cultural mediation and human cognition, and fundamentally and inescapably ideological. Translations and narratives are both marked by an inherent paradox: each purports to give voice to an original text or story, to represent something that precedes the translation or narration itself. However, a source text needs a translation in order to come into being as a source text, and any ostensibly preexisting story or historical event is expressed, described, and conveyed (or translated) only by means of the narrative discourse that claims to represent it. Therefore, translations and narratives also have within them the seeds of their own subversion as each possesses an inherent countertendency to prevent access to that which they claim to recount. Elliott explores this internal paradox by focusing on the Gospel accounts, in which we are presented not only with double translations wherein the utterances of Jesus are translated from speech to writing and from Aramaic to Greek (Aichele), but in fact triple translations whereby Jesus himself is translated into a character, a literary figure, as he is discoursed through narrative. Elliott goes on to consider the implications and consequences of this intersection between translation and narratology in the characterization and employment of Jesus.

In "Postcolonialism, Translation, and Colonial Mimicry," Raj Nadella introduces the crucial issue of colonialism (and its attendant structures) in the struggles over the preferred approaches to translation, caught as they still are between preferences for "literal" and "dynamic" equivalencies in source and target languages. Specifically, argues Nadella, there has not been much focus on the different layers of colonial mimicry that have manifested themselves in the translation process both during and after the colonial era. Suggesting that there is a not-yet-fully explored interconnectedness between postcolonial theory and translation studies, he demonstrates how insights from the former can help foreground layers of colonial

---

1. Understood here as the structuralist-inspired theory of narrative, seen, for example, in the early work of Mieke Bal.

mimicry in Bible translations. Nadella's particular example is drawn from his home in Andhra Pradesh, India. He seeks to explicate issues of culture, subcultures, competing identities, and power as they pertain to Bible translations from English into several South Indian languages, especially Telugu, in the late nineteenth and early twentieth centuries. In this context, one may juxtapose two layers (or types) of colonial mimicry in Bible translations perpetuated by two divergent groups: missionary translators and Indian nationals. Nadella argues that the second layer (perpetuated by Indian translators), which is not usually highlighted by postcolonial critics of South Asian origin, is as colonial in its orientation as the first layer, the focus of many postcolonial critiques.

The response to these four chapters is by George Aichele, "The Translator's Dilemma." Aichele draws upon his immense skills in critical theory, especially the work of Derrida and Benjamin (upon whom Derrida relies), as well as Barthes and Quine. Yet Aichele also has his own preferences, determined heavily by Benjamin's effort to recast the very notion of "literal" translation neither in terms of communicating a message nor of (a) meaning, but in terms of manifesting the text itself. Throughout this endeavor runs a deep desire to forestall the effects of an undesirable logocentrism.

Six of the remaining nine contributions are drawn from various sessions of the Ideology, Culture, and Translation group from 2005 to the present, at both the Annual Meeting and the International Meeting of the SBL. Two (Nielsen and Voth) were first presented elsewhere and commissioned for this collection. The section concludes with a response from John Eipper.

Virginia Burrus's essay, "Augustine's Bible," revisits the ancient dispute between Jerome and Augustine regarding biblical translation, and it does so in dialogue with Naomi Seidman's 2006 monograph, *Faithful Renderings: Jewish-Christian Difference and the Politics of Translation*. Seidman recognizes Jerome's troubling appropriation of an earlier Roman imperialist understanding of translation but nonetheless applauds the famous champion of the *Hebraica veritas* for reintroducing dialogue into the theory and practice of translation while also proffering a more full-bodied understanding of the translator's task. In contrast, Augustine's faithfulness to the Septuagint tends to come across as both unconvincing and unappealing, not only in its transcendentalism (Seidman's main emphasis), but also in its text-critical naiveté, its heavy-handed resort to the authority of ecclesial tradition, and its implicit anti-Judaism. However, in her chapter, Burrus revisits Augustine's claims for the Greek text, as these surface not only in his correspondence with Jerome but also in his *Confessions* and *City of God*. In that light, she then positions herself to complicate the history that Seidman relates: even as Jerome's view of the *Hebraica veritas* colludes with that of the rabbis, so Augustine's particular embrace of biblical translatability aligns him with the thought not only of the Alexandrian Philo, but also of the German-Jewish translator and translation theorist Franz Rosenzweig, to whose work Burrus turns briefly at the end of the essay.

In "'His Love Has Been Our Banner on Our Road': Identity Politics and the Revised Version," Alan Cadwallader considers the revision of the Authorized Version of the Bible, which ran from 1870 until its published release in 1881. That revision generated one of the most bitter instances of political struggles involved in the translation of a sacred book. Cadwallader sets out to examine three aspects of the pluriform political commitments that attached to this Bible translation: the relation between an imperial, sovereign nation and the position of an established church; the integrity and authenticity of denominations within a nation; and the competitive tensions of national and international prestige and responsibility. Each of these aspects exposes how commitments to espoused identities were impressed onto the translation, fueled the dynamics of the translators, and manipulated the structures established to achieve the translation. Through the analytical tools of the politico-literary theories of Umberto Eco and the sociopolitical critique of identity politics initiated by Erving Goffman applied to a range of primary, often unpublished sources, these aspects are analyzed for what they reveal about the interests and conflicts that are hidden from the consumers (and antagonists) of the resultant production.

With Jaqueline du Toit's "Seeing Is Believing: Children's Bibles as Translation Negotiated," we shift focus to consider children's Bibles as visually interactive, child-appropriate renditions of the narrative sections of adult translations of the Hebrew and Greek source texts. Legitimacy for these "Bibles" is founded in their claim to authority as "translation" of the source texts despite obvious adaptation of the adult version of the canon. Du Toit considers the implicit inclusion of visual language in these Bibles despite the aniconistic preferences of the Judeo-Christian tradition. She emphasizes how the visual language interacts with title and text in order to render the biblical narrative appropriate to a child audience. This implies significant adjustment to the interpretation of canon tolerated by the religious tradition because of Ruth Bottigheimer's (1996) observation that children's Bibles historically adhere to societal context rather than textual content. Simplification, addition, adaptation, deletion, and rearrangement therefore happen at will and are regulated most often by the preconceived contemporary societal notions of didactics and entertainment value rather than any adherence to source text. Du Toit's chapter therefore considers the significance of visual translation of the Bible for children and the implicit interaction between text and picture in children's Bibles for our understanding of what a society considers worthy of transfer to the next generation. Much may therefore be deduced regarding the influence and interpretation of the Bible on culture and society by considering the norms and values embedded in the interplay between text and picture in the translation of children's Bibles.

And from children's Bibles we shift our attention to … Greenland, with two contributions: one, a survey by Flemming A. J. Nielsen of the earliest Greenlandic Bible translation, and the other, a critical reflection on the practice of such translation by Christina Petterson. In "The Earliest Greenlandic Bible: A Study of the Ur-text from 1725," Nielsen points out that Christianity was brought to Greenland when the Norwegian missionary Hans Egede arrived in 1721. His attempts at writing Greenlandic constitute the earliest continuous texts written in any Eskimo language. By 1725 he was able to compile a manuscript containing biblical and catechetical texts in an exotic language that had not been described before. Amazingly, the manuscript has been preserved today but has never been published. Egede's tentative efforts, though very pidgin-like, gave rise to a long tradition of translating the Bible into Greenlandic. Biblical manuscripts were produced and copied by hand in great numbers during the eighteenth and nineteenth centuries, but apart from Egede's Ur-text, virtually all of them have disappeared. Printed biblical texts began to appear in 1744. Neilsen's chapter provides a presentation of Egede's manuscript and its background and influence, including the invention of a literary language, the cultivation of new domains in the Greenlandic language, and the beginning of a transformation of the beliefs of an aboriginal culture from shamanism to Christianity.

Following Nielsen's survey, Christina Petterson offers a critical assessment of Bible translation projects in Greenland with "Configuring the Language to Convert the People: Translating the Bible in Greenland." Petterson retraces the steps of those first missionaries to western Greenland in 1721, who were met with a harsh, barren landscape. Dealing with the translational questions surrounding concepts like "God" and "sin" would be difficult enough without the added challenges posed by such seemingly simple texts like Matt 7:16 (with its references to grapes and thorns, figs and thistles) and Rev 5:5–6 (with its description of a lion that is also a lamb). But translating the Bible into Greenlandic meant more than finding adequate words to fix the meaning of the biblical text. As in so many other colonial contexts, it was a later step in a process of conversion and control. *Preceding* the actual translation was what Aichele above calls an "intermedial translation" of the Greenlandic language, namely converting it to a medium of writing, in its particular Western linear and alphabetized inflection. Translation of the Bible set the coordinates within which resistance was possible, and established new parameters for truth. *Following* the translation, then, are the social and cultural upheavals of this intrusion of writing, in terms of class formations and constructions of gender resulting from the education and labor politics of the colonial administration. Set within this framework, Petterson addresses the practice of translating the Bible and other religious texts into Greenlandic and its cultural implications. First, she focuses on the politics of language, that is, the hierarchical relationship between Danish and Greenlandic and the cultural implications inherent in this difference. The second issue is that of Greenlandic religious practice. What happens to this cultural aspect when it meets a dominating monotheistic worldview and religious practice, and what are the cultural consequences of this meeting?

From Greenland we move to Yiddish translations of the New Testament in a study by Naomi Seidman, called "'A Gift for the Jewish People': Einspruch's *Der Bris Khadoshe* as Missionary Translation and Yiddish Literature." As Seidman points out, the earliest known Yiddish translation of the New Testament appeared in Kraków in 1540. From then on, Yiddish translations of the New Testament and other publications designed for missionary work among Yiddish-speaking Jews continued to appear throughout the seventeenth and, especially, eighteenth centuries, along with other material designed to help Christians understand Europe's Jews through the medium of their language. But the most sustained efforts to proselytize Jews through New Testament translations occurred in the context of the much broader phenomenon of the nineteenth- and twentieth-century project of disseminating the Bible first to the poor, in inexpensive editions, and then throughout the world, an outgrowth of the late-eighteenth-century evangelical revival. In the two centuries since 1804, when the British and Foreign Bible Society was founded, the Bible in whole or part was translated under the auspices of an international range of Bible societies into more than a thousand languages. This history, as Homi Bhabha has suggested in his reading of the intersections between the missionary and colonialism projects, evinces not only the triumphant and wondrous bestowal of the Holy Book, but also the deferrals and anxieties of its colonial reception "in which it is repeated, translated, misread, displaced."[2] But some Jewish languages, via their Hebrew components, could also provide a sense of recovery, as translators willing to leave behind the familiar and canonical language of Luther's Bible (and the resulting "missionary Yiddish") and mobilize a more correct and "Jewish" Yiddish would eventually discover. Such an embrace of the Hebrew component of Yiddish was not fully realized until the mid-twentieth century, with the 1941 publication of *Der Bris Khadoshe* by Henry (Chayim) Einspruch in Baltimore. Einspruch's translation, unlike earlier versions, left German behind, taking not Luther or his Judeo-German and Yiddish revisers as his model, but rather the norms of literary Yiddish and, more specifically, the great modernist translation of the Hebrew Bible by Yehoash (Solomon Blumgarten), which appeared in 1926. Seidman's contribution traces some of the internal developments in the sociology of Jewish conversion to Christianity that played a part in Einspruch's linguistic choices.

We have decided to publish Esteban Voth's essay, "Masculinidad en la Traducción de la Biblia en Latinoamérica," in Spanish, with an abstract in English. Despite the immediate limitations posed to those who do not read Spanish, the rationale for our decision is tied directly to the theoretical underpinnings of this volume. Publishing Voth's essay in Spanish highlights and crystallizes, in the most salient and concrete way, the complex issues of ideology, cultural identity, and the role of the reader-translator woven throughout this collection. Whereas the other chapters speak variously *about* these issues, Voth's essay, both in its subject matter and by its very language and inclusion in the volume, *embodies* these issues in a unique way. Whether and how individual readers choose to deal with this untranslated work will immediately position each in a certain way in relation to the questions raised by the other authors. In other words, Voth's essay points up the inescapable, ever-present task of translation that must *always* be undertaken. For Voth, the practice of translation is never a neutral enterprise. More specifically, he addresses the issues of Bible trans-

---

2. Bhaba 1994, 102.

lation and masculinity in translations of the Bible used in Latin America by focusing on six Spanish Bible translations. These come from different religious traditions and represent different theories of translation. Yet precisely because males have dominated the practice of Bible translation, variations on an underlying masculine ideology are clearly present in all of the translations studied. In order to illustrate this point, Voth also presents a case study based on the most recent Bible translation published in Latin America (*Traducción en Lenguaje Actual* [2003]). Based on the findings, Voth's study makes a plea for all translations to be revised bearing in mind the presence of what might be called a "masculine hegemonic influence" in Bible translation. It is his contention that translations of the Bible can be improved and thus be made more "gender friendly."

Finally, Matt Waggoner offers a philosophically nuanced contribution—with a distinct Hegelian "other" present—in "Is There Justice in Translation?" For Waggoner, the theory and practice of translation runs thick with layers of social meaning and political myth. It necessitates attention to issues of difference and identity, host, home and the other, identity, plurality, assimilation, cultural consumption, incorporability, origin and genesis, and various kinds of cultural and political fantasies that mark the desire to speak to the other, to be spoken by the other, or to make the other speak. Translation tinkers with what the Hegelians call the politics of recognition—that is, the risky, uneven process in which self-consciousness is, not without difficulty, confirmed by seeing oneself in another, being seen by another, or being seen through the eyes of another. And it is for that reason that translation is subject to many of the same ethical dilemmas as the Hegelian narrative: To what extent is the other merely the occasion and the material for the fashioning of the self? To what extent is the other consumed in the process of self-fashioning? To what extent does translation harbor, in a life-and-death way, fear of otherness? Or, to what extent does or might translation acknowledge that otherness is constitutive of the self, something without which there can be no self? In the same way that the productive ambiguities of Hegel's narration of selfhood in relation to otherness have contributed so richly to the self-reflection of modern identity (the identity of selves, cultures, races, genders, nations, etc., but also to the identity of the modern), so too is the project of translation implicated, consciously or not, in a whole set of inquiries into modern identity and the constructions thereof. Against the backdrop of issues of contemporary global multiculture, this essay engages the question, What are the ethical stakes of translation work?

In light of the enticing variety of these contributions—from Burrus, Cadwallader, du Toit, Nielsen, Petterson, Seidman, Voth, and Waggoner—one may imagine the challenge presented to the respondent, John Eipper. In addition, Eipper is not a trained Bible scholar; but he has excellent experience in translation, with specialization in nineteenth-century Latin America (especially Mexico), colonial Latin American studies, literary translation, travel literature, and twentieth-century Argentina. All of this is to Eipper's distinct advantage as he weaves his response. On this occasion, we will not say more, hoping that enough has been provided to whet the appetite of the reader.

A rich feast, is it not? Enjoy.

Part 1
Exploring the Intersection of Translation Studies and Critical Theory in Biblical Studies

The Dynamic Equivalence Caper

Roland Boer

About a decade ago I was presenting a paper criticizing the dominance of "dynamic equivalence" among Bible translators. My particular target was Eugene Nida, who I assumed would be on death's doorstep, if not already past it (he was born in 1914). However, at the end of my paper, I got the fright of my life: Nida himself stood up to ask me a question. A decade later I would like to return to that unfinished critique, especially since the ghost of Nida still haunts me.[1]

Dynamic (or functional) equivalence, as is well known, focuses on the message. Everything may be sacrificed—words, syntax, grammar—as long as the essential content of the original text is rendered in an acceptable way in the target language. You may pour the water from a bucket to a cup, but the water remains the same. To my knowledge, dynamic equivalence is the dominant method used by both the various Bible Societies and Wycliffe Bible Translators, especially with translations into indigenous languages. Yet there are some problems with this theory and practice. The main problems are as follows:

(1) There is a fundamental paradox at the heart of dynamic equivalence: it uses what is regarded in certain circles as an "unfaithful" translation technique in order to be "faithful" to the text. This paradox may be broken down into two steps: (a) Dynamic equivalence is not particularly new, for it picks up on the old distinction between metaphrase and paraphrase and opts for the latter; (b) however, it seems new within Nida's

---

1. I have also been prompted to rethink some of these issues since my *Last Stop before Antarctica*, in which that initial paper found its place as a chapter. It has recently appeared in a revised edition (Boer 2008).

context, since dynamic equivalence is a conservative evangelical appropriation of paraphrase that challenges the assumption that a "literal" translation (metaphrase) is the more "faithful" one.
(2) Dynamic equivalence has an instrumental view of form. The form of a language is not merely a container for a message.
(3) Dynamic equivalence follows a gnostic incarnational model: while the "Word" remains the same, it may move from body to body.
(4) The "message" of the Bible becomes a pure expression of the commodity form and as such is a symptom of globalized capitalism.

I will deal with each point in turn, but first a brief outline of the theory itself and the crucial figure of Eugene Nida.[2]

Background

Nida's influence is due to an extraordinarily active long life and a tireless program of publication, promotion, and advocacy (between the time of writing and publication, he died at the age of 96; if he were an athlete, one might be forgiven for suspecting a long program of performance-enhancing drugs). I would like to highlight two factors within Nida's extensive bibliography, namely, his strictly technical works on linguistic theory and a very evangelical stream of publications focused on the needs of the mission field and the need to convert people to Christ. In the first category we find books on morphology (1949), descriptive syntax (1951), English syntax (1966), componential analysis (1975a), semantic structures (1975b), and even a New Testament lexicon (Louw and Nida 1989);[3] while

---

2. The following section is a summary of Boer 2008, 136–43.
3. Nida is the best known of a handful of characters from the Summer Institute of Linguistics (SIL)/Wycliffe Bible Translators who have set about giving some linguistic depth to the task of translation. Two others are William Cameron Townsend, who first established SIL, and Kenneth Pike, who developed tagmemics (1964, 1982). Claiming to provide nothing less than a theory of human language, tagmemics seeks to provide a theoretical understanding of the structure of language from its smallest to its largest components. So tagmemics follows the increasing complexity of language from morpheme to stem to word to phrase to clause to sentence to paragraph to discourse itself. Assuming that human beings are pattern-bearing beings, tagmemics searches in

in the second we can dig up anthropology for Christian missions (1954), learning foreign languages (1957), a translator's commentary (1947b), a collection of wholesome anecdotes from the mission field (1952), or indeed the memoirs of an almost fossilized Nida (2003). As a motivation for his work in linguistics and Bible translation, it is well nigh impossible to miss the evangelical drive to convert the heathen: "The Bible is the message of life because it reveals the Living Christ who gave His life that we might live. This is the book which must be translated, published, distributed, and read in all the languages of earth" (Nida 1952, 177).

The passionate preacher and highly accomplished linguist come together in the single great idea of Nida's life work: dynamic equivalence as the key to the "science of translating." Already the focus of a relatively youthful thirty-three-year-old Nida (1947a), the idea gains richness and nuance over the next forty years (Nida 1964; Nida and Taber 1969; Nida and Louw 1992). While most of us struggle to have one genuinely new idea in our lifetimes (on rare occasions someone like Henri Lefebvre might have such an idea every decade), Nida has been both energetic in developing the idea and in promoting it in the key Bible translation bodies, so much so that by and large it has become translation orthodoxy.

But what exactly is dynamic equivalence? Here is Nida: "Translation consists in reproducing in the receptor language the closest natural equivalent of the source-language message, first in terms of meaning and secondly in terms of style" (Nida and Taber 1969, 12). Despite the formidable armory of linguistic detail, the basic idea is disarmingly simple. What the translator needs to do is to seek equivalence between the experience of current receptors and those of original receptors. Once we can discern what the first readers and hearers thought and felt, then we can seek to recreate that impact on the target audience of the translation.[4] The great enemy is formal equivalence or formal correspondence, where one

---

each language for a system of labeled patterns that parallel the system of intuitively felt patterns used by speakers and hearers.

4. In the handbooks for Bible translators, Nida does develop his theory in response to criticism and new developments. So he moves from "closest equivalence" as a mean between literal translation and the translation of ideas (Nida 1947a, 12, 130–48), through a search for the golden mean between literal and free translation (Nida 1964: 22–26), to a focus on content at the expense of form, for meaning is found, he argues, in content (Nida and Taber 1969). The sophistication of Nida's position is generated by a mass of linguistic detail.

pays undue attention to replicating the form of the original and adapting the target language to it. Both receptors and message suffer (Nida 1964, 165–77; Nida and Taber 1969, 22–24).

In the day-to-day task of translating the Bible, dynamic equivalence is also termed "meaning-based translation." Not a bad descriptor, for the purpose of translation is not a wooden literalness but the conveyance of the truth of the text, which in practice allows a significant degree of variation from the literal text in order to gain the meaning. A favored metaphor is that of a vessel and its content: the language is then the vessel in which the gospel message is contained—the message remains the same, its truth timeless, while the vessel or container may be changed: "We can think of a story or a message as being like one cup of water. Different languages are like different containers. I could pour the cup of water into a glass, into a billy can, or into a bottle, but the water would not change; it would still be the same no matter what I poured it into" (Kilham 1991, 2).

Paraphrase with a Twist

We should never discount the effect of sustained promotion of one's ideas within a certain context (Bible translation organizations). When I surveyed (in the late 1990s) translators of the Bible into Aboriginal languages in Australia, the overwhelming sense was that dynamic equivalence was brand new. More than one translator told me that it was still a struggle to get people to accept dynamic equivalence.

The problem is that dynamic equivalence is not a particularly new idea. Nida has merely given new names—dynamic versus formal equivalence—to an old Greek distinction between metaphrase and paraphrase. While the former has come to designate word-for-word translation, the latter is one that renders the translation in a meaningful form, even if it is at some distance from the original in terms of syntax and grammar. Schleiermacher picked up this distinction and gave it a twist in his 1813 paper "On the Different Methods of Translation." He described these two options as a process of either moving the writer toward the reader or of moving the reader toward the author (his preferred option). In other words, either the reader or the author is primary. If the reader, then one adapts the text to make sure the reader can understand it (paraphrase); if the author, then the reader must adapt to the shape of the author's text (metaphrase). A third way of setting up this opposition is in terms of transparency versus fidelity, where a transparent (or free) translation should be perceived by the reader as though it was written in her or his own language, while a faithful (or literal) translation seeks to render the source text as accurately as possible without adding to it or subtracting from it.

While most translations mediate between these two poles, we can map out the history of translation in light of tendencies to go one way or another. For example, the popular mode of translating into English up until the early nineteenth century was to favor paraphrase. The key was to render the text in a style that would suit the readers. So the translator freely left out passages, added words, and generally shaped the text as he or she saw fit (one might say "creatively"). Two outstanding examples are John Dryden's translation of Virgil in the late seventeenth century and Alexander Pope's long effort with Homer in the early eighteenth century. There was an undercurrent that wished for more metaphrastic translations, especially since the recovery of Classical Greek and Latin during the Renaissance, but it really did not come into its own until Benjamin Jowett's translation of Plato in 1871. This metaphrastic or literal translation became a benchmark for later translation work.

It is not difficult to see where Nida fits in this potted history: he seeks to recover an older practice of paraphrase from the nineteenth century and earlier. He favors paraphrase over metaphrase, transparency over fidelity, moving toward the reader rather than the author. So he wants to place a "no go" sign over formal equivalence, which tries to render the original text "word for word" (*verbum pro verbo*) at the expense of the syntax and grammar of the target language. Dynamic equivalence (or "*functional equivalence*" as it is sometimes called) sets out to convey the basic content of the source text, and if it is necessary to sacrifice the structure of the original, then so be it.

So why is Nida seen as such an innovator? The key actually comes from a comment my father made many years ago. At a gathering, someone produced the widely popular Good News Bible and he warned, "You shouldn't use that Bible translation." When he was asked why, he responded, "It's a paraphrase and not faithful to the original." Now, my father follows a conservative Reformed position (over against a radical Reformed position; see further Boer 2009). For him, a translation must be literal in order to be *faithful*. No paraphrase or transparency for him; what we seek in Bible translation is metaphrase and *fidelity*. I have emphasized "faithful" and "fidelity" for a reason, since the terminology itself gives us a clue. In an opposition like transparency and fidelity, the terms themselves are loaded. So a translation that sticks as closely as possible to the original language is a faithful rendering of that original. Soon enough we have an equation: metaphrase/author-directed/fidelity/literal translation is faithful and true; paraphrase/reader-directed/transparent/free is unfaithful and untrue.

My father's comment highlights the context in which Nida has moved since he answered that altar call as a young man to accept Christ as his savior. Not merely an assumed religious faith, it is one that has enough drive to it to get people to commit to a lifetime of translation activity. Orthodox, conservative, evangelical, call it what we will, but in that context, translation must be *faithful* to the original Hebrew and Greek. And that means metaphrastic, author-directed, and literal. In this context, Nida's approach becomes an innovation and a challenge. The twist was to shift the values of the terms themselves: a *faithful* translation is in fact paraphrase, reader-directed, and free. What everyone in Nida's own context thought was faithful is not so. And the argument Nida brought to bear was a classic evangelical one: we need to get the message of the gospel (assuming we know what that message is) across in our translation so that people will give their lives to Christ. It is above all a question of content, of the message, and not of its medium or form. So one must adapt the form in order to ensure that the message goes through.

Instrumental Form

So far I have argued that what Nida presents is not particularly new, or rather that it is new given the assumptions of his context. More substantially, there are further problems with Nida's method: it has a very instrumental view of form; it relies on an incarnational model that is decidedly gnostic.

Nida has not been without his groupies or detractors. For example, among the former we find Philip Stine's *Let the Words Be Written* (2004), which reads like a preemptive eulogy, or Ma's more expository study (2003). Others have been less impressed. Already in the 1970s, in the second volume of his massive *Pour la poétique* (1970–1978), the literary and cultural critic Henri Meschonnic criticized Nida's approach as a mechanized distortion of the translator's art and task. From a feminist and postcolonial perspective, Sherry Simon (1996, 132) has dismissed Nida's "neo-colonialist evangelical" Bible translations and projects. Above all, Willis Barnstone, a literary critic and translator of encyclopedic scope, takes a (Walter) Benjaminian line and argues for the importance of form. For Barnstone (1993, 62–63), anyone who argues that meaning is located in the content, without thought for "the sound, style, tone and form," is completely off the mark.

Barnstone is the touchstone for my discussion in this section, since he has indeed hit on something in Nida's theory and practice—an instrumentalist understanding of form. Crudely put, Nida sees the form of a language (its syntax, grammar, style, lilt, unique sounds, and complexities) in two ways: as a means or instrument to achieve communication or as a hurdle to overcome. What counts is the communication of the message. If the form of a language can be an instrument in that process, then well and good; but if not, then it becomes a problem that must be tackled and solved. In translation, we must work on the shape of the target language so that it faithfully communicates the message of the original Greek or Hebrew. It may require some filing here, some welding or hammering there, but ultimately we should be able to make each instrument work for us.

The difference between Nida and someone like Barnstone does not merely turn on the issue of paraphrase and metaphrase. There is also the image of the translators: are they artists, sensitive to intuition and the muses, or are they skilled craftsmen who have a job to do? Does Nida stand before a canvas with a paintbrush in hand waiting for inspiration, or is he a woodworker who must construct a table or chair by a certain date for a fee? I hardly need to answer these questions, for Nida is a craftsman first, artist a distant second.

However, this is part of Nida's appeal, for his approach seems like sheer common sense. Of course, language is used to communicate. Of course, we want to communicate a message. Of course, we want to be understood when we learn a new language. Of course, we want the Bible, or any translation we might set to work on, to make sense. This is why Nida offends literary critics and other translation specialists: this commonsense craftsman has little time for the useless pursuits of literary critics with their attention to style, sound, structure, and the shape of language. That is for those with time on their hands, not for those with the urgent task of translating God's Word.

For these reasons, asserting that the form is important and that any literary critic worth his or her salt knows it to be so has little critical impact on Nida's approach. An easy counter to this argument is that Nida and others who follow his method pay extraordinary attention to form, albeit for the sake of making sure the message comes through loud and clear. Instead, we might want to look at a favored move of the Russian formalists. In their effort at defamiliarizing (*Ostranenie*) texts, the formalists would shift the old values attaching to the relation between form and content. So the form is not an instrument for the content to appear, but vice versa: the content is the means for the form. We do not search for the best form—say, speech or essay or YouTube video—in order to say what we want to say. No, we search for the best content so that a chosen form may be used. In order to bring out the full effect of defamiliarization, let me use the example of the gospel (an example close to Nida's heart). The literary genre of the Gospel was not created and used by the early church in order to convey the message about Jesus Christ; instead, the message about Jesus Christ was the means used to create the genre of the Gospel. Or if we take the sermon: it is not the instrument used to convey a timely message to a congregation; rather, the uplifting message is the instrument used to highlight the form of the sermon. These examples might seem overdone and run against the commonsense approach of someone like Nida, but their value is to make us stop for a moment and rethink what is going on.

Gnostic Incarnations

In that spirit, let me switch tactics. Instead of assailing fortress Nida from the outside, I would like to put on my disguise and slip inside in order to spy on what is going on. That disguise is none other than theology. In other words, I want to make a theological point: Nida's model of dynamic equivalence makes use of a gnostic Christology.

I am not the first to point out that translation, especially Bible translation, relies all too often on a christological model: like the preexisting and eternal Christ, the message(s) of the Bible must become a written text in a particular language at a specific time and place in order to be known by us. But now the model expands beyond its original. Christ was incarnated as one man at one time and one place. The Bible was incarnated in more than one language, for the original "flesh" of this "word" happens to be in Hebrew, Greek, and a smattering of Aramaic. Once we have this plurality, more are possible—hence translation, the perpetual reincarnation of the message(s) of the Bible.

In Bible translation, this problem is usually put in terms of the opposition of form and content, where one is the flesh of the text and the other the word of the message. Nida sides clearly with content over against form. Indeed, the form must be changed if that is necessary to convey the content correctly to the receptor. Or as he puts it: "Anything that can be said in one language can be said in another" (Nida and Taber 1969, 4). This focus on content, which is where meaning (the "Word") is located, means that form has virtually no role to play in the production of this message.

The problem for Nida is that had he been alive in the early centuries of the Christian era when one council after another hammered out the core doctrines of the church (usually under imperial pressure for a unified ideology), he would have voted with the gnostics. Why? His theory of translation assumes a definable, clear, and pure message that may take on many different languages without being tainted by them. So also the gnostic Christ inhabited the body of Jesus only to depart this outer casing at will when the going got tough (the usual point is the crucifixion, where the body dies but the spirit of Christ escapes).

I have nothing against the gnostics per se, except that they were not the most astute politicians and thereby lost the crucial battles. But it is a problem for a theological conservative like Nida. If we are going to use incarnational models for translation, then is it not better to use one that assumes the more orthodox unity of flesh and spirit, of body and soul? Or in terms of translation, the form of the text washes over into content so that the content itself is inconceivable without the form. But then so is the form unthinkable without the content, which is really what the Russian formalists were trying to tell us. Certain types of content require a particular form so that the content in question may appear in the first place (for example, it is difficult to write "Dear such and such" at the beginning and "Yours sincerely" at the end without using the form of a letter).

I must admit that I have surprised myself, arguing for the value of a rather orthodox Christology since it provides a better model for translation. At the least, I like it because it gives me much more leverage against Nida's gnostic model of dynamic or functional equivalence. As to what we might do with orthodox Christology, I would suggest that it may well be a specific language that may itself be translated into a number of others, but that is another argument (see Boer forthcoming).

Conclusion: Empire and the Commodity Form

I have argued that we can understand the apparent innovation of Nida's dynamic equivalence in terms of his context. In a conservative theological environment where "faithful" translation means sticking to the original text as closely as possible (metaphrase), the argument that metaphrase is bad translation and paraphrase is faithful will seem innovative. However, it is really just a variation on the long-held distinction in translation theory between paraphrase and metaphrase. More substantially, Nida faces difficulties with his instrumental view of form and with his gnostic christological model of translation, where the content of the message (soul) can move freely from one language (flesh) to another without being affected by that language.

But a more fundamental question in all of this is that we have an opposition in the first place, between paraphrase and metaphrase, which in turns hinges on a distinction between form and content. When pressed, anyone who holds to these oppositions will say that they are only ideal types, or perhaps two ends of a spectrum, and that translation is usually a mediation of the two. But what if we try to think outside the opposition in the first place?

We might do so in two ways, one historical and the other economic. I cannot help notice a comparison between the missionary work of the nineteenth century and the missionary translations of the twentieth. In the same way that the great wave of missionary endeavors in the nineteenth century rode on the back (often uncomfortably and with much ambivalence) of British imperialism, so also the vast push for translation in the later twentieth century rode the lumpy back of U.S. imperialism. Nida's dynamic equivalence is an excellent complement to that imperialism, coupled as it was with untiring fieldwork enabled by cheap and rapid transport.

However, the economic argument is much more substantial than the historical one, even though they overlap.[5] The period in which Nida was working, which coincided with an exponential leap in the work of the Bible societies, was also the period when the commodity form finally saturated the globe. Now, the possibility of a commodity is predicated on equivalence between vastly different items. For example, a piece of linen, a coat, a pair of shoes, and a Bible all become equivalent to one another by becoming commodities, a relationship that is mediated by the commodity of money. In this fashion, everything becomes infinitely exchangeable. So also with the resolute focus on the singular message of the Bible (again, assuming one knows what it is): it is infinitely exchangeable, moving from one language to another with more or less ease. That

---

5. A useful exercise would be to map the changing patterns of translation theory and practice in light of economic patterns.

message is not to be hindered by any local uses (the distinctive sounds and shapes of a language), for it is above all an exchangeable commodity. That such a theory should arise during the emergence of a fully globalized economy is no accident.

Translating from This Place: Social Location and Translation

K. Jason Coker

From 2006 to 2007 I was the project coordinator for the building of a child development center, medical clinic, kitchen, and water well for AIDS/HIV orphans in the Western Province of Kenya. This area of Kenya is one of the most devastated parts of the country in relation to AIDS/HIV. The poverty is overwhelming and the solutions seem out of sight. So, to my amazement, when I asked many of the locals what they needed most and how we could be helpful for them, many told me that they needed Bibles. Of all the things that our group was prepared to do, this did not seem to be the greatest issue. However, their desire for the Bible was evident, so we decided to get Bibles for the people in that area that wanted them. The question then arose about translation. In Kenya the official language is English and the national language is Swahili, but the local language for the Busia area is Luhya. None of us could find a Luhya translation of the Bible, so we attempted to get Swahili Bibles. After considering the costs of Swahili Bibles, it was simply cheaper to buy English translations. Then we were faced with the issue of what English translation to purchase. Do you get something easy to read, considering the language barrier? Do you get something more literal, considering religious biases? Do you get the cheapest you can find, considering the economic issues? The economic, religious, and linguistic became inseparable. It was this experience that prompted this study.

Bible translation has always been and continues to be a text-centered enterprise. This preference for text rather than target culture evidences an imbalance of power between translator culture and local culture. The explicit missionary activity within translating the Bible into non-Western languages has gone hand-in-hand with Western imperialism for centuries and, in many cases, continues to do so. The need to have a legitimating text for authority at least goes back to Erasmus's Greek New Testament. Once this text for authority was fixed in modernity (NA^{27} and/or UBS^4), it could be used by the same forces that created the text to legitimize their own position of authority. One could say this about the KJV and the NRSV. This is even more the case with missionary Bible translations into non-Western languages. The Bible, once produced, is used to authorize and legitimize the missionary and the missionary's culture. In this way, Bible translations have been used to authorize Western societies' domination/conversion of non-Western cultures. There are some attempts on the part of modern Bible societies to move beyond this kind of Christian imperialism, but this seems to be more of an exception than a rule.

In 1995 Fernando Segovia and Mary Ann Tolbert's first edited volume *Reading from This Place* was published, and it made a profound impact on the field of biblical studies. Segovia's introduction to the volume mapped the course that the overall project would traverse. Segovia outlined the discipline of biblical studies and described four major umbrellas that subdivided the field: historical criticism, literary criticism, cultural criticism (1995, 6–7), and cultural studies (1995, 28–31). If one not familiar with biblical studies read Segovia's chapters, one would think that all of these subdivisions were equally accepted and had equal status in biblical studies. Indeed, one would imagine that historical criticism was passé and antiquated.[1] In any case, Segovia's "description" of cultural studies is important. Indeed, I would argue that Segovia is not simply describing this subdivision; Segovia is writing-into-being or creating this new umbrella within biblical studies. For Segovia, this last and best manifestation of biblical studies moves from a text-centered hermeneutic to one that concentrates on a flesh-and-blood reader. Instead of an objective, real reader who has the capacity to let the text (the biblical text) speak for itself, Segovia recommends a subjective, personal reader who does not ignore his or her cultural location but emphasizes his or her cultural place as the locus for authentic and legitimate hermeneutics; thus the title *Reading from This Place*. For Segovia,

---

1. Segovia goes so far as to say that "while historical criticism may be said to be on the decline, both literary and cultural criticism are clearly on the ascendancy" (1995, 7).

The project represents an attempt, in the light of the emerging sociocultural pluralism and globalization in the theological world in general and biblical interpretation in particular, to address in a systematic and sustained fashion such fundamental issues as the role of the reader in biblical criticism, the complex relationship between the task of interpretation and the social location of the interpreter, and the consequences of such discussions for the future of biblical pedagogy and theological education. (1995, 32)

I will explore what Segovia's work implies for the field of Bible translation. Primary issues in Bible translation have revolved around what the original author/editor wrote and how best to convey/translate that in a modern (con)text. Theories of dynamic equivalence and literal translation have been the major concern. A shift in emphasis from the text to the translator, as Segovia proposes in biblical studies, can radically challenge the historical preoccupations of Bible translations. Decentering the text, focusing attention on the social location of the translator, and emphasizing translation as a place of cultural interaction and production between text and translator can offer new possibilities for Bible translation. In short, this would mean "translating from this place."

Segovia's proposal rests heavily upon the postmodern critique of objectivity. Postmodern epistemology is best described by Jean-François Lyotard's brief and popular statement, "Simplifying to the extreme, I define postmodernism as incredulity toward metanarratives" (1984, xxiv). This incredulity began to take place when the promises of modernity simply did not happen. Instead of the world getting better through technology and progress, the post–World War II experience simply seemed unbearable. Gina Hens-Piazza agrees, arguing that "the incredulity [of postmodernism] stems from the realization that these 'big stories' have deceived us. They have made promises they couldn't keep. They set themselves up as templates that in the end don't orient history or define human destiny. When set against the events of this century, their inherent fallacies are disclosed" (2000, 162). Confronted with the reality of the Enlightenment's failed project, Thomas Docherty concludes, "Not only has knowledge become uncertain, but more importantly the whole question of how to legitimize certain forms of knowledge and certain contents of knowledge is firmly on the agenda: no single satisfactory mode of epistemological legitimation is available" (1993, 165). This epistemological crisis of legitimation substantiates the postmodern move into the political sphere.

Postmodernism exposes the powers that lie underneath modernity's philosophical foundations. Philosophical foundationalism's claim to truth was simply a rhetorical device used to gain power. Again, Hens-Piazza is helpful: "Antifoundationalism strives to unseat the power-wielding of foundations in systems, cultural paradigms, [and] governing bodies" (2000, 165). This is the political movement of postmodernism. By exposing the primary motivation of modernity as power, postmodernism seeks to unravel this power discourse for a more ethical solution. Taking a specific kind of knowledge and legitimation typified in modernity and projecting it into a totalizing scheme politically destroys any form of otherness. Homogeneity as some form of normalcy, which is constructed by those in power, is the ultimate goal. Postmodernism shows how this hegemonic discourse is self-serving and powerfully oppressive.

Since I am using Segovia's postmodern concept of cultural studies as a model for Bible translation, I need to detail his argument with more precision as it relates to translation. The turn toward Segovian cultural studies is a turn toward a "critical study of texts *and readers*" (2000a, 30; emphasis added), which is a departure from the text-centered disciplines of historical criticism, literary criticism, and cultural criticism. This development calls into question the construct of a neutral and disinterested reader. The neutral and disinterested reader is firmly situated in the scientific, thereby universal, rhetoric of the academy. Objectivity and impartiality were to be achieved through scientific methods; particularity and personal contextuality were obstacles to be overcome. This goal was achieved through rigorous academic training; thus the production of a professional reader or (biblical) scholar.

The process, however, was incredibly idealistic. To think that a human being could become objective, unbiased, impartial, disinterested, and neutral in a field that was ingrained in the Christian religion was naïve at best and "colonialist and imperialistic" at worst (2000a, 30). Objectivity, nonetheless, is still rigorously defended by champions of historical criticism and other "scientific" methodologies. The problem with a passion-impaired reader is not the fact of objectivity, but what that ideological, objective reader masks. In other words, a scholarly reading, interpretation, or exercise in hermeneutics passed as a historical and scientific retrieval or reconstruction of a past reality. Since these interpretations were objective, they could be applied universally. The result is an objective and universal "fact" about a biblical text.

In reality, however, these interpretations were always personal and social constructions rather than reconstructions. They were laced with bias and subjectivity that supported a certain agenda but were masked with the façade of biblical scholarship. Who were these objective, neutral, impartial, and universal scholars? They were, for the most part, highly educated white Western (clergy)men (2000a, 37). Segovia argues that "objectivity and impartiality were cover terms for Europeanization, given the thoroughly Eurocentric contours and orientation of the discipline" (2000a, 31). Given this masked bias, biblical studies as a body of knowledge was completely packaged within an ideological location. To become a biblical scholar was to become a highly educated white Western man; as Segovia suggests: "To become the ideal critic, therefore, was to enter into a specific and contextualized discussion, a Eurocentric discussion" (2000a, 30–31).

Segovia's exposé of Eurocentric readings that dominate the field of biblical studies paves the way for "other ways of reading." In other words, if the field of biblical studies is rooted in a certain Eurocentric social location, then that opens the door for analyzing other social locations as loci of meaning. The biblical text would read differently under a different sociocultural lens such as an Afrocentric women's lens. This is, in fact, the intent of Musa Dube's edited volume *Other Ways of Reading: African Women and the Bible* (2001b) As identity is foregrounded in this/these hermeneutical approach(es), the biblical text is problematized and transgressed. The social locations of the readers are placed on the same level as the biblical texts and new opportunities and ideas emerge. According to Dube,

> The volume, by offering postcolonial feminist strategies of resistance, seeks to create a space in which women are empowered against the shackles of patriarchy and imperial oppression at various levels and in various forms. It suggests new methods of reading and new interpretations, and it proposes other canonical texts that deserve to be read and heard outside the imposition of imperial culture. By so doing, the volume assumes a postcolonial stance, for it challenges the authority of the Bible and Western methods of reading; it points to a thousand other canons and methods of reading. (2001a, 17)

Dube's efforts embody Segovia's second point about hermeneutics:

> Real readers lie behind all models of interpretation and all reading strategies, all recreations of meaning from texts and all reconstructions of history; further, all such models, strategies, recreations, and reconstruc-

tions are seen as constructs on the part of flesh-and-blood readers; and all such readers are themselves regarded as variously positioned and engaged in their own respective social location. Thus, different real readers use different strategies and models in different ways, at different times, and with different results in the light of their different and highly complex social locations. (Segovia 2000a, 41)

Segovia is not arguing for another "real" objectivity in biblical studies; he is arguing for honesty regarding one's own identity and how that effects meaning production. The identity of the biblical scholar, once described, is then the critical apparatus through which the Bible is interpreted. According to Stephen Moore, this concentration on the reader of texts, as well as texts, offers the most significant challenge to hegemonic discourse in biblical studies:

Within the realm of contextual hermeneutics, biblical scholarship as a disciplinary practice threatens to crumble and come apart, it seems to me, even more than it does within the realm of deconstructive biblical criticism. And it comes apart precisely in order to be reformed as something other than what biblical scholarship originally was, which is to say—among other things, and somewhat reductively no doubt—a white European ideology. (2007, 25)

Examples of Segovian biblical cultural studies have flourished in the past decade and a half since the publication of *Reading from This Place. Interpreting beyond Borders* (Segovia 2000b), *Reading the Bible in the Global Village: Helsinki* (Räisänen et al. 2000), *Other Ways of Reading* (Dube 2001b), *The Bible and the Third World* (Sugirtharajah 2001), *The Bible in a World Context* (Dietrich and Luz 2002), *Reading the Bible in the Global Village: Cape Town* (Ukpong et al. 2002), *Global Bible Commentary* (Patte 2004), and *Reading Other-Wise* (West 2007) are just a sampling of what has been published in the wake of Segovia's work.

Bible translation, although a very different field than biblical studies, has been deeply affected by biblical studies with regard to an objective and impartial reader. This issue of the objective and impartial translator, however, has not preoccupied Bible translators and Bible societies as much as it has scholars who remain in the purely academic guild. Semiotic issues tend to be more prevalent among Bible translators, although the theory of dynamic equivalence certainly dominates the field. There continue to be semiotic questions, but they all come from the perspective of dynamic equivalence. Based on this theory, the material text of the Bible does not have primary meaning. The text only contains or holds the meaning. The meaning of the text is there to be taken by any who can read. In this case, the meaning of the text is there to be taken by Bible translators. Translators, then, take that meaning, an extratextual meaning, and place it into another container language or receptor language. In the process of translation based on dynamic equivalence, there is a conviction that no violence is done to the meaning of the Bible. To use George Aichele's analogy, the meaning of the Bible is like whiskey in a bottle (2001, 61). You can pour the whiskey from the bottle (the Greek text) into a glass (the receptor language) only if you are a qualified bartender (translator).

On the other hand, should a target text reflect the source text's materiality in such a way as to fulfill it? Aichele argues for a more literalist approach: "Literal translation reproduces the uncertainties of the source text's meaning, not the interpretations that would resolve them. ... The value of literal translation lies, not in infallible transmission of a message, but rather in supplementation of the source text" (2001, 72). Although Aichele's argument rightly cautions translators who uncritically engage dynamic equivalence theory, both theories continue to concentrate on the text or the meaning of the text. In the lived experience in Western Kenya, however, it is worth remembering that translation deals not only with texts, but with people, as Anthony Pym notes:

> In a word, when translating, we should communicate with people (intimate second persons), not just with texts (third persons). That lesson is so valuable that I teach it at the beginning of every translation course. And I teach it all the more when the course is on technical translation, localization, translation technology and the like. Wherever our work processes and perceptions seem most caught up in networks of things, one must make at least the pedagogical effort to insist on the people. That is hard, of course, and all the harder when the things include pay packets, deadlines, and instructions that show no awareness of language, culture, or indeed translation as human communication. (2007, 2)

Neither of the two prevalent theories of translation takes into consideration the identity of the translator. For centuries, the most important part of the process has been the text or the meaning of the text. Once the emphasis is rearranged and taken off the meaning of the Bible and placed on the translator, the whole process is changed. Aichele's critique of dynamic equivalence is important at this point:

> The text is believed to be more authoritative when presented in the language in which it was first written than it is in any translated version. This is especially true of scholars, who are usually expected to master the original languages of the texts that they study. Scholars suspect that translation of the text means transformation of the message, that something essential may have been lost or changed in the translation process. Scholars know that translators are thieves. (2001, 64)

But what are they stealing? I am not sure if they are thieves, but translators certainly keep many secrets. One secret is that the position of translator is a position of incredible power. The meaning of the Bible exists with the translator in a phenomenological way that is beyond text or extratextual. When the translator begins to write, the Word, especially in missionary contexts, becomes text. The Bible, then in the receptor language, begins to legitimize the position of the translator.

The act of translation always implies cultural interaction. As Pym rightly observes, "The simple fact of translation presupposes contact between at least two cultures, and does so in relation to language, the social activity that perhaps most effectively and insidiously weaves complex relations of cultural identity" (2000, 1). In the end, translations are achieved by translators, who deserve to be the object of scrutiny. Translators must work from an intercultural perspective due to the overwhelming imbalance of power. Pym places translators directly within this intercultural space: "Since no abstract argument can happily situate them [translators] in one culture or the other, we must admit the working hypothesis that translators operate from the intersections or overlaps of cultures, in what we shall call 'intercultural' space" (2000, 2). From the standpoint of Bible translation, the translator may be in a much different position culturally than a translator not dealing specifically with the Bible. In other words, Bible translators from Western centers who have been seminary trained do not necessarily share any cultural or linguistic identity with target cultures/languages.

This context raises a question: Who are these translators? In many cases, if not most cases, the translators are white Western men. White Western men are the conduits for the Bible in many non-Western places. Within the field of Bible translation, however, this is not a problem since the white Western men are also objective and impartial, which is a less religious way of saying they are faithful to the biblical message. Cultural ideology and cultural imperialism are masked by the myth of objectivity. Here it becomes clear that the translator is not just pouring whiskey from a bottle into a glass. In translation, the translator is distilling *his* own whiskey.

By exposing the ideological dimension in Bible translation, we are positioned to make Segovia's move. What would it mean to *translate from this place*? In other words, what would a local Bible translation look like? Instead of a *Global Bible Commentary*, what would a global Bible look like? By using the identity of a Bible translator from the receptor language as a critical apparatus for translation, the Bible itself would literally read differently. R. S. Sugirtharajah gives a great example of how this might read by focusing on olfaction or the sense of smell as an important part of translation. In the NRSV, Isa 11:3 is translated, "His delight shall be in the fear of the LORD." According to Sugirtharajah, this passage would read, "He shall smell in the LORD," if it was translated literally (2001, 189). Sugirtharajah argues that

> such a translation causes uneasiness among cultures which fail to see a potent link between odor and discriminatory powers. God discerns through the senses of smell and taste just as much as through the oral and visual. In African traditional religions this is a common practice. In these religions there is a Chief Sniffer, whose role is to sniff every entrant at the worship with a view to checking whether the intentions of the worshipper are good or evil. Some African independent Churches have instituted the role of a Chief Sniffer. ... Because of the disuse of olfactory language among contemporary commentators (white, Western men), there is a reluctance among them to accept the idea of a God or Messiah who would discern by a sense of smell. The Hebrew Bible is full of olfactory images, olfactory language and olfactory metaphors of knowledge. The current Western hermeneutical paradigm is heavily biased towards a visual mode of knowledge and equates seeing, especially with seeing of the text, with knowing. African culture, like the Hebrew, is free of this exclusively textualist and visualist paradigm and is in an advantageous position to appreciate the Isaian and similar passages in the Bible. (2001, 190)

It is clear that someone from a culture where olfaction was important would be able to understand this passage in a way that would be challenging, if not impossible, for a Westerner. Here is where identity and epistemology become one and the same. What constitutes a body of knowledge in one culture could be incomprehensible in another. In a relationship between cultures where there is an imbalance of power, one culture will be dominated. The epistemological aspects of that culture will be suppressed so that the dominant culture can control the public body of knowledge. Bible translation has contributed to this type of epistemological imperialism at least since William Carey's mission activity took him to India, where he was involved in nearly forty Bible translations by the early nineteenth century.[2]

Although not dealing with Bible translation proper, Maarman Sam Tshehla reveals this type of unidirectional movement within the academy in general: "I must translate experiences from my remote world in a manner that the guild will approve of, although the guild hardly encourages me to squeeze academic assumptions into the discourse of my mother-tongue world in my vernacular. The process is unidirectional, and in cases where I have to choose between my remote tribe's ways and academic practices, the former usually goes under" (2003, 172). The truth of Tshehla's statement should ground the work of translators in multidirection. In other words, the target culture should have as much to say about translation as the translator. This multidirectional approach would attempt to answer Tshehla's rhetorical questions:

> Where are instances in which those who have "always" been on colonialism's receiving end set out to study the customs of the technologically advanced (big-brother type) tribes? Those who have tried it know that it is like running in shifting sands, like a mirage—the rules and the playfields shift faster than anyone with limited resources (for no fault of her own) can keep up with. One might add that it is as impossible as the likelihood of cadavers, ants, or plants ever studying human beings and having their research findings celebrated by the academy. (2003, 173–74)

Focusing on the social location of the translator as a critical tool for translation systematically changes the locus of power when the translator is a local. This would not only take Musa Dube seriously when she says, "Inevitably, the assertion (whites have the land; blacks have the Bible) challenges Western readers to be aware of their history of hegemonic power and to scrutinize their current interpretations to avoid repetition of the

---

2. Carey is important to the history of modern Bible translation since he is commonly known as the "father of modern missions." Carey celebrates his Bible translation accomplishments in a letter to Thomas Baldwin from 1816: "The number of languages into which the sacred Scriptures are translated, or under translation, are nearly forty" (1817, 65).

victimizing of non-Western races" (2000, 16), but it would also empower local scholars to begin translating from and for their own culture. This is becoming a practice at least in some places and in some Bible societies, where local scholars are trained in the biblical languages and translation theories so that Bible translations will actually come from the local culture.[3] For instance, at the Conference on Bible Translation hosted by the University of West Indies in Cave Hill, Barbados, David B. Frank presented a paper dealing specifically with the cultural dimensions related to translating the Bible into Saint Lucian Creole (2004). Although Frank is an educated white male from North America, many of the principal translators who were part of the translation team were local Creole-speaking Saint Lucians. This model is not the way Bible translations have happened in the past, and it is not the way Bible translations happen in the present, for the most part. It is an attempt, however, to move in the direction of a Segovian critical studies model for Bible translation. This movement is one that places authority in the hands of local scholars, and it is a move that is long overdue.

This reiterates my desire for an intercultural space that is multidirectional. Tshehla voices this proposal. As a native Sesotho speaker and a brilliant academic, he argues that

> this immediately raises the important question of the quality we are to expect from the Sesotho Bible if, unlike the Afrikaans Bible, its effective translators are not mother-tongue Sesotho speakers. Without intending to be ungrateful and unappreciative of the missionaries and Bible society toils for the indigenous peoples, all I am asking is, When are the latter going to stop being dependent? Why must it be acceptable that—in spite of the Bible being among them for over a century—there are not mother-tongue Sesotho translation consultants yet? The simple answer is, in a word, apartheid or colonialism. But things cannot be that simple. Are Sesotho speakers so brainwashed as to believe either that English or Afrikaans Bibles (in their multiplicity) are a sufficient means of access to theology or that they cannot themselves cope with the enormous demands of learning the original biblical languages and translation theory and skills? (2003, 180–81)

---

3. Summer Institute of Linguistics International is one example of a Bible translation organization that attempts to seriously engage local culture in an attempt to produce an "accurate" Bible translation.

Empowering local Luhya people in the Western Province of Kenya with training in biblical languages and translation theory, as well as training Bible translators in the Luhya language, may be a first step. However, locating a Luhya Bible scholar should precede everything. This would follow Dora R. Mbuwayesango's advice when she "calls for a move from translating the Bible through European languages such as English, and instead to working directly from the Hebrew and Greek texts" (2000, 75). In this process of multidirectional training, relationships are fostered. Building these relationships of mutual trust is paramount to the project. Mutuality and multidirectional movement is the key. The Western "we" must not only listen to and consider Luhya advice, it must act on it to ensure multidirection. This is evident in Tshehla's comment:

> So with regard to the quality of the vernacular Bible, the verdict is provisional and indecisive. The efforts of missionary translators are admirable, although the time has come for insider-translators (preferably working together across the language divides) to take matters further. This will ensure both the preservation of the cultural values as well as enable the most natural presentation of the material while simultaneously allowing the insider-translator to be at home in her own mother tongue as well as in any other. (2003, 183)

An intercultural multidirectional translation with, for, and by the Luhya would not only have results that would be meaningful, but the whole process from beginning to end could be transformative. The product would be much greater than just a Luhya Bible. The main question focuses on authorizing agencies. Are Bible societies or Bible translators willing and able to work in this manner? Lyotard reminds us that "postmodern knowledge is not simply a tool of the authorities; it refines our sensitivity to differences and reinforces our ability to tolerate the incommensurable" (1984, xxv). Using Segovia's critical apparatus, Bible translation can be a place where cultures come into dialogue with each other (both ancient and modern) in profound ways. This cultural interaction, however, cannot be a one-sided affair that simply propitiates Western colonialism. "Translating from this place" focuses on interaction rather than exploitation. Dialogical, cultural interaction that uses Segovia's suggestions for translation can be a useful tool for translators to work together ethically on Bible translations. In a global village, those with power must always be careful how it is used. Contextual translation will not bring this utopian concept to past, but it can be one step in that direction. In comparison to how Bible translations have been conducted in the past, contextual translation is not only a step away from traditional, hegemonic missionary discourse—it is an intentional and revolutionary leap in a different direction, a direction toward translating from this place.

Translation and Narrative: Transfiguring Jesus

Scott S. Elliott

> A text is a machine conceived for eliciting interpretations. ... Interpreting means making a bet on the sense of a text, among other things. (Eco 2008, 6)

> The only difference between the original and the translation is that the translator's referent is visible, a text against which the translation can be compared, and the author's original is invisible or at least unarticulated, the text of so-called reality or some elusive, mediated, perhaps banal, conception of that reality. (Gentzler 2008, 34)

> Almost any textual feature can be renegotiated at the local or global level to reconfigure the relationship between participants within and around the source narrative. (Baker 2006, 135)

Translation Studies, Narratology, and Discoursed Creatures

Since its emergence following World War II, the field of translation studies, like so many other academic disciplines, has undergone significant expansion, increased diversification, and critical shifts in focus. Its scope has broadened to incorporate theories and methods from a range of fields and disciplines related to and influenced by the work of translation. No longer concerned primarily or solely with equivalence or fidelity, modern translation studies now attend to frames of reference, ethics, ideology, identity, and so forth. The result of this diversification and reformulation is a field rife with potential and bursting with energy, but also one difficult to pinpoint. As one writer puts it, "T[ranslation] S[tudies] is not a single field but a composite, interdisciplinary network (some say tangle) of data, methods, theories, and hypotheses from fields as diverse as cultural studies, modern language studies, post-colonial studies, gender studies, cognitive linguistics, anthropology, sociology, brain research, semiotics, and media and communications studies" (Hodgson 2008).[1] In a word, the role of translation in the processes of human cognition, identity formation, and cultural mediation is rapidly taking center stage.

Narratology—once the structuralist-inspired theory of narrative discourse attending to matters of nature, form, and function regardless of medium[2]—has experienced similar shifts over the same period. What began as a "scientific" enterprise fueled by the "rage for order" that marked the period of its rise, classical narratology has given way to postclassical narratologies that focus on a variety of areas in which narrative plays a fundamental role (e.g., in constructions of gender, identity, culture, history),[3] not merely as a genre or an instrument of representation, but

---

1. Cf. Gentzler 2008, 1–7. Hodgson identifies six foci or recurring themes amid all the diversity in recent translations studies work: (1) "the ubiquity of translation"; (2) "the target [versus source] orientation"; (3) "the role of audience understanding"; (4) "a concern with the ethics of translation"; (5) "an understanding of translation as cultural mediation rather than as simply literary production"; and (6) a broadening definition of what counts as translation leading to "an inclusive concept of translation that brings together a wide-ranging set of phenomena including literary, Bible, audio-visual, multimedia, technical, legal, and scientific translation, as well as film dubbing and subtitling, and conference interpreting, both consecutive and simultaneous."

2. New Testament narrative criticism, as it is presently conceived, has no clear parallel in "secular" literary theory. Narrative critics draw on certain elements of "secular" narratology to explicate and interpret the Gospels. But they also emphasize the finished form and fundamental unity of the text, and they endeavor to read biblical narratives as the implied reader. In other words, they treat narrative as a rhetorical device wielded by an (implied) author to portray his subject and to convey his message. Correct understanding depends on properly accessing this message, and therefore, despite their critiques of historical-critical methodologies, narrative critics continue to draw heavily on historical information. See Moore 1994, 131. See also, e.g., Rhoads 1982; Malbon 2008; Powell 1990; Resseguie 2005; and The Bible and Culture Collective 1995, 70–118.

3. See, e.g., Rimmon-Kenan 2002, 134–49; Bal 1997, 220–24; and Cobley 2001. "Postclassical narratology" is a term coined by David Herman and subsequently picked up by others. See, e.g., Herman (1999, 2–3): "Narratology has moved from its classical, structuralist phase—a Saussurean phase relatively isolated from energizing developments in contemporary literary and language theory—to its postclassical phase. Postclassical narratology (which should not be conflated with poststructuralist theories of narrative) contains classical narratology as one of its 'moments' but is marked by a profusion of new methodologies and research hypotheses; the result is a host of new perspectives on the forms and functions of narrative itself."

as a discourse that produces and fashions what it purports to render. In the words of one author, speaking specifically of postmodern narrative theory, narratology has moved "from discovery to invention, from coherence to complexity, and from poetics to politics" (Currie 1998, 2, 6).[4] That is, narrative theory has become increasingly concerned with narrative as a particular mode of discourse, an unstable rhetoric rife with intertext and never perfectly in control of the story it ostensibly tells (O'Neill 1994).[5] Hence there has surfaced an invigorating assortment of interdisciplinary combinations, such as feminist narratology, cognitive narratology, cultural narratology, and others. Many of these reorientations have come as a result of the same things that prompted the aforementioned shifts in translation studies, for example, recognition of narrative's ubiquity and of the inextricable and symbiotic relationship between readers and text.

The purpose of this article is to explore the intersection of translation and narrative discourse in relation to Bible translation, and particularly with regard to literary characters. Roman Jakobson identified three types of translation: intralingual, interlingual, and intersemiotic. These entail rewording or paraphrasing within the same language, rendering a text from one language to another, and interpreting verbal signs in terms of a nonverbal sign system,[6] respectively. To these, George Aichele adds a forth type of translation that he labels intermedial, which involves the translation of speech into writing (2001, 61–63). It is this fourth type that I want to take up here.

Aichele notes that the New Testament Gospels are already translated texts in their "original" state. They render in Greek the words Jesus historically spoke in Hebrew or Aramaic, and although traces of the Hebrew and

---

4. Cf. Cobley 2001, 171–200.

5. To be sure, this represents only one version of contemporary narratology, namely, poststructuralist narratology. Several other variants of what has been labeled "postclassical narratology" exist, among them, cognitive narratology, feminist narratology, and cultural narratology. See, e.g., Herman 2003; Page 2007; and Nünning 2004. Admittedly, some of what one finds listed under headings like "postcolonial narratology" and "queer narratology" appear to have a very tenuous relationship to narratology as traditionally conceived, stretching the term considerably and shifting significantly the emphases of narrative analysis.

6. Intersemiotic translation is not, of necessity, limited to the transition between verbal and nonverbal sign systems. Intersemiotic translation, or what Eco will refer to as "intrasystemic interpretation within other sign systems" (2008, 102–4), is any "transmutation" wherein (ostensibly identical) content is rendered in different signs.

Aramaic remain in the Greek text, no original Hebrew or Aramaic text is available. On one hand, this would be an "ordinary" instance of interlingual translation. On the other hand, however, Aichele points out that "a double translation" has occurred. Not only have Hebrew and Aramaic words been translated into Greek, but speech has been translated into writing (2001, 66). I think there is another dimension to this intermedial translation. In the Gospels, Jesus himself is translated into a character, a literary figure, as he is discoursed through narrative. In this third translational trajectory, it is not only the utterances that have been transcripted into written dialogue, but the person himself has been transfigured into a character, a "paper person" (Bal 1997, 115), a "creature of discourse" (O'Neill 1994, 41). In the process, we are left again with an absent and inaccessible original.

In the New Testament Gospels particularly, but also in the Epistles, as well as in the narratives of historical reconstruction that biblical critics relate and the narratives of theological reflection and homiletical discourse proclaimed from pulpits generally, the figure of Jesus is variously characterized. Questions concerning the identity of the "real" Jesus and of how, if at all, the narrated Jesus differs from the historical man have consumed biblical critics for decades. Such questions are grounded in the same conceptual understanding as the source and target dichotomy that, until recently, was so central to translation studies and practice. But narration is a translational act, an act of reading fully executed to the point of writing (O'Neill 1994, 135). In the process, any "original" or "source" ostensibly lying behind the narrated or translated text, any person, event, or supposed story that either claims to recount, is in fact lost and reinvented in the very act of re-presenting it. Neither narratives nor translations provide us with unmediated, unproblematic, or transparent access to their source; rather, they are themselves the entirety of what we have available to us. The narrative is not something "in" the written text. What has been translated in the Gospels is not a preexisting, easily locatable, stable, autonomous "story"; rather, as translations and transfigurations, the Gospels reflect interpretive experiences that can never be perfectly recreated. Any effort to uncover and extract the thing that is thought to be behind the narrative or the translation will only result in another act of telling/translating.[7]

---

7. As O'Neill puts it, "The world of story, what really happened, is and must

On the surface, the Gospel of Mark tells a story about a character named Jesus whose narrative life begins[8] at the moment when he sets out teaching publicly and gathering followers and continues until he is put to death and placed in a tomb. Below the surface, one might argue that it tells other stories as well, whether historical, theological, allegorical, and so on. But no matter how similar the story told looks to anything historically verifiable, anything we claim to know as true, anything counting as reality, it is fundamentally and inexorably a narrative. The point seems obvious, but casual and critical readers alike often overlook it. George Orwell's novel *Nineteen Eighty-four* provides a useful illustration. The city of "London" in which the story is set only seems more real than the larger super-state of "Oceania" of which it is a part because there is a homologue of the *Nineteen Eighty-Four* "London" in our world, but both are equally storied within the narrative discourse. Perhaps someone will grant that this is easy to accept in an obvious case of fiction. But how does one distinguish, within the narrative of Mark, for instance, between "the Mount of Olives opposite the temple" (13:3) and "a deserted place" (1:35; 6:10, 11, 31, 32, 35)? The degree of precision that accompanies one description while absent from another no more guarantees its actuality. And if this is true of places, it is equally true of characters because both occupy and operate on the same narrative level. Therefore, when we attempt to distinguish between purely literary characters, historical persons, and divine entities, for example, we

---

remain not only an abstraction but also essentially inaccessible to entities external to it. We can never penetrate as readers into this world. Any attempt to isolate the story from its discourse simply results in another *telling* of the story. All we can ever do as readers, other than theoretically, is *paraphrase*, *re*-tell, provide another discourse" (1994, 36). To be sure, it is not my intention to deny the referent altogether, or to say that everything is only language/text. Rather, the point, in part, is that while narratives and translations may not provide the direct access they purport to offer, they no less affirm the things they claim to represent for certain readers (e.g., those who position themselves as "ideal readers"). Insofar as the past or reality is only available to us through language and narrative, such discourses—be they historical reconstructions or novelistic representations—are at once *both* histories *and* fictions. See Burnett 2000; Clark 2004; and Thomas 2003, 1–13 and esp. 92–97. I am grateful to Eric Thurman for his help in clarifying this point.

8. Markan "beginnings" is a complicated issue. Mark's Gospel offers no origins for Jesus, and it disguises its own beginning by marking it with an ambiguous and multidirectional ἀρχή that, in part, explicitly ties the figure of Jesus into a particular trajectory of reading.

run up against both the way a story's discourse (i.e., its narration, its telling) always potentially undermines the story and prevents it from being told, and we manifest our role as readers actively engaged in writing.

If the Gospels are translations of a now absent original, and if translations are no longer primarily assessed in terms of fidelity, then something is lost or overlooked when we talk about whether or to what extent the Gospels reflect, represent, and portray Jesus (or the disciples, the religious leaders, Jews, Romans, even the early church, gospel communities, etc.) accurately. Because the figures that populate the Gospels—real or otherwise—come to us through narrative, they are forever inseparable from discourse and narration. This is not only because they come to us in specific narrative discourses (e.g., the Gospels in the case of Jesus), but because we encounter, understand, and conceive of them narratively. They are not simply creatures of *a* discourse, but are rather discoursed creatures.

"Faithful Unfaithfulness"

Patrick O'Neill identifies translation as a specific instance in which "the story of the literary text is taken up and reshaped by readers who also function simultaneously and very overtly as writers" (1994, 132). Referring again to Jakobson's categories, O'Neill states, "in the end translation, whether interlingual, intralingual, or intersemiotic, is in all important ways simply another name for reading—which in very important ways is another name for writing" (135). The author summarizes in broad strokes three approaches to translation practice. He begins with traditional models that were based on a sort of master-servant relationship between original texts and their translations, or between original authors and their translators, the latter never being on equal footing with the former. The goal was transparency on the part of the translator, which O'Neill suggests reflects a wider understanding of reading in general wherein language itself was to be as transparent and unobstructing as possible in order to allow free access to an author seeking to express her or his unique work. More recently, theories of translation have come to share in common the notion that "all translation [is] essentially compound discourse, discourse about other discourse" (139). The consequence of this metatextual model is the displacement of authority and originality, which now no longer rest solely with a "source text" but are resituated in the interactions of individual texts and readers. "A translator ... under the new theoretical dispensation," writes O'Neill, "is nothing more or less than a fully consistent reader, a reader with the courage of his or her convictions" (140). Finally, it is also possible to think about translation within a poststructuralist framework. In an intertextual model, the person or object translated, or the referent that a translation purports to represent, be it, for example, the figure of Jesus or the Gospel of Mark, in our case, is "an entire shifting *system* of potentially endless variable readings, the *sum*, that is to say, of all the translations and readings of [Jesus or Mark] that have ever existed or will ever exist in any language" (140; emphasis original). In this model, "the locus of authority is dispersed, disseminated, diffused throughout the entire textual system" (140).

Just as O'Neill arrives at translation by way of narratology, translation theorists also are incorporating elements of narrative theory into their reflections on translation. I am drawn especially to the recent work of two translation studies scholars, both of whom eagerly explore the implications, consequences, and possibilities of reimagining the role of translators and the act of translation, particularly with regard to identity formation and textual subversion.

Mona Baker (2006) recognizes that in every act of translation competing narratives intersect and overlap at various levels. Treating narrative not solely as stories we tell but as "the principal and inescapable mode by which we experience the world," she observes that narratives are "constructed— not discovered—by us in the process of making sense of reality, and they guide our behavior and our interaction with others" (169). Elsewhere she notes, "people's behavior is ultimately guided by the stories they come to believe about the events in which they are embedded" (3). In the process, each reshapes, relativizes, and conditions the other. The potential for silencing or, alternately, vocalizing another narrative is ever present in each translational act. She therefore attempts to analyze the subtle shifts that take place in personal and shared narratives in the process of translation, the inescapably political ramifications of those alterations, and the translator's role and responsibility in negotiating between fundamentally incompatible narratives. Conflict enters the picture because every narrative attempts to supersede others by implicitly claiming to better describe and interpret that which it claims to represent.[9] The crux of Baker's argument throughout the book is that "translators ... face a basic ethical choice with every assign-

---

9. Cf. Lincoln 1989. Lincoln explains that myth (as a discourse) can be employed in a variety of ways in order to change the nature of existing social formations: "among other possibilities, one might struggle to deprive an established myth of its authority; one might agitate for the elevation of a lesser narrative to the status of myth; or one

ment: to reproduce existing ideologies as encoded in the narratives elaborated in the text ... or to dissociate themselves from those ideologies, if necessary by refusing to translate the text ... in a particular context at all" (105).

Edwin Gentzler (2008) also explores translation as a specific form of writing and cultural production. Gentzler surveys a variety of instances, including even "translation phenomena that occur but may not be defined as such" (2), to demonstrate the fluidity of translation, its perpetual open-endedness and incompleteness, and the complex ways in which translation is always already at work in every act of reading and of cultural mediation. Gentzler repeatedly draws attention to instances in which translators act quite openly and creatively as writers to subvert the narratives they translate. According to Gentzler, these translators seek "not a reconstitution of any given original, but rather the construction of a parallel fiction, a play, or performance of that story that complements, supplements, and creates similar but new openings for interpretation in its re-versioning" (34). He points to such examples as Jorge Luis Borges, for whom "the only difference between the original and the translation is that the translator's referent is visible, a text against which the translation can be compared, and the author's original is invisible or at least unarticulated, the text of so-called reality or some elusive, mediated, perhaps banal, conception of that reality" (34); and to Suzanne Jill Levine, whose "*sub*versions" attempt to convey "'latent truths' inherent but not explicit in the original" using a strategy of "faithful unfaithfulness" (34–35).

For both Baker and Gentzler, the question is one of how translation intersects with identity formation. They are concerned not only with what is translated, but also with what is *not* translated, and with what is always potentially translated. In other words, they are concerned with remainders and supplements. At the heart of the matter is the inescapable problem of selection, the very same issue that is also a primary mark of narrative discourse (Chatman 1978). Turning again to the New Testament Gospels, here we have a literary character by the name of Jesus. Select traits and characteristics, words, and behaviors ascribed to him are incorporated into the narrative to serve the purposes thereof. In other words, the narrative dictates the figure. In the very moment that we as readers begin to rewrite the narrative by, for example, surmising reasons for a certain saying or

---

might modify the details in an accepted myth's standard narration or advance new lines of interpretation for it" (27).

action, or imagining emotional reactions, or inferring history—in a word, participating by interpreting—we are actively translating the figure into a person, while simultaneously resituating that figure into another narrative, which is itself inextricably connected with our own identities. Literary characters and we ourselves are always subjects in the making.

The translations produced by the translators that Baker and Genztler describe reflect unrepentantly appropriated texts, which seem to confirm what O'Neill said about translators being fully consistent readers with the courage of their convictions. These are readings that demonstrate their regard for the source text by their willingness not to faithfully preserve it but to fully engage and refashion it in ways befitting its afterlife in a new context.

Transfiguring Jesus

What would Bible translations look like that take the Gospels themselves as translations and that understand translation to be an opening for subversion, an act of reading put to writing? My response to this question centers on the figure of Jesus as a narrative character. Translated and transfigured into a character occupying a story, the "real" Jesus is lost. We cannot back-translate in order to check the rendition against the original. As translations of Jesus and snapshots of various reading experiences, the Gospels invite—even necessitate—additional translations and adaptations that openly and vigorously appropriate the character of Jesus and diverse readings of him, both ancient and modern, in service to innumerable ends, such that the entire intertextual network factors into every figuring of Jesus. What this means, in part, is that we must attend to translation phenomena not always identified as such.

Hence contemporary Jesus novels represent a potentially fruitful starting point. The works of Nino Ricci (2002), Anne Rice (2005, 2008) and even Gerd Theissen (1987) all reflect, in both essence and function, somewhat ironic and paradoxical, but no less noteworthy, "Gospel imitations." Indeed, they could be said to reflect the natural end of both narrative- *and* historical-critical quests to embody the ideal reader. In these novels, historical fictions (or fictional histories) of Jesus' life are narrated to readers in order that they might better understand who Jesus really was. I am not necessarily recommending we attempt that sort of contextual presentation. Nevertheless, to evaluate these novels on the basis of whether or to what extent they are faithful to the Gospel accounts of Jesus' life is to miss the point (though their authors might beg to differ). Such an evaluation is both unwarranted and misguided. These novels rewrite, in an ironic and paradoxical fashion, the Gospels themselves, and in so doing imitate, mimic, and at times even parody the Evangelists themselves (and certainly their canonical authority), while (unwittingly) destabilizing their accounts.

Similarly, the graphic novels of author-artists like Steve Ross (2005, 2008) and J. T. Waldman (2005) represent intersemiotic and intermedial translations that take advantage of the opportunity afforded by the genre to mix text and image in ways that are both novel and complex. That few would identify these productions as translations only highlights the extent to which traditional understandings of translation persist.

Transfigured into a narrative character, Jesus is forever changed. Further translations of him and of the stories surrounding him, therefore, will always be simultaneously both similar and different. The referent is not Jesus the person, a historical man, but rather Jesus the figure, a fluid, literary "creature of discourse." Although Jesus is irreversibly created in and by narrative, the figure cannot be allowed or forced to remain fixed within any single narrative thereafter.

Postcolonialism, Translation, and Colonial Mimicry

Raj Nadella

Translation studies in the area of biblical studies have generally been characterized by an explicit focus on the issue of dichotomy between "literal" and "dynamic" equivalencies in the process of transferring meaning from source language to target language. While such focus is not without merit, translation theorists and biblical scholars with keen interest in translation studies have not given sufficient attention to the various ways in which the translation enterprise has historically intersected with, and has been impacted by, colonialism, its ideology, and its attendant structures. Specifically, there has not been much focus on the various types and layers of colonial mimicry that have manifested themselves in the processes involving translation of Christian Scriptures into non-Western languages during and after European colonialism.

Suggesting that there is a not yet fully explored interconnectedness between postcolonial theory and translation studies, in this essay I demonstrate how insights from the former can help foreground layers of colonial mimicry in Bible translations in Andhra Pradesh, India. I explicate issues of culture, subcultures, competing identities, and power as they pertain to Bible translations from English into several South Indian languages, especially Telugu, in the late nineteenth and early twentieth centuries.[1] Here I juxtapose two layers (or two different types) of colonial mimicry in Bible translations perpetuated by two divergent groups: the first by missionary translators and the second by Indian translators, who either belong to dominant caste groups or have a bias for their linguistic traditions. I argue that the second layer of colonial mimicry (perpetuated by Indian

---

1. Telugu is the primary language in Andhra Pradesh, my home state.

translators), although generally not highlighted by postcolonial critics of South Asian origin, is as colonial in its ideology and orientation as the first layer, the focus of many postcolonial critiques. Examples of colonial translations—by both the missionaries and Indians—highlight various layers of colonial mimicry at work in the translation enterprise.

Familiar Complaints: The Unhappy Native Informants

A complaint one encounters frequently in postcolonial discourse pertains to cultural insensitivities, linguistic shortcomings, and hegemonic tendencies in the Bible translations that were undertaken by Western missionary societies during, and after, the colonial era. Scholars like R. S. Sugirtharajah have rightly called attention to the suppression of native languages, linguistic concepts, worldviews, and ideas in those translations. For instance, Sugirtharajah laments the introduction of foreign terms as well as lack of a prominent role for Sanskrit terminology and linguistic concepts in missionary translations of biblical texts into Indian languages (1999, 87–91). Highlighting the colonial nature of these missionary translations, these critics have called for indigenization of translation processes. In this case, the suggestion is to make greater use of native concepts and terms, specifically terms and phrases from Sanskrit and other dominant regional languages as redeeming alternatives to Western linguistic concepts introduced by colonial translations. On the one hand, their critique is aimed at exposing a form of colonial mimicry in the translation enterprise perpetuated by the missionaries. On the other hand, however, the alternatives they suggest amount to a different type of colonial mimicry, one that has little to do with the colonial powers or Western missionary societies. Furthermore, their proposals fail to highlight that the use of Hindu/Sanskrit terminology as well as concepts from other dominant Indian languages is yet another form of colonialism, one that is homegrown. To put it differently, Hindu/Sanskrit concepts might be native in relation to English, but they are colonial in relation to subaltern, marginal dialects and ways of speaking, thinking, and living.

There is another, related issue in the context of Bible translations in South India that has not received sufficient attention: the twin processes of according privileged status to the dialects of dominant communities while excluding several marginal dialects in Bible translations. In this case, the processes of privileging and exclusion are perpetuated by the natives themselves. It is a form of colonial mimicry carried out by the previously colonized, but now liberated, natives. In what follows, I will define and highlight different types of colonial mimicry in the context of Bible translations within India.

Translation and Colonial Mimicry

It is pertinent to foreground the distinction between the two different types of colonial mimicry often discussed in postcolonial discourse. Of these two different concepts that have been disseminated by Homi Bhabha and Frantz Fanon, Bhabha's notion of colonial mimicry is the mimicry (or the act of reproducing) that is carried out by the colonizers. It is what the colonizers seek to recreate in their likeness. A key example in this category is the much discussed attempts by Thomas Macaulay to create "a class of persons, Indian in blood and colour, but English in taste, in opinions, in morals, and in intellect" (1952, 729). Macaulay hoped that this class of people from among the natives would "refine the vernacular dialects of the country, ¼ enrich those dialects with terms of science borrowed from the Western nomenclature, and ¼ render them by degrees fit vehicles for conveying knowledge to the great mass of the population" (729). His goal was to create a class of people who were almost (but not quite) as good as the British, "a subject of a difference that is almost the same, but not quite" (724). Bhabha describes this kind of mimicry as "the sign of a double articulation, a complex strategy of reform, regulation and discipline, which 'appropriates' the other as it visualizes power" (1994, 86). In a similar vein, Gayatri Spivak refers to this phenomenon in terms of "subject-constitution" (1990, 13). It is a process whereby one seeks to produce a replica, albeit a slightly lesser one, of oneself.

Fanon's notion of colonial mimicry, the second type, is also very colonial in nature, but it is not undertaken by the European colonizers. Instead, it is an imitation and replication of colonial structures among, and by, the colonized. It refers to the attempts of the colonized to imitate the colonizers. "The Negro wants to be like the master," Fanon argued (1967, 221). In highlighting the effects of colonialism on the native mindset, he astutely observed how the colonial condition creates in (the) colonized communities a desire for culture and power of their colonizers. While Bhabha's concept of mimicry refers to mimicry (or replication) by the colonizers, Fanon's concept refers to mimicry of the colonizers by the colonized. It is an imitation and appropriation of the colonial mind-set by those in the colonies in order to become acceptable to the colonizers and to exercise power over others in ways the colonizers do. Both these types of mimicry manifested themselves during the translation enterprise.

If one applies this distinction to Bible translations in South India, in the first type of mimicry several British missionary societies, which undertook translation of English works into Indian languages, seem to have approached the process with the assumption that English literature had the potential to transform Indian languages. Their goal was to introduce superior linguistic ideas to Indian readers and to their languages. It was an attempt to reproduce Western, English ideas in native languages. On the second level of mimicry, Indian nationals, while resisting missionary attempts to anglicize Indian languages and Bible translations, introduced a new form of colonial translations by positing linguistic concepts from dominant communities as normative. Both these phenomena were evident in the Bible translation projects in Andhra Pradesh in the late nineteenth and early twentieth centuries. Yet the postcolonial critics of Indian origin, who frequently highlight the oppressive aspects in the first layer, do not sufficiently highlight the problems in the second. Furthermore, some of the proposals these critics have tabled in order to address those shortcomings in the first layer amount to an implicit endorsement of colonial tendencies in the second layer.

The First Layer in Colonial Mimicry

Two major phenomena were characteristic of Telugu Bible translations the Western missionaries had undertaken: introduction of neologisms and the process of homogenization.

Neologisms as Colonial Instruments

Western missionaries in Andhra Pradesh introduced neologisms and new concepts into Telugu translations of the English Bible, including instances where Telugu equivalents—literal or dynamic—were readily available. Most of these neologisms were employed in lieu of, and seemingly for the purpose of replacing, existing terminology for certain popular religious concepts in that region. For instance, missionaries introduced the word *krupa* to convey the notion of grace even though the existing Telugu word *prasadam* could have sufficiently conveyed the concept of grace. An obscure Telugu word, *rakshana*, rather than the familiar term *moksha*, was used to translate the Christian concept of salvation. The biblical concept of predestination was translated as *punar nirnayam* rather than as *karma*, a popular concept in Hindu (and Indian) religious discourse. In a similar fashion, *papam* took the place of *dosham* as the Telugu equivalent of transgression or sin.

One can suggest, with some supporting evidence, that the introduction of these neologisms by Western missionaries was an attempt to cleanse Indian languages, Telugu in this case, of native religious influence. Since words like *prasadam*, *moksha*, and *karma*, which are of Sanskrit origin, had arrived into the Telugu lexicon with some non-Christian religious baggage, missionary translators in the nineteenth and twentieth centuries appear to have deemed it important to replace them with virgin, untainted words that would convey their "superior" religious concepts. Seen this way, on one level, the introduction of neologisms in Bible translations was a religious and cultural move. On a different level, it was a political and colonial move as well. Replacing existing Telugu words with neologisms can be described as an attempt by the missionaries to impose English concepts and ways of thinking on the natives. An implication was that Telugu forms of speech were rudimentary and that existing Telugu terminologies were inadequate to convey the sophisticated Christian concepts that only English words were capable of communicating. The issue here is not so much the incompatibility between two systems of language that necessitated creation of new terms but a perceived inferiority of an existing language system as well as inadequacy of native terms to convey complex Western ideas.

As many have observed, translations of religious texts are driven by ideology and political agenda (Bassnett and Trivedi 1999). It is therefore essential that any conversation about translations look into the questions of who the translators are, what their agenda is, what means they have employed, and to what effect. In this case, since English was the language of the colonizers, while Telugu, the supposedly inadequate language, was the language of the colonized, the invention of neologisms by missionary translators foregrounds issues of culture and power. English, the source language, is seen as the donor language while Telugu, the target language, becomes the recipient. The former is the benefactor, the latter is the beneficiary. English is the giver not just of content/text, but also of new and superior ideas and ways of thinking (that were sorely lacking in Telugu). Telugu becomes the simulacrum, a copy of English, the original. English is the master language, not just the *master's* language, which introduced Telugu-speaking people to a whole new world and enabled them to think beyond their (rigid) cultural boundaries and to perceive the superior Christian (Western) truth. In this approach, the process of translating texts from English into Telugu is seen not as a mutual transaction or as a symbiotic process between two languages and cultures of similar value and importance, but as one-way traffic whereby one language spoke, while the *other* sat at the feet of the master language and listened.

Homogenizing the Heterogeneous

During the colonial era, especially in the late nineteenth and early twentieth centuries, British colonial powers in India embarked on a process of consolidating tiny kingdoms into major regions in order to make it convenient for them to govern. This political process of consolidation of native territories was mimicked, on a different level and in a somewhat different fashion, by British missionary translators, who attempted to homogenize Indian dialects. It appears that their goal was to replace the numerous Indian dialects with a few common, mainstream languages that would facilitate efficient growth of their missionary movement. Such a process would also facilitate easier translation and dissemination of Scriptures. Hindi happened to one of those mainstream languages.

In *Postcolonial Criticism and Biblical Interpretation*, Sugirtharajah aptly observes that since the British rulers and missionary Bible translators perceived the presence of multiple languages and dialects in India as an impediment to rapid expansion of colonial rule and missionary work, respectively, they strived to homogenize those languages (2002, 158–62). Their efforts aimed at achieving homogenization had layered effects on the Indian society. On one level, as Gayatri Spivak's essay "The Burden of English" (1993) points out, such efforts led to an imposition of English for imperial convenience. On another level, Hindi, which was hitherto not spoken in several parts of India, especially in the southern part, was introduced as a national language purportedly for national unity. On a regional level, because some local dialects were often replaced with mainstream languages, those efforts resulted in the loss of certain local dialects and autochthonous expressions. In the southern part of India, although the Bible was translated into all four major regional languages, missionary translators promoted Sanskrit as the core language, even as they avoided use of Sanskrit words that had explicit religious (Hindu) connotations. They streamlined the four South Indian languages—Telugu, Tamil, Kannada, and Malayalam—by substituting numerous key words and unique expressions in those languages with seemingly untainted Sanskrit words—or with Sanskrit neologisms—in a manner that sent several unique, ancient expressions into oblivion.

Such a pattern of homogenizing languages and undermining local expressions resonated with the Indian nationalistic agenda of "unifying" different languages for the purpose of creating a sense of "national unity."[2] It was one agenda on which the British colonial powers, missionaries, and the Indian nationalists concurred. Given the key role Bible translators played in streamlining the four South Indian languages, their decision to privilege Sanskrit vocabulary, which they considered untainted,[3] resulted not just in the invalidation of ancient expressions in non-Sanskrit languages but also in the loss of unique worldviews behind those expressions. Another important aspect of this issue is the question of how, and to what extent, the privileging of Sanskrit has forced South Indians to think in terms alien to their language and whether it amounts to linguistic colonialism.

The Second Layer of Colonial Mimicry

As Sugirtharajah has aptly observed, translation has traditionally been a tool of colonization aimed at converting the natives to the British ways of thinking and articulating the Divine. He notes that "since the invader and the invaded spoke different languages and practiced different religions, translation played a crucial role in enabling the colonizers in conquering and converting the other. A virtual hagiography has emerged around missionary translations, describing the trying conditions under which these early translators toiled" (2002, 156). Seen this way, with some notable exceptions, the work of the colonial Bible translators was at least as political as religious in terms of its actual effect.

Postcolonial scholars, who call attention to the colonial nature of Bible translations undertaken by Westerners, generally make a twofold proposal aimed at attenuating, and possibly reversing, the effects of the colonial mimicry perpetuated by the missionaries: (1) They call for a return to the Hindu/Sanskrit worldview that was vilified by the missionaries. As I have

---

2. That such a lofty goal never materialized is another matter.

3. Missionary Bible translators were careful not to employ Sanskrit words that were commonly used in the religious context of Hinduism. Those words were considered to have come with unwanted religious baggage.

observed above, some critics bemoan the absence of an authentic Hindu and Sanskrit worldview from Bible translations and posit Hindu/Sanskrit words and texts as redeeming, postcolonial alternatives to imperialistic texts and translations. Since the British missionaries suppressed certain Sanskrit words with Hindu religious connotations, a return to those words would be a right step in the direction of undermining colonial legacy. (2) Some of these critics also condone modern Bible translators' practice of employing major Indian languages like Telugu, Kannada, and Tamil in the regions where they are the dominant languages. Rarely do they highlight the need to employ marginalized dialects and linguistic concepts of subaltern communities like those in the Telangana region of Andhra Pradesh. Nor do they call attention to the oppressively hierarchical relationship between the dominant Indian languages on the one hand and the marginalized Indian languages and dialects on the other. While Hindu and Sanskrit concepts are native and noncolonial in relation to the British missionary and political establishments, they are hegemonic and colonial in relation to subaltern dialects and ways of living within India. Although Sanskrit is an Indian language, it is a language popularized and spoken primarily by the Brahmins, the dominant community in the Indian caste system. Sanskrit is also the sacred language of classical Hinduism, the religion of the dominant communities.[4]

In the context of such hierarchical relationships between various languages within India, the aforementioned proposals from postcolonial critics (to make greater use of Sanskrit and other dominant Indian languages) amount to a type of colonial mimicry, akin to the one described by Fanon. They amount to an intranational mimicry that differs from the mimicry perpetuated by the British colonizers. Their proposals would amount to replication of colonial structures by the previously colonized. Furthermore, use of Sanskrit as the standard language in a uniform fashion attributes a notion of inferiority to other, less popular Indian languages. Such an effort also replicates the colonial practices of otherizing certain ways of thinking, articulating, and living.

This type of colonial mimicry continued, and still does, on a regional level as well. Translation efforts undertaken by Indian mission groups have often privileged the dialects and linguistic concepts of dominant regions

---

4. I am making a distinction between "classical" and "popular" versions of Hinduism. In this context, the term *popular* has a derogatory connotation.

and communities, especially in Andhra Pradesh. Bible translators in Andhra Pradesh generally prefer a version of Telugu spoken in the coastal districts, the more affluent and politically influential region of the state. By employing the coastal Telugu dialect in their translations, the translators have posited it as the standard, normative, and superior version of Telugu in Andhra Pradesh. Such an approach has amounted to marginalization and otherizing of other versions of Telugu spoken in other regions. Furthermore, Telugu Bible translators in the twentieth century have usually privileged terminology and dialects generally used by dominant communities and caste groups. In doing so, they have condoned claims of superiority made by some subcultures over others, some dialects over others, within the same regional and cultural context. Finally, the very enterprise of literary translation in Andhra Pradesh, with its emphasis on written communication and printed texts, devalued the oral communication practices among certain subaltern communities.

Conclusion

Postcolonial critics of Indian origin have addressed issues of British colonialism and Bible translations primarily from the perspective of the dominant communities in India. However, they have not paid sufficient attention to the ways in which subaltern ways of thinking and articulating the Divine were suppressed not just by Western colonial powers and missionaries but also by dominant communities from within India. Some of the proposals put forward by these critics, with the goal of attenuating the effects of colonialism, could themselves amount to colonial mimicry. Their proposals are postcolonial in relation to both the British colonial powers and the colonial interests among the missionaries, but not necessarily in relation to the subaltern communities. An authentic postcolonial proposal for Bible translations in the South Indian state of Andhra Pradesh would have to be threefold: (1) translating biblical texts into Telugu using peripheral dialects wherever relevant and avoiding the influence of both English and Sanskrit on Telugu translations; (2) transmitting the Bible by resuscitating the rich oral traditions of subaltern communities; and (3) presenting the content of the Bible in ways that would resonate with and find relevance in subaltern cultures.

The Translator's Dilemma:
A Response to Boer, Coker, Elliott, and Nadella

George Aichele

> All true language
> is incomprehensible,
> like the chatter
> of a beggar's teeth. (Artaud 1976, 549)

I want to thank Scott Elliott for his invitation to respond to the papers given at the Ideology, Culture, and Translation panel in the 2008 Society of Biblical Literature Annual Meeting in Boston, and again for inviting me to respond to published versions of some of those papers in this volume.

To Roland Boer's description of dynamic equivalence, I would add only that this approach to translation is profoundly logocentric. As Jacques Derrida says, for logocentrism, "reading and writing, the production or interpretation of signs, the text in general as fabric of signs … [is] preceded by a truth, or a meaning already constituted by and within the element of the logos" (1976, 14). In other words, meaning or truthful content is quite distinct from any textual embodiment. Because dynamic equivalence favors the signified thought or content of a message at the expense of the signifier, it is logocentric.

In discussions of translation theory, dynamic equivalence is usually opposed to formal equivalence or "literal translation." As Boer notes, if any actual translation were purely dynamic, we might no longer recognize it as a translation at all, and if it were strictly literal, it would be incoherent, because languages never match up "word for word." In reality, there are no purely literal or purely dynamic translations, but this binary opposition is useful in our thinking about translation, as a way to compare actual translations as more or less literal or dynamic.

Dynamic equivalence is only possible if someone knows how the original readers understood the text, and while that is not exactly the same as knowing how the historical author understood the text, as a historical or epistemological problem it is practically the same. This is the preference of Schleiermacher (whom Boer cites). However, literal translation has no interest in what the author or any reader ever understood the text to mean. As its name implies, literal translation cares primarily about the signifier, as Walter Benjamin makes clear:

> a translation, instead of resembling the meaning of the original, must lovingly and in detail incorporate the original's *mode of signification*. ... This may be achieved, above all, by a *literal rendering of the syntax* which proves words rather than sentences to be the primary element of the translator. (1968, 78–79, emphases added)

Translation always involves a tension between the two texts—a physical, inter-textual tension. Benjamin says that a translation is "transparent" when it "allows the pure language, as though reinforced by its own medium, to shine upon the original all the more fully" (1968, 79). In other words, transparency is not the manifestation of meaning, according to Benjamin, but rather the manifestation of the text itself, through its translation. Translation always involves a tension between the two texts—a physical, inter-textual tension.

Because of this, I appreciate Boer's comments on the metaphorical loads borne by the words *transparency* and *fidelity*, for they clarify points of contention between these two views of translation. Benjamin also describes as "fidelity" the "longing for linguistic complementation" between the words of the source text and those of the target text. In contrast, Eugene Nida calls for both transparency and fidelity, but Nida's "fidelity" is not verbal-syntactic harmony between two physical texts, but the spiritual faithfulness of the target text to "Christ." The practitioner of dynamic equivalence in biblical translation must claim to know already what "the message of the gospel" is, for otherwise that translator could not do her job. As the story of Pentecost makes clear, Christianity has always been in love with the "spirit" of the Scriptures, which is the signified, Christ (Acts 2:36).

However, because literal translation is not logocentric, it allows no binary opposition between spiritual signified and fleshy signifier, and therefore it is not congruent with either orthodox incarnational or heretical gnostic theologies. Benjamin's ideal of literal translation is the interlinear version of the Scriptures (1978, 82): word *by* word (not word *for* word), flesh against flesh.

K. Jason Coker also criticizes ideological (Western imperial missionary) dimensions of translation, but I think that his analysis of the need for an authoritative text could be better nuanced. For example, his initial remark about the expense of the Swahili Bible translation as opposed to a cheaper (but less reader-friendly?) English one deserves more consideration, especially in light of Boer's concluding comments on "empire and commodity form" (21–23). It costs money to translate and publish a text, and that requires the involvement of publishing houses and attendant capitalistic motivations. In addition, nearly all of us, not just Africans, are the heirs of "missionary" translations. (Do not Jerome, Wycliffe, and Luther qualify as missionaries, even though they were also natives?)

Coker chastises translators who think that "the material text of the Bible does not have primary meaning" (31), but I reject the claim that "material text" has any meaning at all. We are most likely to perceive this meaningless materiality when we cannot read the text, either because we cannot read or do not know the language or alphabet, or because of some interference, such as lack of sufficient light or smudged ink. I am not sure how the materiality of a text might be "fulfilled" (31), as Coker says, but perhaps he means something like Benjamin's notion of "linguistic complementation" (1968, 79). The translator transforms this materiality, which gets more or less hidden behind the logocentric veil of meaning, for even the most literal translations succumb to the desire for meaning.

Coker groups together dynamic equivalence and literal translation as both concerned with "what the original author/editor wrote and how best to convey/translate that in a modern (con)text" (27). That statement ignores important differences between dynamic equivalence and literal translation. Coker also observes, "What constitutes a body of knowledge in one culture could be incomprehensible in another" (33); but if some "body of knowledge" referenced in a biblical text (for example, "the Lord is my shepherd") is incomprehensible to a translation's recipients, then isn't that precisely the sort of problem that dynamic equivalence addresses? This is the issue of "fidelity" or "faithfulness," which is so well laid out in Boer's essay.

To these two approaches Coker contrasts a reader-centered hermeneutic, following Fernando Segovia. Perhaps Coker's point is that meaning does not lie "in" the text itself, placed there by its author, as logocentrism (and dynamic equivalence) supposes. Instead, meaning lies "in" the specific location or context of the reader. With that I have no quarrel, but it seems inconsistent with Coker's mention of "primary meaning" (31), as well as his later emphasis on the importance of the translator, especially the native or "insider-translator" (36). Copyright laws usually treat the translator as the "owner" of the translated text; and, in this way at least, a native speaker of Luya who translates a text is the legally recognized author of the result. This shifts the locus of "the author," but once again the author determines the meaning.

Nevertheless, I second Coker's call to scrutinize the translator. He focuses closely on the role and power of the translator as the one who (re)distributes the meaning of the texts, and this is a very important, and often overlooked, matter. Translators are never innocent. However, Coker suggests that if we replace white male Western translators who embody imperial power with translators from the native populace, then the translation may be freed from its colonialist tendencies. I doubt that things are so simple, and so, I think, does Raj Nadella (see his essay in this volume, and below). Surely shifting the translator from foreigner to native does not simply erase the question of ideology.

Scott S. Elliott intriguingly questions whether narrative involves a kind of translation, in which "the person himself has been transfigured into a character" (42). I agree that to tell a story about an actual person (I assume that this is what Elliott means by "the person himself") involves a kind of translation. Since narrative always belongs to the realm of the signified—that is, the characters, plot, and other elements in a written story, like "the person himself," provide the signifying basis for ideas or mental constructs, virtualities—in this way, every narrative is indeed a translation.

However, this "translation" from the semiotic system that is "reality" (as a largely nonverbal text) into mental narrative (the semiotic system of conscious verbal thought) would be a form of what Roman Jakobson calls intersemiotic translation (1987, 429). The transfer from a writer's thoughts about the person "himself" into a story would then require another translation into verbal language such as speech or writing, and then yet another translation into a reader's thoughts. Every reader is a translator. Elliott calls this "our role as readers actively engaged in writing" (44).

Elliott seems to think that actual events or objects are stories, but that is not so. Instead, in order to understand or even experience such actualities at all, we tell stories about them. Scientific hypotheses are among those stories, as are the conclusions of historians about past events. Indeed, "reality" and "truth" are themselves not actual things, but narratives. Only in a story can the actual become real or true, though then it is no longer actual, but virtual. The relation between any story and an actual event or being is always mediated by the story's signifiers, and thus *every* story is a virtuality that informs our understanding of reality. Every story is always already meaningful. The story's "original," to use Elliott's words, is the physical signifiers that make up the text, *not* some actual extratextual event or person.

I agree that the story is a translation or "transfiguration," as Elliott says, but narrative is not something distinct from text and found in actual things, as a logos that precedes the text and can be transplanted through dynamic equivalence. Instead, story always lies between texts, in intertextuality or the "complementation" (Benjamin's word) that forms their mutual reading and translation. This intertextuality defines what Coker calls the reader's location, or as Elliott says, "our own identities." (47). This is true even of the narrative that connects the author's imaginings, thoughts, or memories of "the person himself."

Finally, Raj Nadella explores the imperialism of "colonial mimicry" in translations of the Bible into the Telugu language. Like Coker, Nadella is less concerned about questions of text or meaning than he is about social location and cultural politics. Nevertheless, the concern plays out differently in Nadella's essay. Here it is not only white Western males who cause the problems, but also the desire of indigenous groups to imitate foreigners. To play a bit with Coker's example, would *any* competent native speaker of Luya who is also trained in the biblical languages be acceptable to provide the desired translation? Would a highly competent Muslim or atheist be preferred to a less competent Christian? Who gets to decide whether a potential translator is truly competent in the necessary languages? Are there no "marginal dialects" (to use Nadella's words) to be considered?

However, if competency is not the sole consideration, then who gets to decide between the candidates, and on what basis? Would factors such as personal qualities, religious commitment, gender, lifestyle, or social class be considered? While I am very sympathetic to reader-oriented approaches to biblical scholarship, one problem that plagues them is susceptibility to purely idiosyncratic factors, and such factors could operate here as well.

Nadella raises another valuable and often neglected question, that of the translation's influence on the target language through vocabulary shifts and homogenization of dialects. I am intrigued by his phrases "virgin, untainted words" and "untainted Sanskrit vocabulary" (53, 55). How can words be untainted? I am thinking here especially of Benjamin's "pure language." Or are these words virginal simply because they have never been used before, because they did not exist before in the target language? In any case, it would appear that the untainted words of both of Nadella's phrases already carry religious or cultural "baggage" (as Nadella says), which would be a perverse extreme of the meaning preceding the text.

Nadella's discussion of mimicry in relation to translation reminds me of Claude Lévi-Strauss's story about a nonliterate tribal chieftain who sees an anthropologist writing in a notebook and proceeds to imitate his behavior, which he perceives as an action of power (1970, 289–93). I think also of those Greek manuscripts of the Jewish Scriptures that transliterate the divine name with Greek letters that resemble the Hebrew Tetragrammaton, but that would sound quite different if spoken. In each case, there is a "literalism" that is so extreme that a totally new (and thoroughly untranslatable) text is created. The materiality of a signifier, rather than its meaning, is reproduced. But is it then still a signifier?

To be sure, Nadella follows a different line of thought. He calls instead for "transmitting the Bible by resuscitating the rich oral traditions of subaltern communities" and "presenting the content of the Bible in ways that would resonate with and find relevance in subaltern cultures" (57). Something like this (or a bizarre parody of it) already appears in American *manga* Bibles and Biblezines, or the extremely specialized editions of the Bible that are increasingly common in popular bookstores, with their highly dynamic equivalencies. Would Nadella's suggestions lead to an explosion of translations in languages, dialects, and idiolects without limit?

I close with a question suggested by a quote from Willard Van Orman Quine, who is sadly overlooked in discussions regarding translation of the Bible. Quine notes that

> a full knowledge of the stimulus meaning of an observation sentence is not sufficient for translating or even spotting a term. … How directly the sentence and its words are associated with sensory stimulation … does not settle whether to posit objects of one sort or another for words of the sentence to denote in the capacity of terms. (1960, 236)

In other words, even the most straightforward, seemingly clear sentence is rife with connotative possibilities.

Quine imagines the case of a linguist who seeks to understand a language previously unknown to the larger world. Perhaps it is a missionary, or even a Bible translator. The linguist must rely solely on native informants and their willingness to confirm by way of simple gestures the linguist's guesses as to what their words and sentences mean. Quine assumes that the natives are willing for the linguist to understand and speak their language. But what if they are trying to confuse or deceive instead? To what extent do assumptions about the desires of people to understand one another, or the primacy of communication as a function of language, guide or misguide our thinking about translation? If we refuse the logocentric assumption, then the "task of the translator" must be to create a target text that is as open to multiple denotations and connotations as the source text is. In other words, the goal is a target text that is as incomprehensible as its source text.

Part 2
Sites in Translation

Augustine's Bible

Virginia Burrus

For Christians, the Bible is characterized by its radical translatability, for Jews by its essential Hebraicness: so goes a familiar account. Yet Jews are also frequently depicted as consummate translators—on the one hand, native informants reluctantly yielding the secrets of the *Hebraica veritas* to the colonizing impulse of Christian exegesis; on the other hand, trickster-ish denizens of cultural borderlands where linguistic identities are both built up and broken down, even as all truths prove duplicitous. Is Yiddish itself not evidence that the boundaries between languages do not hold—and that translation does not merely introduce old texts to new readers but transforms language through its very doubling? These and other complexities attending the representation, theory, and practice of Jewish translation are explored by Naomi Seidman in her 2006 monograph, *Faithful Renderings*, a historically wide-ranging work that demonstrates how the politics of translation is implicated in the production of Jewish-Christian difference, while also foregrounding the role of *narrative* in conveying ideas and ideologies of translation.

The inaugural translation narrative, for both Jews and Christians, is that of the so-called Septuagint, or Seventy, a Greek rendering of the Hebrew Bible said to have been ordered by the Hellenistic king Ptolemy II. The legend, to which Seidman devotes her first chapter, is widely attested in antiquity, appearing first in the fictional *Letter of Aristeas* (ca. 130 B.C.E.), which records both the royal commissioning of the translation from the Jerusalem high priest and its subsequent production via the collaboration of seventy-two hand-picked Jewish elders sequestered on the beautiful island of Pharos for seventy-two days (*Aristeas* 301). Philo later varies the script by describing the translators as speaking prophetically, resulting in the miracle of spontaneous and simultaneous unanimity (*Moses* 2.7.37). His version (introducing what Seidman calls a vertical as opposed to horizontal model of translation) seems to have exercised the most direct influence on patristic writers, though he could scarcely have endorsed all of the conclusions subsequently drawn. Seidman identifies Augustine's rendering in particular with the culmination of "what could be called a Christian translation theory" that strongly privileges the spiritual "sense" of the text over its necessarily transcended "Jewish letter" (2006, 53, 57).[1] For late ancient Christians more generally, the Septuagint becomes the sign of Scripture's transcendence and universal translatability, "a perfect document *despite* its having been composed by Jews," as Seidman puts it (2006, 54). Tellingly, the Talmud records a counternarrative that suggests that the Septuagint is a miraculous *mis*translation intended to deceive Christians while preserving the Hebrew Bible, in all of its *un*translatability, for Jews (2006, 63–64).

Seidman's presentation of the history of Christian appropriation of the Septuagint focuses on the mobilization of sexual tropes, especially the trope of virginity, in which the purity of the Greek text and the authority of its translational choice *parthenos* (for *'almâ* in Isa 7:14) coincide. She notes: "The fourth century saw the discourses of virginity and translation at their closest convergence; by the turn of the fifth, the two courses had dramatically diverged." Seidman rightly credits the Christian biblical translator Jerome with having "first opened the gap between (Western) Christianity and its 'perfect' Greek Bible" (2006, 70).

Though she does not dwell on this point, Augustine was among those who resisted Jerome's efforts, remaining faithful to the Septuagint as if to a virginal bride, even as Jerome cast aspersions on the purity of a text long since both corrupted and corrected—corrected, famously, by Origen's marked-up edition. Augustine's reframing of the legend of the Septuagint's auspicious origin represents not only a high watermark for the christianization of this particular translation narrative but also (in hindsight) its end, at least for the Latin-speaking west. For Augustine's defense of the Septuagint as a perfect translation comes wrapped in another translation narrative, in which the Septuagint is, finally, positioned almost as ambivalently as in the Talmud. This enveloping narrative, which is generated by Augustine's contentious and well-publicized correspondence with Jerome,[2] pertains to the production of an authoritative *Latin* translation.

---

1. On the Septuagint between Jews and Christians in antiquity, see also Rajak 2009, esp. 278–313.

2. On the likelihood that both Augustine and Jerome collected and circulated

It may be read as a story, among other things, of chastened "chutzpah," as Alfons Fürst puts it: "Trotz seiner Ignoranz [that is, Augustine's] beweist er da eine beträctliche Portion Chuzpe" (1999, 144).

To read it thus, however, is to allow Jerome to control the coauthored script. In an initial response to Augustine's repeated epistolary queries, he warns, "Do not because you are young challenge a veteran in the field of Scripture." Jerome further elaborates the assertion of his own seniority:

> I have had my time, and have run my course to the utmost of my strength. It is but fair that I should rest, while you in your turn run and accomplish great distances; at the same time (with your leave, and without intending any disrespect), lest it should seem that to quote from the poets is a thing which you alone can do, let me remind you of the encounter between Dares and Entellus [cf. *Aeneid* 5], and of the proverb, "The tired ox treads with a firmer step." (*Epist.* 68 [402])[3]

When he first writes to Jerome in Palestine in 394 or 395, Augustine is about forty and still relatively new to the presbyterate of Hippo; but he is a forty-eight-year-old bishop of growing reputation by the time Jerome responds with these words in 402. Moreover, Jerome *may* have been no more than seven years Augustine's senior. (His birth date is difficult to establish.) If so, his scripting of the forty-eight-year-old Augustine as youthful, impudent, and *chutzpadik* becomes all the more striking—a foolish Dares, doomed to defeat, playing opposite Jerome's elderly but stalwart Entellus. That contemporary scholars are not typically inclined to question this representation may betray the fact that most are heirs of the doctrine of the *Hebraica veritas* upheld by both Jerome and the rabbis, but not by Augustine.[4] Even Seidman, who recognizes Jerome's troubling appropriation of an earlier Roman imperialist understanding of translation (2006, 72), nonetheless credits him approvingly with reintroducing dialogue into

---

at least the first part of their correspondence in their own lifetimes, thus quite self-consciously producing a narrative for public consumption, see Hennings 1994, 71–76.

3. All translations in this essay are mine, unless otherwise indicated. Readers may, however, avail themselves of the English translations of the Jerome-Augustine correspondence, together with interpretive apparatus, in White 1990. For the Latin edition of Jerome's letters, see CSEL 54–56; for Augustine's letters, CSEL 34, 44, 57, 58; for Augustine, *On Christian Doctrine*, CCSL 32; *Confessions*, CCSL 27; *City of God*, CCSL 47, 48.

4. That the scholarly consensus runs heavily in Jerome's favor in this particular case is supported by Fürst 1999, 144 n. 383, 145 n. 390.

the theory and practice of translation while also proffering a more full-bodied understanding of the translator's task: "translation rests for Jerome on the painful and frustrating acquisition of an utterly foreign tongue, and it is not the transcendent mind but rather a resistant throat that 'channels' the Hebrew word" (2006, 70). In contrast, Augustine's faithfulness to the Septuagint tends to come across as both unconvincing and unappealing, not only in its transcendentalism (Seidman's main emphasis) but also in its text-critical naiveté, its heavy-handed resort to the authority of ecclesial tradition, and its implicit anti-Judaism.

It is nonetheless worth revisiting his claims for the Greek text, as these surface not only in his correspondence with Jerome, but also indirectly in his contemporaneous *Confessions*, as well as his later *City of God*. Having done so, we will be in a position to further complicate the history that Seidman relates: even as Jerome's view of the *Hebraica veritas* colludes with that of the rabbis, so too Augustine's particular embrace of biblical translatability aligns him with the thought of both the Alexandrian Philo and the German-Jewish translator and translation theorist Franz Rosenzweig, whom Seidman discusses in a later chapter and to whose thought I will myself turn very briefly at the end of these remarks.

* * *

We can begin with Augustine's first letter to Jerome, in which he tactfully introduces reference to the Septuagint translation via the indirection of rhetorical apophasis:

> I say nothing of the Seventy, regarding whose harmony in mind and spirit, surpassing that which is found in even one person, I dare not in any way pronounce a decided opinion, except that in my judgment, beyond question, very high authority must in this work of translation be conceded to them. (*Epist.* 28.2.2 [394/395])

If he will "say nothing of the Seventy," "not daring in any way to pronounce a decided opinion," he has nonetheless already protested that he "cannot marvel enough" at the notion that "anything should at this date be found in the Hebrew manuscripts that escaped so many translators perfectly acquainted with the language." Underlining his conviction regarding the translational saturation of the Hebrew text, Augustine subsequently brings the Septuagint more directly into his argument:

I am more perplexed by those translators who, though enjoying the advantage of laboring after the Seventy had completed their work, and although well acquainted, as it is reported, with the force of Hebrew words and phrases, and with Hebrew syntax, have not only failed to agree among themselves, but have left many things that, even after so long a time, still remain to be discovered and brought to light. Now these things were either obscure or plain: if they were obscure, it is believed that you are as likely to have been mistaken as the others; if they were plain, it is not believed that they [the Seventy] could possibly have been mistaken. (*Epist.* 28.2.2)

Writing almost a decade later (by which point Augustine has reiterated his challenge),[5] Jerome responds sarcastically: "on the same principle, no one would ever venture to speak on any subject after others have pronounced their opinion, and no one would be at liberty to write anything regarding that which another has once handled, however important the matter might be" (*Epist.* 75 [404]). Indeed, Augustine's argument does seem susceptible to just such a critique. Moreover, as Ralph Hennings observes, his narrative does not jibe with the facts: "Since Jerome is the first Christian theologian who wants to prepare a complete translation of the Old Testament from Hebrew into Latin, the question arises, which translators Augustine means" (1994, 113).[6] As Hennings goes on to note, Augustine's emphasis on the lack of unanimity of the translators in question might seem to point toward the anonymous translators responsible for the diverse and inconsistent Latin translations in circulation in his day; however, these are Septuagint-based translations, precisely what Augustine is calling for, so that his critique of Jerome seems ill served by such a reference. Alternately, Hennings also suggests, he might be referring to the Greek translations of Aquila, Symmachus, and Theodotion; however, these are translations from the Hebrew to the Greek while Jerome is attempting not a Greek but a much-needed Latin translation, which again suggests that Augustine's critique misses its mark.

I would suggest that the ambiguities are the result of Augustine's deliberate displacement of the Septuagint narrative onto a reimagined scene of Latin translation. In undertaking to retranslate the Hebrew anew, Jerome

---

5. See *Epist.* 71 (403).

6. "Da Hieronymus der erste christliche Theologe ist, der eine komplette Übersetzung des Alten Testamentes aus dem Hebräischen ins Lateinische anfertigen will, entsteht die Frage, welche Übersetzer Augustinus meint."

is, in Augustine's view, indeed placing himself among such misguided translators as Aquila, Symmachus, and Theodotion—never mind that they translated into Greek and he into Latin. Attempting vainly to improve upon an already perfect translation, he is doomed to contribute to inconsistency and discord rather than to the harmony of textual spirit. Jerome is the one with real chutzpah—challenging all seventy-two elders! Therefore, his translations will merely add to the confusion already existing among the multiple, fragmentary Latin renderings: as Augustine describes the situation in a subsequent letter, "for the variations found in the different codices of the Latin text are intolerably numerous" (*Epist.* 71.4.6), noting elsewhere, "for the translations of the Scriptures from Hebrew into Greek can be counted, but the Latin translators are out of all number" (*Christian Instruction* 2.11.16). If he wants to produce a harmonious and authoritative translation, Augustine insists, he ought not to begin with the impenetrable Hebrew, fully legible only to Jews, to whom even Jerome must appeal for confirmation. Rather, he must return to the font and guarantor of biblical translatability—the Septuagint.

Augustine thus positions the Septuagint as the necessary double of the Hebrew text—not merely the original and most perfect translation of Scripture but the manifestation of Scripture precisely *as* translation, revelation, or testimony. Much as there is one divine Son, a perfect image of the Father, so too there is one inspired *interpretatio*, a perfect rendering of the biblical text. As Augustine puts it later, in book 18 of the *City of God*, "the church has received the Septuagint *as if it were the only one* [*tamquam sola esset*]." Not only does its authority exceed that of all other Greek translations; it is also the touchstone of the truth of all translations "from Hebrew into any other language." Elaborating on Philo's doctrine of inspiration in that same work, he continues:

> For the same Spirit that was in the prophets when they delivered those messages was present in person in the seventy men also. ... And the Spirit could say that very thing in different ways, so that though the words [*verba*] were not the same, yet, when they should be properly understand, the same meaning [*sensus*] should shed its light through them; and it could omit or add something, so that from this too would be shown that this is not a work of human servitude that bound the interpreter with the words [*verbis*], but rather of divine power that replenished and guided the mind of the interpreter. (*City of God* 18.43)

Passages such as this one suggest to Seidman (as well as others whom she cites and follows) that Augustine, anticipating Saussure, places a "bar between signified and signifier, between divine message and Jewish medium," freeing the Christian Logos by incarcerating the Jewish letter. Seidman notes further that this theoretical move is ominously paralleled by ancient Christian versions of the Septuagint legend in which the Jewish translators are represented as imprisoned in ascetic cells. She here links Augustine's version of the Septuagint legend with that of Epiphanius, claiming that both of these Christian writers "not only imprison the Jewish translators" but "also convert them into (involuntary) monks" (2006, 56, 59).

While it is true that Augustine follows Philo in emphasizing that the translations of the Seventy were made in isolation from one another ("each sat separately") so as to highlight the miracle of the "marvelous, astonishing, and clearly divine agreement [*consensus*] in their words [*verbis*]," he does not (to my knowledge) anywhere invoke the architecture of incarceration, described by Epiphanius with such elaborate care. Rather, as we have seen, Augustine's translators are said explicitly *not* to be bound or enslaved by the Hebrew, and they meet nonetheless with perfect accord not only of meaning (*consensus*) but also of Greek words (*verba*) (*City of God* 18.42–43). In other words, Augustine's rendering of the legend lacks both the ascetic zeal and the passion to control and harness Jewish knowledge discernible in Epiphanius's work, as in Jerome's.[7] It reflects instead an emerging theory of biblical interpretation that, as Mark Vessey puts it, "offers to shift the ethical conditions of acceptable or 'successful' exegesis from the realm of asceticism to that of love or charity" and that does so in fairly explicit resistance to Jerome's own attempt to establish, on Origenian foundations, a "'science of Scripture' ... that was at once philologically and ascetically rigorous." Refusing Jerome's *scientia* (his *Wissenschaft*, I am tempted to translate), Augustine, argues Vessey, reframes biblical interpretation as a version of literary conversation: "the joint work of two or more human beings gathered in the presence of God, as an *actus conferendi* or 'conference' performed in the spirit of charity" (1986, 59, 53, 69).

The *Confessions*, written during the same period as Augustine's correspondence with Jerome regarding his translations, offers a window onto this larger hermeneutical project. The text does not refer explicitly to the

---

7. See Jacobs 2004, 44–51.

narrative of the Septuagint, but it does include an alternative narrative of biblical translation—or perhaps rather of its failure. Musing in book 11 on the inaccessibility of Scripture's author, Moses, Augustine remarks on a simple fact: "He wrote and he departed, passing hence from you to you, and he is not now before me." He continues, contrafactually:

> For if he were, I would grab him and entreat him and for your sake beg that he reveal these things to me, and I would offer the ears of my body to the sounds bursting from his mouth. And if he spoke in the Hebrew language, he would beat against my senses in vain and he would not thereby touch my mind in any way; but if he spoke Latin, I would know what he said. But how would I know whether he spoke the truth? (*Confessions* 11.3)

Augustine here gives imaginative body to his yearning to know and love God "from the mouth" of Moses. Yet the scene is as agonistic as it is intimate, and his desire remains unfulfilled even in fantasy. Moses the writer is first imagined to speak "in the Hebrew language" (*hebraea voce*), the eruptive sounds assaulting Augustine's ears without touching his mind. Were Moses, however, to speak Latin, an interpretive dilemma would still remain: How would Augustine know whether he spoke the truth? The issue is clearly not authorship in the usual sense, for Augustine does not question Moses' authority as divinely inspired scribe any more than he doubts that Moses wrote in Hebrew. Nor is the issue translation per se. The issue is, rather, true interpretation—which will be the subject of much of book 12 of the *Confessions*.

To put it more precisely, Augustine has here identified both authorship and translation with interpretation: for Moses *to speak* truly is for Moses *to be read* truly. In the absence of his graspable and audible body, only the elusive text remains. Its interpretation takes place "in the inward habitation of thought," where (contra Jerome) truth is "neither Hebrew nor Greek nor Latin nor barbarian" but is uttered "without organ of mouth or tongue, without clang of syllables," Augustine asserts (11.3). Such interior cognition, paradoxically, seems to invoke and indeed require externalization in an interpretive community—whether an angelic host,[8] seventy Jewish elders, or (closer to home) Augustine and the readers to whom

---

8. "For they always look upon your face, and there they read without syllables in time, what your eternal will enfolds" (*Confessions* 13.15).

his *Confessions* issues an invitation to exegetical dialogue. The goal is not to compete and exclude by claiming to grasp Moses' original and singular intent, Augustine insists (again, contra Jerome), but rather to increase and multiply the possible meanings of Scripture, the semiotic depths of which will never be fully plumbed. "Let truth itself provide *concordia*, in this diversity of true opinions," he urges. "Let us love each other" (12.30). As Vessey observes, "The ground on which Augustine rejects an imaginary conversation with Moses is the ground on which he joins in an imaginary conference with his readers" (1986, 69).[9]

The *Confessions* thus points toward a dialogical hermeneutics that illumines not only what Augustine desires from his (ultimately disappointing) epistolary exchange with Jerome, but also what attracts him to the legend of the miraculous consensus achieved by the seventy *interpretes*—an *actus conferendi* on a grand scale indeed. To be sure, "each sat separately" (*City of God* 18.42). But so too do he and Jerome sit separately, never in fact meeting in the flesh. Augustine can nonetheless assert confidently, at least in his early letters, not only that he imagines himself intimately familiar with Jerome's unseen visage but also that "you love me [*me ... diligis*], both of old through the communion of spirit by which we are knit to each other and more recently through what you know of me from the mouth of my friend." Augustine's friend, Alypius, has visited Jerome, and Augustine himself is joined to Alypius by a union of the heart—*concordia*—so profound that they are two in body but only one in soul (*Epist*. 28.1.1), he assures Jerome. The play between spiritual intimacy and physical distance is mediated by expressions of physical intimacy: when Alypius saw Jerome, asserts Augustine, "I saw, but with his eyes," and Jerome now loves Augustine "from the mouth [*ex ore*]" of Alypius. When the language of spiritual union is echoed in his immediately subsequent description of the Seventy as possessing "greater *concordia* of either judgment or spirit than if they were one person" (*Epist*. 28.2.2), Augustine invites comparison, even identification, with such a harmonious interpretive community. By this point, the verticality initially inscribed by Philo onto the narrative of translation has been firmly crossed by the horizontal dimension of human conversation. Tellingly, it is not "from the mouth" of Moses but "from the mouth" of a friend that the gifts of love and truth arrive.

---

9. Vessey continues: "The third chapter of book eleven of the *Confessions* marks the end of Augustine's apology against Jerome and the beginning of one of the greatest conversations in history" (1986, 70).

As we have seen in the *Confessions*, Augustine links the dialogical context of interpretation with the polysemous character of Scripture. In a work written just a few years later, he asserts more programmatically that "all divine Scripture is twofold [*bipartita*]"—that is, able to be read either figuratively (*secundum figurarum ... intellectum*) or as a faithful account of historical events (*secundum fidem rerum gestarum*) (*Gen. litt.* 1.1.1). His debate with Jerome yields still another insight: the hermeneutical doubling of Scripture is matched by the doubling of the scriptural text itself; for if one text can generate more than one (version of the) truth, so too can one truth generate more than one (version of the) text. By the time he writes book 18 of the *City of God*, the Septuagint becomes not so much the guarantor of scriptural translatability as the instantiation of scriptural multiplicity. When Augustine rests his defense of the Seventy on the claim that Greek and Hebrew versions are faithful to the same spirit, he does not understand that spirit to be separable from its written incarnations, any more than breath is separable from the sound it conveys: *all* of the words, Greek and Hebrew alike, must be preserved. "Anything in the Hebrew text that is not found in that of the seventy translators is something which the Spirit of God decided not to say through the translators but through the prophets. Conversely, anything in the Septuagint that is not in the Hebrew texts is something which the same Spirit preferred to say through the translators. ... Both are one and divine." From this perspective, editions of the Septuagint (e.g., Origen's) that mark the passages where the Greek differs from the Hebrew do not correct a flawed or corrupt translation but rather embody the manifold character of Scripture (*City of God* 18.43–44). Divergence adds depth of meaning by generating a multiplicity of imaginative worlds.

The book of Jonah provides an interesting case. With regard to the plant that shades Jonah in 4:6, Augustine insists that the Septuagint-based rendering of "gourd" be maintained as a legitimate option, as this is how his own Latin-speaking African congregations know and love the story—even if the Hebrew refers to "ivy" or some sturdier vine-like shrub (*Epist.* 71.2.4; cf. Jerome, *Epist.* 75.7.22). Apparently less locally controversial, but also potentially more theologically significant, is the difference between the Hebrew text's announcement at Jonah 3:4 of a forty-day period within which Nineveh will be destroyed and the Septuagint's allowance for a mere three-day space: here Augustine is able to enjoy and profit exegetically from both versions (*City of God* 18.44).

Not despite but because of its posited textual, linguistic, and hermeneutical instability, Augustine's Bible emerges into history as infinitely expansive and ultimately elusive—it enters as the book that, as Vessey suggests, is "in fact absent and *yet* to come" (2007, 272), "a book beyond anyone's capacity to read or write," in Philip Rousseau's suggestive paraphrase of Vessey's Mallarmean point (2007, 9). This book both is and is not Jerome's Bible, or the rabbis'.

* * *

I suggested at the outset that Augustine's understanding of biblical translatability has affinities with the thought of Franz Rosenzweig. Let me here return to that suggestion briefly, by way of conclusion. Rosenzweig was a keen reader of Augustine and was not only familiar with *Confessions* and *City of God* (Ciglia 2004), but also (late in his life) aware of Augustine's debate with Jerome about the Septuagint.[10] My interest lies, however, not so much with how Augustine's writings might once have influenced Rosenzweig's as with how Rosenzweig's theoretical insights may now illumine Augustine's.

Translation was a concept, as well as an activity, that occupied Rosenzweig for much of his life. Seidman quotes the following lines from a letter that he wrote in 1917, at age thirty:

> Translating is after all the actual goal of the mind [*Geistes*]; only when something is translated has it become really *audible*, no longer to be disposed of. Not until the Septuagint did revelation become entirely at home in the world, and as long as Homer did not yet speak in Latin [*lateinisch*] he was not yet a fact. In a corresponding way, also translating from person to person.[11]

As Barbara Galli has argued, this striking passage cuts to the heart of a philosophy of translation that Rosenzweig would continue to develop in subsequent years, which included, first, the writing of his magnum opus, *Star of Redemption*, and subsequently, his translations of the twelfth-century Hebrew poems of Jehuda Halevi and, in collaboration with Martin Buber,

---

10. On February 2, 1928, Rosenzweig writes Catholic church historian Joseph Wittig, requesting sources for the debate: "It was a great surprise to me that the *Itala* [LXX-based Latin translation] was played against Jerome, very similarly to how later Jerome was played against Luther, and now Luther against us" (1979, 2:1179).

11. Letter to Rudolf Ehrenberg, October 1, 1917, cited by Seidman 2006, 156, from the translation of Galli 1995, 322.

of the Hebrew Bible.[12] As the early letter already indicates, for Rosenzweig the Bible is not the Bible—Homer is not Homer[13]—until it has been received by another language. Paradoxically, writing becomes fully a "fact" (*Tatsache*)—or "act-thing" as Rosenzweig elsewhere parses the familiar (and also philosophically weighty) German word[14]—only by losing its singularity. Necessarily a multiplicity, a text emerges *as a text* dialogically, through the temporal processes not of mere writing but of interpretation, translation, response.

Indeed, at base, translation *is* dialogue or communication, for Rosenzweig; conversely, dialogue *is* translation. When successful, translation transforms languages and cultures. As Rosenzweig phrases it in "Scripture and Luther" (1926), a true translation is a one-time "miracle" involving the mating of the spirits of two languages:

> The time for such a *hieros gamos*, for such a Holy Wedding, is not ripe until a receptive people reaches out toward the wing-beat of an alien masterpiece with its own yearning and its own utterance and when its receptiveness is no longer based on curiosity, interest, desire for education, or even aesthetic pleasure, but has become an integral part of the people's historical development. ... A good translator will translate the foreign book into something indigenous.[15]

---

12. As Galli phrases it and goes on to demonstrate: "All the components of Rosenzweig's philosophy of translation are concentrated here" (1995, 322).

13. My primary concern here is with the question of biblical translation. However, Augustine might have felt much the same about Homer as well. In a well-known passage in *Confessions*, he describes how, as a boy, he hated the hard work of secondary-language acquisition and the alienating process of reading in a tongue other than Latin: whereas the bewitching tales of Virgil drew him in all too easily, reading Homer's Greek was a torturously unsatisfying experience to which he was driven only by the threat of beatings, though he recognized that its language and tales must have been as seductive for Greek-speaking boys as Virgil's were for him (1.14.23). It seems to me possible that Rosenzweig has this passage in mind when he refers in the 1917 letter to Ehrenberg to the Septuagint and the latinization of Homer as prime examples of translation as an act of rendering a text audible.

14. See Rosenzweig 2005, 260: "It is not the thing [*Sache*], it is not the act [*Tat*], it is only the fact [*Tatsache*] that is secure against falling back into Nothing."

15. Cited and translated by Galli 1995, 341. Note that Rosenzweig also frames the point in the opposite way, insisting that translation should transform and renew language by bringing something foreign into it: the task for one who translates into German is "not to Germanize what is foreign, but rather to make foreign what is German" (1995, 170).

For Augustine, as we have seen, the composition of the Septuagint is just such a miraculous, transformative *hieros gamos* of Hebrew and Greek, a reception of the Hebrew by the Greek that makes the Bible a *Tatsache*— and also "something indigenous" to Christian culture. Its effects on the latinization of the Christian Bible cannot, then, be ignored. He seems inclined in his early letters to Jerome to view the translation as displacing the original, in his later *City of God* to emphasize rather the fundamental multilingualism of the biblical text, in conjunction with its spiritual unity. If the earlier stance has affinities with Rosenzweig's conviction that translation is what renders a text audible and is thus privileged, the latter resonates with Rosenzweig's claim in the "Afterword" to his Halevi translations that "there is only one language." The dialogue of familiar communication ("translating from person to person") expands into the dialogue of languages and cultures that renders all borders potential gateways of transformation. Thus:

> One can translate because in every language is contained the possibility of every other language; one may translate if one can realize this possibility through cultivation of such linguistic fallow land; and one should translate so that the day of that harmony [*Eintracht*] of languages, which can grow only in each individual language, not in the empty space "between" them, may come. (1995, 171)

To be sure, Rosenzweig sustains his faithfulness to the Hebrew as the particular language of the Jewish Bible, and Augustine his suspicion of a Hebrew text that he views as fully legible only to Jews.[16] But both of them are also drawn irresistibly by the power of translation, closely linked to a capacious dialogism pitched to overwhelm not only the exclusive claims of a professionalized exegetical elite, but also the very boundaries of lin-

---

16. Rosenzweig worries, moreover, that Augustine's location of truth in God, rather than Scripture, compromises his commitment to a multiplicity of meanings. With reference to *Confessions* 12.24.33, he writes: "Here lies the whole relationship of Christianity to the Scripture. The Scripture *contains* truth, but the human recognizes it in *God*, not in the Scripture. The question of the true meaning of the word of Scripture is left in suspense, not as with us eliminated (through the theory of multiple meaning); that is, in Christianity the (singular) meaning is the historical origin of truth, which, however, is recognized (in God) independently thereof; with us the Scripture is the lasting site of the discovery of truth" (*Paralipomena*, February 7, 1916; cited by Ciglia 2004, 228–29).

guistic, cultural, and religious difference. Instead of the promised purity of *Hebraica veritas*, we may discover that there is nothing but the shifting borderspeak of *Yiddish varhayt*—which is where Seidman begins and ends her book. Yet that claim too risks an infelicitous idealization. After all, Yiddish is a dying language, as Seidman notes mournfully; having become burdened with too many unspeakable secrets, it now must bear its own translation. Instead of the promised purity of *Hebraica veritas*, we discover *what*, then? Translations, interpretations—an ongoing conversation about the book that is too vast to be either written or read by anyone.

"His Love Has Been Our Banner on Our Road": Identity Politics and the Revised Version

Alan H. Cadwallader

"His Love has been our banner on our road." This is a line from a hymnlike poem composed by Edward Bickersteth.[1] It was offered by private printing to his fellow members of the Company for the Revision of the Authorized Version of the New Testament.[2] The engineered warmth of self-congratulations among the twenty-four members was occasioned by the conclusion of the second draft revision in late 1878.

It had been a long haul of almost nine years since the work of revision began in the Jerusalem Chamber of Westminster Abbey. There had been bonds of friendship forged between members of the company who had come from different Christian confessions, such as that between the Methodist William Moulton and the Anglican Brooke Foss Westcott.[3] There had been some semblance of reconciliation or at least appeasement between combatants such as Henry Alford, Joseph Blakesley, and Frederick Scrivener forged over their common interest in grammar, text, and

---

1. Bickersteth did hold a minor claim to the combination of bishop and poet (Aglionby 1907). He had published a poem to launch the revision in 1870 in *The Guardian*, July 6, 1870 (p. 804).

2. *CUL Ms Add. 9739 Resolution of Friday Dec. 13, 1878, day on which concluded Second Revision*, Robert Scott Papers, folder 3. Archival and manuscript abbreviations are from Cadwallader 2007.

3. Moulton to Westcott April 30, 1897 (*Adelaide Theological Library* [Rare Books and Manuscripts]). Moulton writes of his "abounding gratitude" to Westcott for his "guidance, help and friendship." This was cultivated through the years of work on the RV New Testament, the RV Apocrypha, and regular correspondence. See Westcott to Moulton's son, February 22, 1898 (Methodist Archives, Moulton Collection [University of Manchester, John Rylands Library] II.483).

translation.[4] Almost two years later, the actual finale to the work of revision—the "third revision" as Westcott called it[5]—was celebrated by a service of prayer organized at St. Martins-in-the-Fields by the vicar, the Reverend W. G. Humphry, also a member of the New Testament committee.[6] By the time the formally authorized revision was published in February 1881, its preface declaimed the manifest unity, collegiality, and harmony exhibited among the many members of the committee (Ellicott 1881, xi). The public identity of the group that was presented to its authorizing body and its potential readership was of a common cohort that had fulfilled its charge.[7] That same body "HUMBLY presented to HER MOST GRACIOUS MAJESTY QUEEN VICTORIA" a vellum-bound copy contemporaneously with the presentation of the work to the two houses of the sponsoring body, the Convocation of Canterbury in the Church of England.[8]

Yet the delay of two and a half years following Bickersteth's premature celebratory conclusion of the project, the noneucharistic liturgy held at a London parish church—and a Church of England establishment at that—the combination of sovereign and ecclesial body, even the very protestation of unity, indicate on closer examination fissures in the monolith of amiable equanimity about the project. The delay of two and a half years was in part due to an honoring of a compensatory salve to determined American ambitions to have an input into decisions about matters of translation; the noneucharistic liturgy held away from Westminster Abbey avoided a repeat furor over Nonconformist and Unitarian participation in the work of translation that had threatened to scuttle the project before it began in 1870; the conjunction of monarch and ecclesiastical institution pointed to a major problematization of the role of the Established Church in relation to the state, exacerbated by the refusal of Prime Minister Gladstone to provide legislative or financial backing to enhance the authority of the revision (Cadwallader 2013).

---

4. Samuel Newth, "Minutes of NT Revision, Nov. 8, 1870–July 19, 1872," *BL* Add. 36279, fol. 69.

5. Westcott to Hort July 12, 1880 (*CUL* Ms Add. 6597, fol. 164).

6. *CUL* Ms Add. 9739, Robert Scott Papers, "List of Leaflets Containing Resolutions and other printed papers," printed note dated November 12, 1880.

7. This was actively cultivated by a number of its members, such as Westcott ("Notes on the Critical Study of Holy Scripture," *LPL* 1401, fol. 5–6; see also Westcott 1903, 1:402)

8. *CUL* Ms Add. 9739, Robert Scott Papers, "List of Leaflets Containing Resolutions and other printed papers," resolution dated November 11, 1880.

These three aspects—the relation between an imperial, sovereign nation and the position of an Established Church, the integrity and authenticity of denominations within a nation, and the competitive tensions of national and international prestige and responsibility—highlight in magnified proportions Umberto Eco's insight that translation is not merely about the familiar polarities of source text and target audience. It is about the politics of negotiation about the end-translation, the means by which that point is reached, and the pragmatic factors (time constraints, publication agreements, etc.) that constantly impinge upon decision making (2003).

Eco allows that any translation is enclosed by the "horizon of the translator" (2003, 143–44); but crucial to this is the ideological formulation of personal and group identity, not merely of translation technique. It is a constant and powerful shaper both of positions adopted and promoted in the process and, ultimately, of the final product. Inevitably, in a body as diverse in its membership as the New Testament Revision Company and as subject to strident appeals for expansion, the translation is not merely a compromise but a victory of one position over another, complex and multilayered though it may be. F. J. A. Hort may have lamented that the work among so many members was inevitably full of compromises,[9] but eight Nonconformists, and they from different traditions (including the Unitarian G. Vance Smith), were always to be subject to a prevailing influence, even when their suggestions were accepted. A translation then is both a result and a key reinforcement of a particular identity that has become highly politicized in the process of translation. In this sense, language, even the language of a translation of Sacred Scripture, becomes, as Erving Goffman recognized, a most important player in the subtle business of asserting a position for an individual or group within society (1972, 28). Moreover, as he also argued, the admission of a minority identity relies upon the minority's underlying embrace of the dominant (what he called "Normal") position, even if it be done tactically. The sheer agreement by the eight to serve on the translation company was already an acceptance of the terms of reference laid down by the administrative body (convocation) of the Established Church of England. Accordingly, without any objection, they welcomed the (Anglican) archbishop of Canterbury into

---

9. Hort to Rev. W. C. Bishop, January 17, 1882 (*CUL* Ms Add. 6597, fol. 179); Westcott thought similarly: Westcott to Hort July 12, 1880 (*CUL* Ms Add. 6597, fol. 164); cf. Scrivener 1883, ix. See generally Norton 1993, 179.

the Jerusalem Chamber whenever he felt so inclined to drop in to see how the men were doing.[10] Such an ease of access was allowed no one else, including heads of other churches, even if any attempted it (which they did not).

These two prongs of analysis then, the politics of negotiation and the politics of identity, provide a heuristic device to retrieve and explore the tensions, conflicts, and interests of those involved in the project called the Revision of the Authorized Version. Both are not without limitations or criticism, especially as they may leave unnoticed the fundamental relationship between the literary product and the ideological defense or rationalization of an established position. This provides a relevant transition to the first of the three fields of exploration: the relation between an imperial, sovereign nation and the position of an Established Church.

The Relation between an Imperial, Sovereign Nation and the Position of an Established Church

The critique of the Authorized or King James Version (KJV) actually began within a few years of its publication, and it was reprised many times prior to 1870, both by those who felt alienated by its (paraded) legislative authorization and, later, by those concerned at its inaccuracy (Trench 1859; Lightfoot 1871; Eadie 1876). The American revisers were keen both to show the shortcomings of the Authorized Version and to present their scholarly acumen, already on display in an earlier American revision of 1862–1865, as sufficient for the task of revision (Members of the American Revision Committee 1879). Concern about accuracy became of paramount importance in the mid-nineteenth century as the Established Church felt its influence waning. In some measure, it was held that scientific and skeptical attacks were made the more substantial because of a failure in scientific precision in one of its basic texts, both in its form as translation and in the Greek *Vorlage* on which it relied. "Faithfulness"— one of the key commitments required by the church resolutions that established the committees (Ellicott 1881, x)—was interpreted in the direction of supposed literalness, sacrificing whatever musicality was asserted of the KJV (Westcott 1901, 170, 171). This scientific precision in establishing the Greek New Testament and mimetic literalness in translation were held by

---

10. Newth, "Minutes," *BL* Add. 36279, fol. 29.

some on the company to be principal weapons in the defense of the belief of the ordinary English-speaking Christian against the destabilizing spirit of the age (Westcott 1901, 167). As such, it was considered to be a major contribution to the well-being of the nation and therefore a fulfillment of the role of the church in its *established* position—that is, the service of the nation, its declared character and its perceived providential purpose in the world (in terms of both election and mission). Certainly all these points were raised in welcome to the RV by the editor of a leading London newspaper and supporter of Broad Church views, *The Guardian* (November 16, 1881, 1628–29). They well illustrate David Simpson's observation: "Definitions of national character must be seen as rationalizations of the various political processes whereby the nation-states of Europe were trying either to come into being, to maintain themselves, or to extend their territories and their imagined moral superiorities. Each defines itself in terms of, and usually at the expense of, the others" (Simpson 1993, 41). His larger macrocosmic interpretation needs to be complicated, however, since political positions were also rehearsed in smaller measure *within* the boundaries of nation-states.

Unity and common adherence were fundamental anchorage points for this purpose, although the specifics of both were vehemently debated. Those who were ultimately appointed to the Old or the New Testament company, whether Churchmen or Nonconformist, were already inclined to a broad understanding of unity, namely that the work of translation was to be for the benefit of the whole nation.[11] The dean of Westminster took a leading role in the invitations that were sent throughout the United Kingdom to ensure that scholars from all Christian traditions were represented. This included an unsuccessful attempt to lure John Henry Newman onto the New Testament company.[12] It was known that he, with other members of his Oratory, had begun work in 1857[13] on an English version of the Vulgate (Ward 1912, 1:418–19). His stated reason for his refusal to the 1870 invitation—that he was not a scriptural scholar—belies this, and the manuscript of his earlier revision survived until he burned

---

11. The emphasis on "one nation" and unity of all ranks and classes is a common motif in the discourse of the time; see letter of "T.F." to the editor, *The Guardian*, January 17, 1872 (p. 82).

12. *CUL* Ms Add. 9739.3 (Scott papers).

13. See *The Weekly Register*, September 26, 1857; and *The Guardian*, August 3, 1881 (p. 1095).

it in 1877 (Ward 1912, 1:423). Newman does hint in his letter of decline that there were other reasons (Dessain and Gornall 1973, 25:136). He had been quite wounded by the demise of his own translation project (Ward 1912, 1:427–28). Congregationalist, Baptist, Presbyterian, Methodist, and Unitarian scholars did accept, but Newman's refusal denied any Catholic representation on the revision for the nation.

Even so, when it came to the mechanics and product of translation, the commitment to unity was manifest and was understood substantially as univocal uniformity. A Greek word was to be translated uniformly by a single English word; a distinction between the aorist and the perfect in the Greek verbal system was similarly to find expression in English grammar in the conformity of one to the simple past and the other to the compound form; the presence or absence of the definite article in the source was to be observed in the target text. Westcott argued successfully that where there were Synoptic parallels, the Matthean form that had been translated first determined the form in the other Gospels.[14] Whatever criticism of this approach may have come from members of the company—and some of the Nonconformist scholars were hesitant about the rigidity—became invisible in the final result and in the eventual scrupulosity of members in adhering to what became the accepted principle of translation technique. It was not that these applications of uniformity were uncontested at the time (Moon 1882); even Westcott's own son would later concede that the "aoristization" of the translation was not only clumsy but also inaccurate.[15]

According to others, however, unity was not necessarily to be found in a common production of a major new, even more accurate, text. There were two other conceptions of unity reverberating at the time, related but yet distinct. The first was a recommitment to that which was past. The sheer longevity of the hold of the KJV was a major element in the argument that English identity was substantially formed in and upon the language and cadences of that translation. The leading liberal politician, William Gladstone, used the well-publicized division in the Established Church over the merits of a revision of an authorized version to argue against any state involvement.[16] Edward Cavendish in the War Office was similarly con-

---

14. Minute Book of the Revised Version New Testament Company, June 27, 1871 (*CUL* Ms Add. 6935, fol. 301).

15. Letter of (Frederick) Brooke Westcott to the editor, *The Times* March 22, 1912.

16. W. Gladstone to A. Stanley (dean of Westminster) May 4, 1870, *BL* Add. Ms 44318, fol. 94.

cerned about the project's demonstrated capacity to foster disputes.[17] "The hectoring tone of Mr. Gladstone" about the Revised Version (RV), as one reviser termed it,[18] effectively stalled the effort to make the RV a buttress to the relations between the government and the Established Church. Gladstone himself wrote, "The English nation, while they retain their senses, never can assent to such a substitution as this" (Matthew 1990, 200). The default to the KJV promoted the position of the more conservative wing of that church in its tenacious grip on the past as the strategic means to deal with the challenges of the present. The same model of preserving the supposed purity of the past as the means of securing national and ecclesial identity unleashed a strident objection to the presence of Nonconformists in the work of revision.[19] The objection hit fever pitch when the Communion service held in the Henry VII Chapel at the Abbey was opened to all, including the Unitarian minister, G. Vance Smith. Petitions were mounted against the involvement of "teachers of other sects,"[20] cries of heresy riddled the newspapers and pulpits, objections were brought to the the minority houses of convocation, one member resigned from the Old Testament company,[21] another soon followed from the New Testament company (Merivale 1898, 457–62) and the whole enterprise was on the verge of collapse (Cadwallader 2007). So vehement became the recriminations that, more than once, *The Guardian* newspaper tried to stop unrelenting debate in its pages.[22] The bishop of Manchester (James Fraser)

---

17. Edward Cavendish to Stanley, May 10, 1870: *CUL* 6946, "Letters to the Revised Version New Testament Company," fol. 4.

18. C. J. Vaughan to Alex Macmillan (the publisher) in *BL* Add. Ms 55113, fol. 78.

19. H. P. Liddon (Canon of St Paul's London) to J. B. Lightfoot, February 21, 1871 (*DDC* Lightfoot Papers). For the public debate, see *The Guardian*, November 23, 1870: "The same principle closes the altar of the Church against the willful Anabaptist, or Presbyterian which closes it against the willful Swedenborgian or Unitarian" (quotation of a Mr. Skinner's letter to the editor).

20. *The Guardian* reported one such memorial containing fifteen hundred signatures (August 24, 1870). The dean of Chichester, John Burgon, was one of the extreme polemicists and one of the better organized for a battle at a national level (Goulburn 1892, 2:45 and n. 9).

21. Canon John Jab had not attended the Communion service, claiming an inability to arrive in time, yet, in a letter to Dean Stanley, had welcomed the chance to receive it together (*The Guardian*, December 7, 1870 [p. 18]). This was a public "graciousness" that masked a disquieted conscience.

22. *The Guardian*, October 10, 1870 (p. 958).

might write: "The united Communion in Westminster Abbey, which some so strangely delight to carp at, but which was a source of lively satisfaction to me, proved the possibility of union in an act of common worship, of those who differ, even widely, on points of dogma. When men can be brought to kneel down side by side, dogmatic differences cannot long continue to sever hearts that own one common Lord."[23] Such an argument had particular force in a climate that included ongoing tensions with the Roman Catholic Church, which in July of the same year had passed the Edict of Papal Infallibility. This had been widely criticized in the English Church's convocation as fatally flawed since the claim to an "Ecumenical Conciliar" decision was a fiction "if Christians from other provinces were not included."[24]

Nevertheless, for the champions of Anglican purity, such double standards in argument were irrelevant. Sectarian and "Socinian"[25] involvement hopelessly soiled the work before it began and steeled the resolve of RV antagonists to influence the direction of the translation (Burgon 1871)[26] and to plot the demise of the text once it was published.[27] The role of the Established Church in relation to the state was deemed to lie most powerfully in the maintenance of its privileged position, whether that be in the work of translation or in controlling participation in common worship. The perceived power of the Authorized Version for the security of the state was nowhere more apparent than in Ireland, where upholding the KJV became a sign of loyalty to the English Crown. Accordingly the common language of unity and union was brandished by sides in open conflict with one another, both of which focused, for and against, on the work of translation of the Bible, both of which were prepared to make use of the denominations (positively and negatively) as weapons in their struggle.

---

23. *The Guardian,* July 20, 1870 (p. 848).

24. *The Guardian,* July 20, 1870 (p. 857).

25. "Socinian," with its associations of heresy, was a status-denigration label applied to Unitarians.

26. Burgon's intent was only stalled by a rapid yet expert refutation by F. J. A. Hort (one of the revisers) published in *The Academy* magazine on November 15, 1871, one day before the company was to deal with the textually troublesome passage of Mark 16:9–20.

27. Throughout the 1880s, a succession of public letters, lectures, pamphlets, and books followed in the wake of the RV.

The Integrity and Authenticity of Denominations within a Nation

The receipt of an invitation by those of Christian traditions categorized as "Nonconformist" did not always meet with a positive response—as we have seen in the case of Newman. Neither was it always offered with unanimity.[28] However, most invitees did accept and saw their involvement as a mark of recognition and an opportunity to advance their constituencies' place as an authentic player in the nation and in the weighty responsibility for the translation of the Scriptures. Their formal identity surfaced explicitly in 1871 at the death of Dean Alford, one of the members of the company. In the momentary interruption to proceedings for the New Testament company to express their sympathies, both the Presbyterian, John Eadie, and the Baptist, Joseph Angus, specifically declared that they "spoke as non-conformists."[29] There was, accordingly, an appearance of unity-in-diversity in the record of condolences.

However, when the harboring of their self-defining identity as Nonconformists came under the microscope of revision of specific verses of the New Testament, the result was quite different. Ordinarily, the gatherings of the company at the Jerusalem Chamber at Westminster Abbey[30] on four to five days every month were the main drive for the translation and were uneventful. Members were expected to come with their notes in readiness for the work—some even forwarded their preparations to the chair (Ellicott) for submission when attendance was impossible.[31] At such

---

28. In the heat of the "Westminster Scandal," a printing of an exchange of letters between the bishop of Gloucester and Bristol (C. J. Ellicott) and the chief organizer of the company, the Very Reverend Arthur Stanley, was privately circulated among the members of the New Testament company. In it, Stanley noted that the members of the convocation were far from unanimous in support for an invitation to Newman or G. Vance Smith: *Printing of exchange of letters between Stanley and the Bishop of Gloucester & Bristol re threatened change to RV Comm. 1871 CUL* Ms Add. 9739, Scott papers, folder 8.

29. Newth, "Minutes" *BL* Add. 36279, fol. 69a.

30. The Westminster dean, Arthur Stanley, was as quick to offer the Abbey's resources as he was to drive the politics of the move for the revision. A place common to the Authorized Version and its revision was touted as one of the symbols of continuity between the two. What London may have lacked in centrality (the archbishop of Dublin was an infrequent attendee), the chamber compensated in its significance.

31. The preparations of J. W. Blakesley (dean of Lincoln) are noted in Newth's

meetings, there was a certain leveling of denominational differences as each member found their respective textual and grammatical observations and translation suggestions challenged, refined, and accepted or rejected.[32] The method of decision was by a vote requiring a simple majority in the deliberations of the first revision draft and a two-thirds majority for any changes made during the second.

However, when an individual felt strongly enough about a verse for translation either in prospect or retrospect, he resorted to a private note, usually printed, which was circulated among the members. The repeated call or demand for privacy and confidentiality ensured that divisions never circulated in public.[33] Nevertheless, within the heady atmosphere of the Jerusalem Chamber, particular denominational or party affiliations did surface, as revealed in the personal notebooks and printed papers of members. Negotiations became intense when the niceties of grammar correlated with the ideology of group identity. Repeatedly, individual representatives of nonestablished denominations reveal how much their identity is either grounded in or sought confirmation from a turn of phrase in the Bible as they argued forcefully for a self-confirming translation. At the same time, the challenge that such individuals made to the Established Church majority on the company is manifest in the counter-arguments and voting patterns that resisted alternate translations. Two examples will suffice.

Joseph Angus, in a privately printed circulation to the members, argued strenuously that the Greek of Matthew 3:11, βαπτίζω ἐν ὕδατι, should be translated "baptize *in* water," not "*with* water" (as also "*in* the Holy Spirit and fire"). He laid out a range of reasons, ranging from Septuagintal usage through the symbolism of Pentecost to the majority of early

---

personal minute books as in the chairperson's possession when Blakesley was late in attendance: *BL* Add. 36279, fol. 27b.

32. The suggestion that the Cambridge triumvirate and especially Westcott and Hort dominated both the proceedings and the result of the translation is simply not borne out by the facts as recorded in the voting patterns written down in the notebooks of Westcott (only Matthew extant) and Samuel Newth (complete). To my knowledge, no other member either recorded the voting patterns (*quaere* William Moulton) or has had their records survive. In fact, at least in the early period, Charles Vaughan was frequently successful in receiving support for his suggestions; Hort often stood alone.

33. See, as but one example, Samuel Newth, "Minutes of NT Revision" *BL* Add. 36279, fol. 65.

English translations.³⁴ This last was a potentially powerful argument given that, in the "Principles and Rules" laid down by resolution of the houses of convocation to guide the revision, the language of revision was to follow as far as possible "the language of the Authorised and earlier English Versions" (Ellicott 1881, xi). But in this case, the KJV rendering of "with" won out against the "in" of Wycliffe and Tyndale's translations. Angus could, perhaps tactically should, have added that in John and in the Paulines, the Established Church's Regius Professor at Cambridge, Brooke Foss Westcott, had accented that the full weight of ἐν should be affirmed (as in the change made to Phil 2:10). His own theology relied in its foundation on the repetition of "in Christ."

For Baptist commitments, baptism by immersion was central (Wosh 1994, 142–45), and Angus, for forty-four years president of the Baptist College in London, was appointed as a learned articulator, indeed ideologue, of the Baptist position (Armitage 1890, 588; Payne 1942, 229, 232). He had written at length about Baptist history and writings and had noted the persecutions that his group had suffered in the past. Baptist identity was bound to the translation of ἐν not as an instrumental but as a locative. However, the sheer weight of numbers of those on the company who were content with the general use of, rather than specific immersion in, water, saw the instrumental retained. Angus's criticism remained marginal, quite literally, as the brief "or *in*" found its way into the marginal note of the second draft and the final published revision. And with this marginalization was placed also his denomination's nonconformity.

Angus was bound by the terms of confidentiality, which had been a condition of participation, to accept the decision. He had felt the full force of rebuff when it was suggested that, at one private lecture, he had breached this binding rule (Cadwallader 2007, 424). Only private papers reveal the conflict over identity, as nothing of this was permitted either in the media release or even in the minutes of revision proceedings kept by the secretary, John Troutbeck. Angus himself had argued that "churches were always independent associations of men as equals" (Angus and Waddington 1862, 8); he may have considered his service on the RV company as an example of this or an attempt to gain it, just as

---

34. *CUL* Ms Add. 9739, Scott, folder 7. *Printed and hand-written suggestions re translations*: "Notes on the Gospel of Matthew by J.A.," note 3. Angus also provided another extended note on the atonement, similarly seeking the clarification of the translation and its formatting so as to accommodate Baptist understandings more sensitively.

he collected autograph signatures on books (especially by eminent non-Baptists) for the Regent Park college library (Whelan 2004). His hard lesson was that at the point of key differences of identity, all his reception onto the company for his criticism of the KJV and his undoubted learning were insufficient to have his particular views adopted. In Goffman's conception of "the stigmatized," the acceptance of the invitation to membership of the New Testament Revision Committee had led to the belief that the Nonconformist invitee was more accepted than he was, a belief that evaporated right at the moment when the unwanted stigma was given particular notice (Goffman 1963, 45–46, 145).

By contrast, the Unitarian G. Vance Smith seemed little disturbed by these issues. He also raised a sustained argument for a translation that was more conducive to his religious affiliation. Romans 9:5 was a heavily debated verse precisely because it potentially held considerable support for Unitarian dogma. The prime debate focused on punctuation. The first revision of the company drafted the rendering, "Christ as concerning the flesh, who is over all, God blessed for ever. Amen." Vance Smith argued for "Christ as concerning the flesh. He who is God over all *is* [or *be*] blessed for ever. Amen"; that is, separating the Godhead from the Christ.[35] One can see clearly the value of one of these options for the Unitarian position.

Vance Smith had been attacked for his sheer presence on the company at the beginning of its life because of his failure to hold to the ancient creeds of Christendom;[36] he had been vilified for his alleged hypocrisy in attending the opening service of Holy Communion, a service held by some to be dependent on adherence to Christian doctrine such as the Trinity;[37] and he was the continued target of belligerents for his failure to admit the full Godhead of Christ.[38] In one letter to the editor of *The Guardian*, he was equated with Jews, whom no one held should be represented on the committee (but see *Hansard* 1870, 100). In another, he

---

35. CUL Ms Add. 9739 Robert Scott Papers, folder 4, "From the Expositor on Rom IX.5."

36. *The Guardian*, August 3, 1870 (p. 912). The charge was also directed in general to some of the other dissenters (*The Guardian*, August 10, 1870 [p. 942]). Angus, for example, had clearly held that creeds, even Baptist ones, were merely representations "in a general way [of] the sentiment of the body" (Schaff 1882, 852).

37. *The Guardian*, August 3, 1870 (p. 911).

38. *The Guardian*, August 18, 1875 (p. 1058), letter to the editor from William White, FSA.

was equated with a "Mahomet" with similar intent.[39] This may have made him seek from the beginning of the company's discussion of Rom 9:5 the compromise position of having a margin option for the alternative that he proposed. He harnessed the same breadth of scholarly argumentation as had Angus; he mentioned modern authorities, Pauline style, Greek syntax, punctuation in ancient manuscripts (even contradicting the authority of Tischendorf), septuagintal precedents, and the more general appeal that marginalia had been allocated in far less contested cases than this. He even pointed out that he had a sizable, though not two-thirds, of the committee with him.

In the final agreement on the manuscript for publication, the innocuous marginal cross-references for Rom 9:5 in the first draft revision gave way to one of the longest marginal notes in the whole work.[40] It included all the options of punctuation and translation that Vance Smith had mentioned. After the publication of the work, Vance Smith held to the commitment "not to breach 'private and confidential' printed upon all the different sections of the work" (Smith 1881a, 917), even though he asserted his right to continue to dissent where he felt it necessary. These statements, it should be noted, were published in the journal *The Nineteenth Century*. The inclusion of his commentary in a non-Unitarian journal was a mark of his growing acceptance in the wider Christian scholarly community. He continued his defense of Unitarian positions (Smith 1881b) but that identity, articulated through his learning, had, it seemed, won a significant wider church appreciation within the United Kingdom. He had accepted the stigma attached to his Unitarian position and in so doing had gained a level of acceptance among those defining and representing "normal" Christianity so as to find a place within the frame (Goffman 1963, 135). For Vance Smith and for the constituency he represented, a marginal note became a major sign of acceptance. For those outside the United Kingdom, the matter was somewhat different. To this I turn.

---

39. *The Guardian*, August 3, 1870 (p. 912); August 10, 1870 (p. 957).

40. The margin read: "Some modern interpreters place a full stop after *flesh* and translate, *He who is God over all be (is) blessed for ever*: or, *He who is over all is God, blessed for ever*. Others punctuate, *flesh, who is over all, God be (is) blessed for ever.*"

The Competitive Tensions of National and International Prestige and Responsibility

In the furor over Vance Smith's inclusion in the revision company and in the Communion service, an effort was made to adjust the resolutions of the houses of convocation that established the project, so as to have him excluded. Dean Stanley led the charge to retain the original wording of the resolution as defending the right of the company to have the presence of a Unitarian scholar. The particular words that he relied upon were that the Convocation Committee for Old Testament and New Testament companies was to "invite the cooperation of any eminent for scholarship, to whatever nation or religious body they may belong."[41] In the same letter, which was printed (no doubt as part of the political pressuring of the New Testament company chair, Bishop Ellicott to revert to the original intent), Stanley underscored the intended breadth of the Revision by adding, "With the express view of carrying out its intention, and in direct reference to it, I have according to the instructions given to me, entered into arrangements, as you know, with the scholars of the USA." Here the argument, it would seem, was that the U.S. scholars were to be in the same position as Vance Smith, that is, full members of the companies with at least declared equality of contribution and voting. Some involvement of the Americans had been proposed by the bishop of Rochester in the upper house of convocation, but the exact terms of this involvement, in spite of the apparent parallel with the instance of Vance Smith, remained in dispute. Indeed, the effort to involve the Americans in a collaborative venture for revision was raised in Parliament. Gladstone expressly opposed American involvement, even though he was no friend of the project in general (*Hansard* 1870, 112). National pride and integrity in the international sphere seems to have weighed more than denominational allegiance for the prime minister.

Nevertheless, by late 1871, an American Revised Version Committee was being formed, though substantially comprising a membership that in England was tagged Nonconformist.[42] The reaction of some in the United

---

41. The resolution was passed on May 3 and 5 by the upper and lower houses of convocation. Stanley made these words the foundation of his lengthy letter to Bishop Ellicott arguing against any proposed changes: Stanley to Ellicott February 9, 1871 (*CUL* Add. Ms 9739, Scott folder 8).

42. *The Christian Intelligencer,* December 14, 1871.

States was to use an argument for American inclusion against Unitarians and Nonconformists but for a Pan-Anglican group. "The proper body to inaugurate such a movement would seem to be," wrote John Antekell of Connecticut to *The Guardian*, "not an English convocation nor an American Convention, but a Pan-Anglican Synod, representing all the English-speaking races. Let Dissent take care of itself—we want a Bible for Churchmen."[43] The Diocese of Illinois in its Synod commented on "the marked exclusiveness of the movement."[44] The issue of membership, at denominational and national levels, continued to be controversial. One Episcopalian priest, in the light of the apparent dearth of Episcopalian biblical scholars, argued strongly in favour of including "the very men who have done most to make American scholarship respectable in England," as helping to make an accurate Bible for all English-speaking people.[45] A similar proposition is heard from Ezra Abbot, one of the members of the American committee.[46] Within a couple of months of the beginning of the American company's work, however, it became clear that the involvement of those outside the United Kingdom was to be at a less influential and adjudicating level.

This is the nub of the relative positioning. In Abbot's letter, there was a desire for recognition by England of the merit of biblical scholarship in the United States. The work of translation was particularly fit for that demonstration. The issue of standing and status lies in the background with the desire by the younger nation to assert its credentials in what was then a crucial arena of play. By contrast, from the English position, there was the undoubted sense of superiority about its education and learning, even when some of the committee, such as Westcott and Lightfoot, had already shared in scholarly enterprises with some Americans. There was, more deeply, a subtle argument that yet preserved English ascendancy. The KJV was the product of English scholarship; it was argued as a consequence that responsibility for the repair of its faults and failures must accordingly lie primarily with the English. Consequently, the American Bible Revision Company was told it was to have no vote on the changes.[47] Matters were

---

43. *The Guardian*, November 23, 1870 (p. 1367).
44. *The Guardian*, October 5, 1870 (p. 1179).
45. *The Guardian*, March 27, 1872 (p. 421).
46. Abbot to Lightfoot January 5, 1872 (*DDC* Lightfoot Papers).
47. The Americans received this notification on October 1, 1873, at their meeting

not helped by what was interpreted by the English company to be repeated instances of "literary piracy."[48]

The American committee persisted in its search for equal standing and recognition. They submitted their revision on a large part of the Pentateuch and the Gospels to enable the English members "to form a correct estimate of the character and merits of our cooperation with them in the joint work." Given the confidence that the old world's scholars would recognize the integrity and worth of their work, they went on to seek clarification of what was declared to be "the unsettled question of our precise status." They declared that they entered on the "trust" of their work "under the impression that we were fellow-revisers, and not simply advisers."[49]

Matters came to a head with the visit of Philip Schaff to England in May 1875. Schaff laid an impassioned and at times manipulative plea before both English companies in June and July. There were warnings of the threat to the success of the work if it became known that the Americans were not fellow *revisers*, but merely *advisers*. He allowed that the English revisers were the initiators of, even the eminent contributors to "this great work." But he also pointed out the imitation of the English in the structure and methodology of the American Revised companies, even speaking of the American inheritance from the English of "a spirit of self-respect and manly independence that will never consent to occupy a subordinate and humiliating position." He reminded them that Scotland, with its independent, Episcopalian polity was in a similar position to the Americans ecclesially yet had the advantage of proper representation. Schaff accented that the American revisers paid their own expenses and added a further monetary incentive: without proper representation, he could not guarantee protection of the copyright invested in the English revision. His plan, however, was that with American representation possessing equal rights of voting, an agreement could be reached that may yet allow a common text with minor variations.

The oratorical flights did not modify the polite firmness of the English. A carefully worded statement was delivered to Dr. Schaff that asserted

---

at Bible House in New York: *CUL* 6946, "Letters to Revised Version New Testament Company," fol. 39.

48. Stanley to Schaff, December 14, 1871; Schaff to Ellicott, January 7, 1880; Thayer to Ellicott, January 31, 1880, *CUL* 6946, fol. 23, 95, 98.

49. Resolution of March 26, 1875: *CUL* Ms Add. 9739, Scott, folder 3. "Resolution of the American Committee."

that the original constitution of the committee and subsequent agreements entered into with the university presses precluded concession to the American appeal. The ambiguity in the resolution about an invitation for "the cooperation of any eminent for scholarship, to whatever nation or religious body they may belong," which had been used to *retain* the Englishman, Vance Smith, with full voting rights on the New Testament company, was the same text relied upon to resist the American claim. The negotiations over the process of translation had become driven by the interests in preserving national identity against the assertiveness and interests of a younger nation, even at the potential expense of the quality of the translation. Even so, for the sake of accentuating a unity across the international span, the American companies found themselves in the preface to the published RV as formed "for the purpose of acting with the two English Companies" (Ellicott 1881, ix). Perhaps there was a desire to shore up the sales of the product as well.

In the aftermath, the veiled threats of Schaff came to naught, in part mollified by the commitment of the English companies to consider suggestions made by their American colleagues. The commitment took more than two years to fulfill, given the erudite, carefully printed responses submitted by the Americans. In spite of the claim by Ellicott in his defense of the Revision before an English audience that there were "singularly few and unimportant" differences in the American recommendations as to text (Ellicott and Palmer 1882, 30), the details of the differences over translation reveal a different story. In Matt 14, as but one randomly chosen example, fifteen American recommendations for changes to the second draft revision were made. Three suggestions were accepted and one further with a variation. This proportion (20 percent) is representative of the entire revision. Ultimately, the American Revision adopted far more of its own recommendations for the American Standard Version, published in 1901; *some* were noted in an appendix to the English RV, a device that ended up accenting the lack of equality across the Atlantic yet a desire to allow a measure of recognition to the Americans. No variant reading from Matt 14 made it into the published appendix.

The noble trust of making accessible to as wide an English readership as possible the Word of God in as pure a form as possible—this was the constant rhetoric of proposal and defense—became in reality a defense of the interests of national identity in such a way as to allow an opportunity by those of more marginal identities to stake a claim for greater inclusion within the nation. That the groups and representative individuals involved made varying gains is itself testimony to the conflicts and compromises involved in the negotiations determining any translation project. More importantly, however, it illustrates that in the instance of the RV, the national identity, to which marginalized groups of that nation and international countries of shared backgrounds alike aspired, held sway on the RV company, retaining control over the process and the outcome. As such, all—marginalized and international groups—were pressed into the service of a barely articulated dominant ideology. The irony was that the hold on the national identity remained more strongly in the text that the RV was supposed to replace. The son of one of the leading scholars on the New Testament Revision Company, Frederick Brooke Westcott, wrote in 1912, "To hope that the laborious version of 1881 will finally win its way is to hope for an impossibility."[50] However, the complexity of struggles over the text for the ideological strengthening of particular identities continued. And though the revision did not become the anticipated supplanter, it had severely shaken the KJV. The resultant fissures in the KJV edifice became cracks that would topple its dominance of the English Bible skyline in the century ahead.

---

50. Letter to the editor, *The Times*, March 22, 1912.

Seeing Is Believing:
Children's Bibles as Negotiated Translation*

Jaqueline S. du Toit

> I should like to mention a problem that is quite specific to children's books: the question of illustrations. One may argue that illustrations are not part of the problem of translation. However, I would like to claim that they pose a very special translation problem, as they convert texts into pictures. (Stolt 2006, 78)

Two challenges to the understanding of children's Bibles form the basis of this chapter. First, appreciating the contribution of "narrative representation" (Kress and van Leeuwen 1996) or "the delicate counterpoint between image and written text" (Lathey 2010, 8) for the enterprise of cross-generational knowledge transfer; and second, the "invisibility" (Venuti 2008) or "transparency" (Lathey 2010, 5) of authors/storytellers/translators of children's Bibles, including how the motivation for such transparency differs from translators' invisibility in secular adult literature as alluded to by Lawrence Venuti.

The reading of images and the preoccupation with visual appeal are important but underappreciated components for understanding the character and purpose of children's Bibles and Bible storybooks. Moreover, the pervasive presence of pictures and illustrations in this genre is tolerated by religious collectives with traditionally strong pretentions to aniconism. In

---

* This chapter represents research conducted as part of a larger project entitled "Bible Interpretation in Children's Literature. The Transfer and Interpretation of Bible (Religious) Knowledge from Diverse Institutional and Parental Sources to Children: Visual and Literary Interplay." The project is funded by the South African National Research Foundation's (NRF) Thuthuka Program. Any opinion, findings, and conclusions or recommendations expressed in this material are those of the author. The NRF does not accept any liability in regard thereto.

fact, the visual attraction of these rich and colorful renderings of the Bible in child-appropriate format is one of the aspects, along with the strong emphasis on the inculcation of societal values and norms, that makes these books commercially viable outside the confines of confessional affiliation and the parameters of religious community.

Different from the popular move in recent years toward attempts at "transmediazation" (Soukop and Hodgson 1999, 3) in the translation of the Hebrew, Aramaic, and Greek source text into alternative media and by means of new technologies primarily intended for an adult audience, children's Bibles have always maintained a close synthesis of picture and text from their medieval inception: "Picture Bibles united summaries to rhymes in conjunction with images. The illustrated Old Testaments published by the Trechsels in Lyons (1538 et seq.) and the Strasbourg *Bible for the Laity* (1540) of Wendelin Rihel were among the first post-Reformation productions of this type." Ruth Bottigheimer (1996, 11–12) continues by elaborating on the purpose of these Bibles: "Rihel wrote that children and simple folk would benefit from the combination of illustration, plot summary, and verse recapitulation whose repetition would fix each story's content in their memory. Such picture Bibles did not offer stories per se, but they began to approach the sustained narrative that would later be found in the Bible stories Hartmann Beyer excerpted from Luther's translation of the Bible (1555 et seq.)."

The combined target audience of "children" and "simple folk" is worth noting. To this day children's Bibles and picture books often aim to serve a dual audience, mostly for reasons of economy and a perceived common intent at evangelizing. The target audience is as much the illiterate and semiliterate adult convert, served by the educational and persuasive presentation of the biblical text, as the child audience.[1] The illiterate or semiliterate child (or lap reader) follows the story by means of accom-

---

1. Cf., e.g., the isiZulu, Afrikaans, and Setswana translations of the English source text, respectively: *Indaba Ebalulekile Kunazo Zonke Ezake Zaxoxwa* (1999), *Die Belangrikste Storie ooit Vertel* (2000), and *Kinane e e Gaisang Tsothle: The Most Important Story Ever Told* (2002).

The broader research project on which this chapter is based makes exclusive use of children's Bible resources readily available in commercial bookstores and online in South Africa. All children's Bibles quoted, unless otherwise indicated, are in either English or Afrikaans, two of the eleven official languages of South Africa. For a discussion of the disproportionate nature of language representation in children's Bibles on the South African market, see du Toit and Beard 2007.

panying pictures while read to by an adult intermediary, usually at bedtime.[2] The children's Bible's perceived ability to serve a dual audience is easily explained in terms of the still prevailing nineteenth-century notion of childhood as an incomplete state of adulthood to which formal and informal education is the conduit. This notion has persevered, especially in religious education, and implies that the child reader is just as much a potential convert as any adult to be persuaded by educational induction into a state of conformity to the social norms ("tradition") of the adult religious collective.

Furthermore, the strong ties children's Bibles have to didactic translation (cf. Lathey 2010, 15–29) have allowed their highly selective adaptation of the source text to be tolerated within religious traditions otherwise strongly regulated by strict adherence to canon.[3] The emphasis on education belies the pretention to entertainment displayed in the colorful illustrations and easy playfulness encapsulated in the visual presentation or "translation" of the medium. Kenneth Taylor's foreword to parents in *Family-Time Bible in Pictures* (1992, 1) is more explicit than most in expressing this: "Young children are wide open to spiritual truth—more than children will be at any later age. Now is the best time to read Bible stories to them." The dual audience and the burden of persuasive purpose inherent to children's Bibles, disguised by the prettifying illustrative presentation, fits within Zohar Shavit's (1986, 64) explanation of texts that do not easily fit within the rigid status categories traditionally assigned to all texts within the literary system: "This status can be described in terms of

---

2. See, e.g., Kenneth Taylor's *Family-Time Bible in Pictures* (1992) with explicit instructions on the back cover on how the children's Bible should be utilized by parents: "Read along and watch the Bible come to life for your children," or the purpose implicit in the title of *Read Together Bible for Young Readers*: "You read to me, I'll read to you. We can read together too!" (Bruno and Reinsma 2007, 7).

3. The sense of discomfort caused by such free adaptation is felt especially within conservative religious communities. As this development has established traction within the broader religious tradition, it has found expression in a new kind of "children's Bible" sold in a child-friendly cover and size (smaller and more manageable for smaller hands to grip) and promising pictures (often grouped together in the middle or end of the Bible, that is, not adjacent to the narrative it illustrates), but containing the full text of the adult translation with no alteration of language register for a child audience. See, e.g., the, *Holy Bible for Little Hearts and Hands: New Living Translation* (2007).

binary opposition: either the text is for children or for adults, either it is canonized or non-canonized."

Children's Bibles and Canon

It is the ambivalent canonical status of these texts that is particularly important for explaining the strong emphasis on assigning children's Bibles the status of translation instead of radical reworkings or retellings of the biblical source text. This despite little evidence of a tradition of consultation of the Hebrew, Aramaic, and Greek source text by authors of children's Bibles coming from the United States and the United Kingdom, where most South African derivatives originate.[4] Instead, children's Bibles find legitimacy for their liberal adaptation of the source text in the claim to authority as "translation" of the source text. This despite the fact that in most instances these Bibles may at most claim to be generous adaptations of an adult mediating English translation of the source text channeled via an American or British children's Bible. The latter is often translated by means of formal equivalence with no alteration to or adaptation of the accompanying images.[5] In order to sustain for their product the status as "translation of," children's Bible authors and illustrators (the combined "translators") go to great lengths to establish claims of close adherence to source text in their rendition of the Bible for children. Hence the fidelity to the adult version implicit in the titles and subtitles of children's Bibles that tend to imply simply a change of register from adult to child, rather than any radical adaptation or abbreviation of the source text. See, for example, Leena Lane and Gillian Chapman's *My Eerste Bybel* (2005a) from the British source text, *My First Bible* (2005b); *The Bible for Little Ones* (2007); *The Beginner's Bible* (DeVries 2007); and *My First Message: A Devotional Bible for Kids* (Peterson 2007).

The impetus to establish children's Bibles' status as translations is the result of the authority bestowed by the religious tradition on a perceived

---

4. For example, the Afrikaans and Sesotho translations (with no accompanying "translation" of format or illustrations) of *The Lion's Children's Bible* (Alexander 1991), *My Gunsteling Kinderbybel* (Alexander 2000), and *Bibele ya Bana* (Alexander 2008), respectively.

5. See Lathey (2010, 113–15) on the distinction between Toury's (1995) "indirect translation" and Dollerup's (1999) use of the term "relay translation." The latter is closer than the former to what is described here.

"faithful" or "true" rendering of the original source text. Thus by claiming strict adherence the same authority for the children's Bibles as purveyors of religious norms from one generation to the next is ensured. Without such a claim to derivative sanction ("God's own words"), these Bibles would lose legitimacy as a didactic medium within the tradition.

The act of retelling (in text as well as accompanying image) is for this reason cloaked in the guise and language associated with formal equivalence (cf. Nida 2000, 161–62). The language describing this approach to Bible translation is also often impregnated with the same truth claims. Thus formal equivalence, or an "essentially literal translation," is defined by an adherent as translating

> the meaning of every word in the original language, understood correctly in its context, into its nearest English equivalent, and attempts to express the result with ordinary English word order and style, as far as that is possible without distorting the meaning of the original. Sometimes such a translation is also called a "word-for-word" translation, which is fine if we understand that at times one word in the original may be translated accurately by two or more words in English, and sometimes two or more words in the original can be represented by one word in English. The main point is that essentially literal translations attempt to represent *the meaning of every word* in the original in some way or other in the resulting translation. (Grudem 2005, 20)

Although no reader of a children's Bible realistically believe that it represents a "word-for-word" translation as here described, the author of the children's Bible may still claim that any adaptation, no matter how radical, is only tolerated in order to render the text more child appropriate. As Shavit (2006, 26) explains for translation of secular children's literature:

> Unlike contemporary translators of adult books, the translator of children's literature can permit himself great liberties regarding the text, as a result of the peripheral position of children's literature within the literary polysystem. That is, the translator is permitted to manipulate the text in various ways by changing, enlarging, or abridging it or by deleting or adding to it. Nevertheless, all these translational procedures are permitted only if conditioned by the translator's adherence to the following two principles on which translation for children is based: an adjustment of the text to make it appropriate and useful to the child, in accordance with what society regards (at a certain point in time) as educationally "good for the child"; and an adjustment of plot, characterization, and

language to prevailing society's perceptions of the child's ability to read and comprehend.

The implicit inclusion of visual language in children's Bibles and the preference for claims to formal equivalence are tolerated by the genre as long as the child version is successfully able to negotiate a claim that any adaptation of the child-friendly "translation" happens purely for the sake of didactics. This implies that the religious tradition may allow significant adjustment to the interpretation of canon because of Ruth Bottigheimer's (1996, 71) observation that children's Bibles historically adhere to societal context rather than textual content. It also reveals the subtle power politics at play in the assignment of canonical status and divine authority to a text by the religious tradition. This is brought about in a deliberate move to hide the visibility of the author in the guise of mimicking translation. In so doing the authors and illustrators of children's Bibles submit to the same hegemony that governs the act of translation, as explained by Lawrence Venuti (2008, 274): "most translators today don't wish to recognize the precise nature of their authorship or even to submit their practice to sustained theoretical or critical reflection." Authors and illustrators of children's Bibles deliberately prefer to pose as mere conduits of meaning for the source text and its implied author, God. By doing this, they are able to negotiate for their product a preferred status within the religious tradition (cf. du Toit 2011).

The Translator's Invisibility in Children's Bibles

> "Invisibility" is the term I will use to describe the translator's situation and activity in contemporary British and American cultures. (Venuti 2008, 1)

> As a result of the peripheral position of children's books within the literary system and the resulting lack of status for translators, translators for children seem to be the most transparent of all. (Lathey 2010, 5)

Children's Bibles, with their combined presentation of narrative in text and picture, are entangled in an intricate power dynamic by which a loosely defined retelling/reworking of a highly selective rendition of the adult biblical source text gained canonical status, and hence authority, in the religious tradition via the careful negotiation of a claim to formal equivalence in the "translation" of the combination of text and picture.

Ewald van Rensburg's (2006) *God's Storybook* is an example of how traditional translator "invisibility" is used to the advantage of establishing authority. Although van Rensburg is the evident author, the title implies a reduced status. Van Rensburg is "translator" or mediator of a collection of stories authored by the Deity to whom the title implies the stories belong. This results in implied divine authorship bestowed on *God's Storybook* based on the traditional understanding of canon. Although in this instance the author's name is found on the front cover, most children's Bibles conform to the invisibility principle to an even greater degree by not acknowledging the translator/author of the children's Bible on the cover of the Bible and only rarely on the title page.

Translator's invisibility is also underlined by appeals to formal equivalence in the child-appropriate rendering of the source text. An example comes from Ken Ham, president and CEO of *Answers in Genesis*–USA and of the Creation Museum in the United States. Ham has authored a broad range of educational material and Bible-related literature available in the museum's bookstore and online. The children's Bibles originating from this source are more explicit than middle-of-the-range children's Bibles in their claims to supposed adherence to the source text. This adherence is a simulation of formal equivalence in order to establish authority for the children's Bible as a vehicle for the transfer of creationism from one generation to the next. *My Creation Bible* (Ham 2006), for example, carries the implicit claim of strict adherence to the source text, the Bible, by an explicit claim on the cover as to the purpose of the book: to teach children "to trust the Bible from the very first verse." This claim of implied faithfulness to the source text ("from the very first verse") is contradicted by the content, which includes a radical truncation to include only the Gen 1–11 stories of creation, Noah's flood, and the tower of Babel, followed by the birth of Jesus and a significantly reduced New Testament.

Translator's invisibility in children's Bibles may be argued to be the result of a deliberate ploy to establish authority for the text within the tradition by means of its implied direct relationship to the source text. The source text, in turn, has legitimacy because of claims to divine authorship and/or sanction. In this sense, the "translated" children's Bibles serve as evidence for an attempt at creating invisibility for both translator and illustrator. But different from Venuti's description of translator's invisibility as a mask for "an insidious domestication of foreign texts" (2008, 12) that leaves English-language translators unrecognized, translator (and illustrator) invisibility in children's Bibles is a deliberate choice. The choice ensures for the children's Bible authoritative status in its guise as a "true" rendition of the adult source text in child-appropriate format where the source text is believed to have been authored, or at least inspired, by God. The concomitant "mystification of troubling texts" (Venuti 2008, 12) is achieved by the selective nature of the renditions in the guise of what is considered appropriate for a child audience.

The Picture and the Text

In light of the above, visual "translation" of the Bible for children often escapes notice entirely. While English children's Bibles originating in the United States or United Kingdom, for example, are regularly translated into indigenous South African languages, the accompanying illustrations are rarely adapted in the South African editions despite huge differences in target audience and target culture. It implies the not unusual, yet erroneous, assumption that visual language is universal and not culture-specific.[6] In fact, the independent status of the illustrations as a medium of knowledge transfer is largely undervalued. Perry Nodelman (1988, 221) furthermore not only acknowledges the independence of visual expression from the verbal equivalent, but describes the relationship between text and image as "combative": "Because they communicate different kinds of information, and because they work together by limiting each other's meanings, words and pictures necessarily have a combative relationship; their complementarity is a matter of opposites completing each other by virtue of their differences. As a result, the relationships between pictures and texts in picture books tend to be ironic: each speaks about matters on which the other is silent." Leaving pictures "untranslated" in translated children's Bibles therefore acts as profound commentary on the devalued appreciation for the potential knowledge transfer to illiterate lap readers for whom the accompanying pictures are the only direct, unmediated contact with the narrative.

The respective Afrikaans and Sesotho translations of *The Lion's Children's Bible* (Alexander 1991), for example, are exact parallels in terms of illustrative placement despite the far more wordy Afrikaans translation of the English intermediary. This means that in the Afrikaans *My*

---

6. Cf. Kress and van Leeuwen (1996, 3): "This means, first of all, that it [the grammar of 'visual design'] is not a 'universal' grammar. Visual language is not transparent and universally understood, but culturally specific."

Gunsteling Kinderbybel (Alexander 2000) one often finds text encroaching on illustrations that disappear underneath writing in order to keep the existing format intact (see, e.g., pages 32–33 of Pharaoh's Dream and the same pages in the Sesotho translation [Alexander 2008]). Accompanying visual presentation in children's Bibles are therefore assumed at most to fulfill the purpose as prettifying mechanisms in order to facilitate the child-friendly format. They are believed to duplicate, for the sake of the lap reader, the text to be read and interpreted by the adult intermediary. Kress and van Leeuwen (1996, 75–76) caution against this assumption: "while both visual structures and verbal structures can be used to express meanings drawn from a common cultural source, we have insisted that the two media are not simply alternative means of representing 'the same thing.'"

Rather, more than mere repetition in an alternative format, illustrations in children's Bibles are aligned to the accompanying text in the same pretention to formal equivalence as was identified in the text. The prevalent hyperrealism of representation typical of the genre poses as the visual rendering of an attempt at so-called word-for-word translation. Clearly defined contour lines (cf. Lewis 2001, 103–4) that highlight characters and objects, for example, tend to imply certainty vis-à-vis vagueness. Hyperrealistic renderings imply faithfulness to "truth" compared to fading, nondescript, or abstract representations of mood implying uncertainty. Color, referred to by Lewis (2001, 104) as the "most basic feature of picturebook pictures," tends to be vibrant, with a strong emphasis on primary colors, especially in Bibles intended for toddlers and younger readers. The obvious purpose is to attract and focus the attention of the juvenile reader. But the symbolic use of color as a visual convention in religious art is already present in children's Bibles, such as the white robe associated with Jesus, purple and gold with Pharaoh, and so forth.

The interrelationship between picture and text in picture books is, according to Lewis (2001, 33), best described as a "composite" of "interdependent storytelling" (2001, 41)[7] that makes sense only if the interchange between image and text is achieved through close proximity. "It is not much use if the two strands [image and text] … are on different pages or

---

7. Riitta Oittinen (2003, 130–31) identified three kinds of functional relationships between the verbal and visual in picture books: supportive (telling the same story through congruence), contradictory (the two versions stand in exact opposition), and simultaneous (a side-by-side doubling of the story in words and pictures).

are so far apart that they cannot be brought together in the act of reading. If the words are on one set of pages and the pictures elsewhere in the book, then it becomes difficult for the two forms of representation to enter into the construction of the story together" (Lewis 2001, 33).[8]

Despite the inherent presumption of repetition between text and illustration implied by the close approximation of text and picture, pictures in children's Bibles have a much broader function. Substitution of narrative by means of illustrative depiction often takes place. In most instances pictures also function to simplify text in an attempt to both engage the lap reader during the act of reading and to adapt the register of an original adult text for the age of the intended target audience. Simplification for the sake of adapting the level of comprehension again has its most obvious parallel in the simplified, translated Bible stories (with pictures) for semiliterate and newly literate adult consumers of missionary Bibles. Thus what Hephzibah Israel describes for missionary translation in nineteenth-century India is equally applicable to contemporary children's Bible production: "For missionary translators, the act of translating the Bible functioned as a medium for defending Christianity and missions both from the attacks of Western rationalists and sceptics and from the superstitious, false beliefs of the East. That the Bible could be translated into any language without loss of meaning served as proof of its divine nature" (Israel 2009, 211). In this manner hyperrealistic presentation reinforces the imperative to a pretention at formal equivalence, hence also the allowed rationalization of a disruption of canonical sequence found in both missionary Bibles and children's Bibles in order to enhance a literalist perception of perceived historical progression in the Bible. The "haphazard canonical arrangement" was considered an impediment to missionary belief in "progressive revelation" best served by the rearrangement of books and stories to fit a chronological retelling of the Bible: "The idea was to offer a comprehensive anthology of stories and messages which embodied the gradual revelation of spiritual truth. This proposed lining-up of the biblical books, they thought, would not only bring out the natural evolution of its basic doctrines but also the historical integrity of the various books" (Sugirtharajah

---

8. Cf., e.g., *Holy Bible for Little Hearts and Hands* (2007). The depiction of Gen 1 is grouped together with a collection of illustrations from the first books of the Bible, but bound into the text in the middle of 1 Kings and thereby devoid of context.

2005, 155). It should therefore come as no surprise that in children's Bibles one often find the same rearrangement.[9]

Conclusion

"Picture books … are unlike any other form of verbal or visual art. Both the pictures and the texts in these books are different from and communicate differently from pictures and texts in other circumstances" (Nodelman 1988, vii), The same quandary posed in the assessment of children's verse for its literary qualities as poetry may be argued to be true for visual depiction in children's Bibles as "art." In this regard Rebecca Lukens (2007, 239–68) makes the important point that the elements present in most children's verse—nursery rhymes, limericks, and nonsense—do not equal poetry. For the same reason the illustrations in children's Bibles do not necessarily equal "art." Rather, as was indicated for the accompanying text, the didactic function of the depictions overrides all other considerations: "Bible illustrations in juvenile books should be examples of attractive visual art, never careless expressions of ready-made, sentimental piety. The pictures should avoid grossly falsifying the historical period depicted. Even if the greatest of artists have almost always painted biblical personalities and settings anachronistically, in the detail of their own times, there is no point in unnecessarily cluttering the child's retentive mind with misinformation" (Phy 1985, 182). Are illustrations in children's Bibles therefore examples of "art"? Should they be? Not necessarily. Rather, they are vehicles for the adult perception of what is appropriate, educational, or entertaining to the child reader. That these illustrations are most often left unaltered as the predominant American and British children's Bibles are disseminated in translation across the world allows for an uneasy disjuncture between text and illustration, but also between one target audience and the next (cf. also Stolt 2006, 78–83).

In pointing to the significance of visual translation of the Bible for children and the implicit interaction between text and picture in children's Bibles for our understanding of what a society considers worthy of transfer to the next generation, one must emphasize the underappreciated relationship of image vis-à-vis the verbal. This is the only part of the

---

9. See, e.g., Lane and Chapman's list of references for where the stories selected are to be found in the Old and New Testaments (2005b, 248–52).

Bible communicated without intermediary to the child audience. And as didactics and the transfer of what is considered normative are central to the exercise, much may be deduced regarding the influence and interpretation of the Bible on culture and society by considering the norms and values embedded in the interplay between text and picture in translation. Because, as Riitta Oittinen (2006, 84) so aptly explains,

> We create texts for different purposes, different situations, and different audiences, so any "text" to be translated is much more than a mere text. It is the unity of the original text in words and pictures, the creators, and cultural, social and historical milieu, and text contexts such as the child images, which mirror our cultures and societies. It involves a whole situation with several different perspectives, and includes what the translator brings to the situation as a human being with her/his own background, language, culture, and gender.

And children's Bibles have proved examples par excellence of the constant negotiation required in making sense of the parameters of religious tradition, and the required need to convey an adult text in child-acceptable format in order to initiate the child into the normative religious tradition.

The Earliest Greenlandic Bible: A Study of the Ur-Text from 1725

Flemming A. J. Nielsen

Printed and Unprinted Greenlandic Bibles

Christianity was brought to Greenland when the Norwegian missionary Hans Egede (1686–1758) arrived in 1721. Already three years later, by November 1724, he was able to produce the earliest Greenlandic translation of a biblical text, Gen 1:1–11:9, and during the following months, a number of New Testament texts were added (H. Egede 1725a, 150). In June 1725, a manuscript containing these and other Greenlandic texts was sent to Copenhagen, capital of the then dual monarchy of Denmark and Norway (H. Egede 1725b). Hans Egede's attempts at writing Greenlandic constitute the earliest continuous texts written in any Eskaleut language.[1]

Egede's translations gave rise to an extensive manuscript tradition since many foreign missionaries and Greenlanders produced such texts during the eighteenth and nineteenth centuries.[2] They were copied and spread in considerable numbers, but very few were printed. It is remarkable that in spite of their tremendous influence on the transformation of Greenlandic culture, most of these biblical manuscripts were lost—or their caches are unknown today—but the Ur-text has been preserved.

The first printed edition of biblical texts in Greenlandic was Hans Egede's son Poul Egede's (1708–1789) translation of the Gospels published in Copenhagen in 1744; in 1766 he printed the entire New Testament.[3]

---

1. A thorough introduction to these languages is Dorais 2010.
2. K. Kjærgaard 2010, 113–25; T. Kjærgaard 2011. It was not until 1857 that a local printing press was established (Oldendow 1957).
3. A full list of Greenlandic books issued before 1880 may be found in Pfaff and Lauridsen 1890, 199–216.

Otto Fabricius (1744–1822), a Danish theologian, zoologist, and linguist, and another pioneer in the field of Greenlandic studies, spent five and a half years as a missionary in the country from 1768 to 1774. He issued a substantially revised edition of Poul Egede's New Testament in 1794 (*Testamente nutak*), reprinted in 1799 and 1827. These editions were funded by the Danish administration. An alternative edition of the New Testament made by the Moravian missionary Conrad Kleinschmidt (1768–1832) was published in 1822 (*Testamentitâk*) and reprinted in 1851.[4]

Conrad Kleinschmidt's famous son Samuel (1814–1886), who was born in Greenland and spent most of his life there, translated most of the biblical books. However, Samuel Kleinschmidt would not risk the premature publication of his New Testament translations, as he saw it, since he did not want to cause unrest in regard to the biblical texts that were particularly familiar to the religious community.[5] Accordingly, his New Testament was not published in his lifetime, but a revised edition came out in 1893 (*Tastamantitâk*) and subsequent revisions in 1912 and 1936. The most recent Greenlandic New Testament was translated anew from Greek and published in 2000 (*Biibili*).

The publication of Old Testament texts progressed much more slowly. In 1822 the first printed edition of Genesis was issued (Fabricius and Wolf), and a number of Old Testament books appeared during the following years.[6] Beginning in 1864, Samuel Kleinschmidt printed a number of Old Testament texts[7] and circulated them among the Greenlandic catechists in order to get their responses (Wilhjelm 2001, 315–16). It was not

---

4. Two Protestant denominations were present in Greenland from 1733 to 1900 when the Moravian Brethren closed down their activities. For a very short English introduction, see Moravians in Greenland 2008.

5. For a brief introduction to the early Greenlandic Bible translations in print and Kleinschmidt's important contributions, see Wilhjelm 2001, 308–25. Wilhjelm's biography of Samuel Kleinschmidt in Danish is exhaustive. A very short English introduction is Holtved 1964.

6. Before Kleinschmidt, Niels Gjessing Wolf published translations of Psalms, Isaiah, and Proverbs (Wolf 1824; 1825; 1828), and the prolific Peter Kragh issued the book of Daniel with apocryphal additions, the book of the Twelve Prophets, Exodus, Deuteronomy, Job, Ezra, Nehemiah, Esther, Ruth, and the Latter Prophets (Kragh 1829; 1832; 1836). The Moravian Brethren issued a translation of Psalms in 1842 (*Tuksiautit*).

7. Kleinschmidt's earliest printed translation was Genesis (*Atuagarssuit* 1864). During the 1870s he issued the rest of the Pentateuch, Job, Psalms, Proverbs, Ecclesi-

until 1900 that the entire Old Testament was printed (*Tastamantitoкaк*), and a new translation was issued in 1989 (*Testamentitoqaq*), with a revised edition in 2000 (*Biibili*).

Greenlandic Bibles containing all canonical books from both Testaments have been issued twice with an interval of a century (*Atuagarssuit* 1900; *Biibili* 2000). The 1900 edition of the Greenlandic Bible was something of a feat, a literary masterpiece, and probably one of the best non-European Bible translations of the day.[8]

Below I shall give a presentation of the Ur-text of this substantial tradition of translating the Bible into Greenlandic and its background and influence, including the invention of a literary language and the cultivation of new religious domains in the Greenlandic tongue.

Christian Beginnings: Norse and Inuit in Greenland

Greenland is geographically situated in North America, but historically, politically, economically, and culturally, this cold and sparsely populated island is closely connected to Europe. Today only 57,000 inhabitants share 2.18 million square kilometers, most of which is an arctic desert dominated by an ice sheet that alone covers 1.7 million square kilometers. When the Norwegian mission arrived in 1721, little more than 5,000 people subsisted in the land.[9] At the end of the tenth century, Norse from

---

astes, Canticles, the Latter Prophets, and Lamentations. A full list of his publications may be seen in Wilhjelm 2001, 273–74.

8. Wilhjelm 2001, 399. From without, it is difficult to catch sight of the Greenlandic Bible. There is no mention of it at all in a work such as Noss 2007.

9. The exact figure is not known. Kathrine Kjærgaard and Thorkild Kjærgaard (2008, 276) estimate it at 5,500, whereas Ole Marquardt advocates the figure 8,000 (2002, 48) or 10,000 at the very outside (2004, 142). We know for certain that in 1789 little more than 5,000 people lived in West Greenland (Gad 1982, 87–88). Circumstances conducive to the growth of the population before this year include the living conditions, which were dramatically improved in the regions where the Europeans settled. However, the same Europeans also brought new diseases that decimated the population from time to time in certain areas. A notorious example is the smallpox epidemic raging in the Nuuk area in 1733–1734 that killed about 90 percent of the population (Gad 1973, 166–70; Marquardt 2004). But not everybody died: "the demographic recovery of the district was so rapid that one is led to suspect that a good many former inhabitants fled the district during the epidemic—and returned to it when it was over" (Marquardt 2004, 141).

Scandinavia settled in the southwestern part of Greenland (Gad 1970, 26–89; Seaver 2010).[10] Apart from the Smith Sound area in the extreme north where traces from the Late Dorset culture indicate its presence from the eighth to the thirteenth century (Appelt and Gulløv 1999),[11] Greenland was uninhabited when the Norse arrived. They remained for around five hundred years, constituting from the beginning a Christian free state run by chieftains. In the thirteenth century, this state became incorporated in the kingdom of Norway. From 1261 to 1814, Greenland remained part of Norway (Gad 1970, 119–21), and the town of Bergen became the link to the Norwegian dependencies in the North Atlantic (Sørensen 2006, 11). Ecclesiastically, Greenland was an independent bishopric from the 1120s (Gad 1970, 62–63). It was the Roman pope's most distant province and represented the first foothold of Christianity in the American hemisphere (Kjærgaard and Kjærgaard 2008, 269).

About two hundred years after the arrival of the Norse, the so-called Neo-Eskimo culture entered the far north of Greenland from the American continent.[12] Eskimo[13] languages are closely related and are today spoken by about a hundred thousand people living in a vast area extending from extreme northeast Siberia through the coasts of North America to Greenland.[14] In the fifteenth century the Norse disappeared from

---

10. For reasons unknown to me, European settlers in Greenland, be they Norse in the Middle Ages or missionaries and merchants in the eighteenth century, are often termed "colonists" or "colonizers," whereas Inuit settlers are called "immigrants."

11. Regarding possible traces elsewhere, cf. Gulløv 2011, 24.

12. Gulløv 2011, 24–25; 2005a. The expansive Neo-Eskimo culture based on new techniques for whaling originated on the Siberian coasts of the Bering Strait and on St. Lawrence Island about 500 C.E. and spread across the Bering Strait and the Alaskan and Canadian coasts during the following centuries; see Gulløv 2005b.

13. I use "Eskimo" as an inclusive term denoting various peoples speaking related languages: Yupiks in the Chukchi Peninsula and Alaska, Iñupiaqs in Alaska, and Inuit in Canada and Greenland. Cf. Jacobson 1995, vii. Archaeologists use the same term when they discuss the pre-contact and early-contact era.

14. Eskimo languages may be subdivided into three branches: Inuit languages are spoken on the northern coasts of Alaska (Iñupiaq) and Canada (Inuktitut) and in Greenland (Kalaallisut); Yupik languages are spoken across the Bering Strait, from the coast of the Chukchi Peninsula (Naukanski Yupik and Central Siberian Yupik) to the southwestern coast of Alaska (Central Alaskan Yupik and Alutiiq Alaskan Yupik). The Inuit languages form a dialect continuum, whereas the Yupik languages are more sharply differentiated and unintelligible to Inuit speakers. The third branch, Sirenikski, comprises but one language that was "discovered" as late as 1895 in two villages

Greenland,[15] and for two and a half centuries the Neo-Eskimos—calling themselves *Inuit* ("human beings")—were the only people in the land.

Norway and Denmark formed a united monarchy from 1380 to 1814, with a shared king from 1397.[16] It was never forgotten that Greenland was a tributary to Norway. After all, the possibility that there were still Norse living isolated in Greenland could not be precluded.

The Second Coming of Christianity

In 1708 Hans Egede was a young, newly appointed clergyman on the island of Vaagen in the archipelago of Lofoten in northern Norway (Bobé 1952, 13–23). One evening in the month of October, as he recalled many years later (H. Egede 1722a, 3), it suddenly crossed his mind that he had once read that there were Christians, churches, and monasteries in Greenland, but throughout the years it had not been possible to learn anything about them from those who had been there for the purposes of whaling and trading. The following year, Hans Egede wrote to his brother-in-law, who had also sailed to Greenland, and asked for information. He received the reply that there were "savages" in Greenland at the Davis Strait, but it was impossible to explore the eastern coasts of Greenland because of drift ice. This relation, Hans Egede wrote, "called forth in me a commiseration for the miserable state of these poor people who in former times had been Christians and enlightened in the Christian faith but who now for lack

---

in the southern part of the Chukchi Peninsula. A few decades later it was virtually extinct—the last speaker of the language died in 1997 (Hallamaa 1997, 189). Eskimo languages are related to the Aleut languages, but relationships to other language families are open to question. See Fortescue, Jacobson, and Kaplan 2010, x; Dorais 1993, 13–19; Krupnik 1991; Fortescue 1998.

15. The causes of their disappearance are much discussed. Rather than looking for strictly internal causes, the matter may be put into a broader perspective and conceived as part of the European contraction in the wake of the plague about 1350 that extirpated a quarter of the population on the Continent. As far as we know, the plague never reached Greenland, but in Norway—then the center of a North Atlantic Commonwealth with the Faeroe Islands, the Shetland Islands, the Orkney Islands, the Hebrides, Iceland, and Norse Greenland—perhaps half of the population died and left space for Norse from the fringes of the Commonwealth in search of milder climes in the land of their ancestors; see T. Kjærgaard 2010, 276–79.

16. Jespersen 2004, 3, 12, 21–22. In 1814 Norway entered into a personal union with Sweden that lasted until 1905.

of teachers and instruction had again fallen into heathen blindness and savagery." He wished he could preach the gospel to them, and he thought the obligation was all the greater because they had at one time been Christians; furthermore, they were of Norse descent and lived in a country subject to the Norwegian crown.[17]

After twelve years of hard work (Bobé 1952, 22–48), Hans Egede managed to procure an appointment as missionary from the Danish king and the financial support from a circle of businessmen in the Norwegian town of Bergen that enabled him to go to Greenland in 1721 as "royal Danish missionary and commissioned chief of the royally chartered Bergen colony in Greenland" (Bobé 1952, 51). Even though the Bergen trading company's service to Greenland was discontinued as early as 1726 and taken over by the Danish Crown (Gad 1973, 51–120), who subsequently allotted a trade monopoly to willing merchants,[18] Egede managed to stay in Greenland for fifteen years. In his capacity of missionary and government official supervised by the Danish Government Department for the Dissemination of the Gospel in Copenhagen,[19] he initiated the Danish-Norwegian resettlement of Greenland in competition with Dutch and English whalers and traders (Bobé 1952, 39–171). Among his important achievements are his linguistic studies and the invention of a Greenlandic literary language.

Written Greenlandic before 1721

The earliest written evidence of the existence of an Eskimo language may be a passage in the *Saga of Erik the Red*, chapter 12,[20] which recounts the adventures of the Norseman Thorfinn Karlsefni on his way back from

---

17. H. Egede 1722a, 3; the passage quoted is from the English translation in Bobé 1952, 22.

18. Gad 1973, 199–234, 273–314, 374–419. Eventually, a national trading company, "Den Kongelige Grønlandske Handel" (KGH; "The Royal Greenland Trade"), exercised the trade monopoly from 1776 to 1950.

19. No other European country had anything like this government department (Collegium de Cursu Evangelii Promovendo). It had been set up in December 1714 in order to administer the missionary work funded by the king regarding the peoples living at the extremities of the then Danish-Norwegian Empire: the northernmost part of Norway populated by the Saami people and the Danish colony in India, Tranquebar (Gad 1973, 17). Eventually, the Greenlandic mission would also belong under the department. For a thorough treatment, see Stampe 1946.

20. The best text is that found in *Skálholtsbók* (Magnusson and Palsson 1966,

"Vinland" to Greenland. He and his fellow travelers break their journey at "Markland" and have an encounter with five so-called Skraellings: a man, two women, and two boys. The precise locations of Vinland and Markland in today's Canada are open to discussion, but the most widespread hypotheses seem to be that Vinland is Newfoundland and Markland the coast of Labrador (Arneborg 2005, 231). The adult Skraellings escape, but the boys are caught. The word *Skraellings* is commonly used in the Icelandic sagas as the name of the indigenous peoples that the Norse met in North America and Greenland. In Greenland, archaeology tells us that the Skraellings represent Inuit and perhaps people from the Late Dorset culture present at Smith Sound until late in the thirteenth century (Gulløv 2005c), but the ethnicities of the peoples encountered in North America are uncertain (Seaver 2010, 62–73). If the identification of the ancient Markland as the coast of Labrador can be maintained, there is every possibility that the Skraellings of Markland might also have been Inuit. In 1905 the renowned Danish Eskimologist William Thalbitzer developed a linguistic argument that this was actually the case (1905; 1913; 1932, 7–8).

According to the *Saga of Erik the Red*, chapter 12, the abducted boys learned "language" (*mál*) and were baptized. Then they told the names of their parents: their mother was called Vethildi and their father Óvægi or Vægi.[21] They also said that the Skraellings were ruled by kings and that they were called Avaldamon and Avaldidida or Valdidida. The saga was put in writing in Iceland during the thirteenth century, and it depicts incidents that may have occurred around the year 1000 (Magnusson and Palsson 1966, 7–43). According to Thalbitzer, the four names may be words of Inuit origin that the author of the manuscripts or the oral tradition construed as personal names and developed into the story of the boys' parents and the kings of the Skraellings of Markland.

The names of the parents, Vethildi and (Ó)vægi, may reflect words corresponding to modern Greenlandic *uatsili*, "just wait a little!" and *uatsi*, "wait a little!" The names of the kings, Avaldamon and (A)valdidida, are also easily recognizable for the Greenlandic ear; they seem to correspond to *avallermut*, "toward the outermost (land)," or perhaps *avallermiut*,[22]

30–31; Halldórsson 1985, 333–38). The citations below are from Halldórsson's edition. For an English translation see Magnusson and Palsson 1966, 75–105.

21. There being two manuscripts with different names; Thalbitzer 1905, 190; 1913, 88.

22. *-mun* is the earlier version of the modern Greenlandic allative case ending

"the dwellers of the outermost (land)," and *avallitit-aa?* "do you mean your outermost?" perhaps meaning "the outermost seen from your location" or "the outermost islands in your country." Thus it is possible that these four names are fragments of conversations between some Norse and two abducted Inuit boys.

Apart from these possible samples of an Inuit language spoken around the year 1000 handed down in the *Saga of Erik the Red*, the earliest list of Inuit words was written down by Christopher Hall, an assistant to the British explorer Martin Frobisher at Baffin Island in 1576. It contains seventeen words that are perfectly intelligible today.[23] The earliest list of Greenlandic words has about forty words taken down by John Davis on an expedition to Greenland in 1586, but his linguistic abilities did not compare favorably with those of Christopher Hall, so some of Davis's words are impossible to explain. But as a whole, the language reflected by the list is clearly recognizable as being Greenlandic.[24]

Three lists of Greenlandic words survive from the seventeenth century. They were compiled on the basis of conversations with three Inuit women abducted from the Nuuk Fiord and brought to Denmark in 1654 (Plank 1990, 309–11). Most comprehensive is a German-Greenlandic list of about seven hundred words known from three manuscripts produced in the late seventeenth and early eighteenth centuries (Petersen and Rischel 1985a; Møller 1985) but not printed until modern times (Petersen and Rischel 1985b). The relationship between this comprehensive list and two short printed ones is not clear, but the latter are independent sources to the conversations with the abducted Greenlandic women (Petersen and Rischel 1985a, 158–59; Plank 1990, 310–11; Thalbitzer 1932, 12–13). The shortest list (about a hundred words) is part of Adam Olearius's *Vermehrte Newe Beschreibung der Muscowitischen vnd persischen Reyse* (1656, 171), and the author states that he himself heard the Greenlanders pronounce

---

-mut (Fortescue, Jacobson, and Kaplan 2010, 488). Regarding the plural inflectional affix *-t*, it has long since been observed that in continuous speech final *-t* was often replaced by *-n*; Fabricius (1801, 14) gives the example *innuïn audlarput*, corresponding to modern Greenlandic *inuit aallarput*, "the men left."

23. Words and interpretions in Dorais 1993, 37–38.

24. The list and an interpretation by Hinrich Johannes Rink may be seen in Markham 1880, 21. A more profound interpretation is Schultz-Lorentzen 1930. Dorais (1993, 39–40) has new interpretations of some of the words. Hall's and Davis's lists are also treated in Thalbitzer 1932, 10–12.

the words.[25] The longer one (about three hundred words) was drawn up by Caspar Bartholin and published in 1673 by his brother Thomas Bartholin in one of the world's earliest scientific periodicals, *Acta Medica and Philosophica Hafniensia*. A son of Thomas Bartholin, whose name was also Caspar, was Hans Egede's preceptor at the University of Copenhagen (Plank 1990, 312; Bobé 1952, 38).

Before Hans Egede departed for Greenland, he had made his own list of Greenlandic words. His sources for doing so were, according to his own account, Olearius's list and some communication with the Icelandic philologist Árni Magnússon. Egede did not specify the kind of communication he had had with Magnússon, but he informed his readers that the words he had learned from the scholar had been published by Caspar Bartholin "in his Actis Medicis," and he regretted that the language had not been studied to a much greater extent when the women abducted in 1654 were still alive (H. Egede 1722b, 39).

In Egede's day, Greenlandic waters had been regularly frequented by European—notably Basque, Portuguese, Dutch, and English—pirates, fishermen, whalers, traders, and explorers for centuries, and a Greenlandic-Germanic pidgin language had evolved. Its Germanic components were Scandinavian, Dutch, Frisian, and German, but we do not know much about it.[26] Egede was confronted with this language before his arrival at the shores of Greenland, when a Dutch boatswain agreed to act as interpreter and pilot for the Norwegians. In a letter to the Bergen Company, Egede wrote that this boatswain had been in the Greenland trade for several years "and understands very well the speech of the savages."[27] However, even if Greenlanders and Europeans of the day were able to communicate, this mutual understanding probably applied only to trading activities.

Hans Egede's Early Study of Greenlandic

Brought up in the Lutheran-Evangelical tradition in the Age of Enlightenment (Hope 1995, 99–146), Egede took it for granted that Christianity should be preached in the local tongue and that the future Greenlandic

---

25. Facsimile of the list in Petersen and Rischel 1985a, 157.
26. For a thorough description and analysis of the surviving data, see van der Voort 1996.
27. Letter from the Greenland Council to the Bergen Company dated July 15, 1721, printed in Bobé 1936, 79.

believers should master the central dogmas and biblical texts in their own language. In defiance of stupendous difficulties, he therefore resolved to learn a language that had not been properly described before, develop a written language, invent words for the foreign religious concepts that he wanted to introduce into the native tongue, teach his audience to read, and instruct them in their new lives as citizens of the United Monarchy of Denmark-Norway and members of the Danish Evangelical-Lutheran State Church. And he began to produce a number of Greenlandic religious texts for the use of the missionaries and their parishioners.

From the word lists produced in the seventeenth century, one may see that in Europe there was a traditional practice of writing Greenlandic words already in Hans Egede's day. Though far from being consistent, his own orthography is very much dependent on the spellings in these early word lists, and the very first sample of Greenlandic writing that has been preserved among Egede's autographs, a word list from 1722, is based on these lists rather than independent field research.[28]

This very early orthography registered a lot of vowel qualities that European ears are sensitive to, but that are not phonemic in Greenlandic. Phonemic, on the other hand, is the length of vowels as well as consonants; both may be short or long. Though the early missionaries—at least Hans Egede's son Poul, who became fluent in Greenlandic as a teenager—and some of their successors must have become aware of these very important features of Greenlandic phonology,[29] they did not let them influence their orthography, so that consonants are written both doubly and singly without consistency. In this, the early orthography shows clear dependency on the tradition of writing established during the seventeenth century. Add to this that Greenlandic contains a few consonant sounds that are foreign to Europeans, most notably an uvular stop (written *q* in modern Greenlandic) and an intervocalic unvoiced palatal lateral (*ll*), for which the missionaries, accordingly, had no graphemes, and it is no wonder that it was very difficult for the Greenlanders to acquire the spellings devised by the foreigners. Only Samuel Kleinschmidt's groundbreaking linguistic description (1851), freed from the categories of Latin and Greek grammar

---

28. Petersen and Rischel 1985a, 158; Bergsland and Rischel 1986, 12–13. The list is printed in Bergsland and Rischel 1986, 49–52.

29. H. Egede 1741, 167: "They have besides many double and unknown consonants, which is the reason that many of their words cannot be spelled according to their manner of pronouncing them."

that had earlier been superimposed upon the language, changed this. He established the proper phonemes of the language, developed new graphemes, and—with some important and problematic exceptions mostly caused by etymological considerations—he allotted one grapheme to each phoneme.[30] Modern Greenlandic orthography is but an adjustment of Kleinschmidt (R. Petersen 1975, 2009).

Regarding Egede's earliest coherent texts, there are a lot of serious grammatical difficulties since the Eskimo languages share a number of features that are foreign to most Indo-European languages. They are of the ergative type, that is, the subject in a transitive sentence has its own case that differs from the case of the subject in an intransitive sentence. If the case system is not properly understood by the speaker, it becomes very difficult for the listener to sort out who does what to whom, so this is not only a matter of conventions. The verbal inflection is highly complex, distinguishing between transitive and intransitive forms. Transitive verbal forms have markings for both subject and object, but most verbs may be used only transitively or intransitively, their meaning changes according to their being used in either way. Another problem is that relative clauses, so common in Indo-European languages, are difficult to transform into sentences that are meaningful in Greenlandic. Most complicated, from an Indo-European perspective, is the extreme polysynthetic character of the language that allows nouns and verbs to transform and grow into complex one-word sentences (*uninngavimminiiginnarallarpoq*, "he just stayed for a while in the place where he was," John 11:6) by adding up to ten or twelve successive affixes to a radical according to rules that have still not been described adequately (Fortescue 1980; Trondhjem 2007, 8; the aforementioned word is based on the verb *unippoq*, "he has stopped"). It is even possible for separate parts of some derived verbs to govern different elements in the sentence that they are part of (Langgård 2002); if the cases are not used correctly when such verbs are employed, utter confusion is brought about as to who causes whom to do what.

As will be seen, grammatical pitfalls abound when Europeans try to express themselves in this language. The grammatical problems were unavoidable given the stage of linguistic science in Hans Egede's day. Not only did Egede have to learn a language that had not been described before, he also had to cultivate new domains for this language. However,

---

30. For a thorough assessment of Kleinschmidt's grammar, see Nowak 1987.

the Greenlanders of his day were in the habit of communicating with Europeans, and a pidgin language for the purpose of barter did exist. Even though we do not possess any coherent texts in this pidgin language (van der Voort 1996), it seems reasonable to assume that it did not differ much from Egede's early texts. In fact—in spite of obvious difficulties—the locals soon learned to understand the missionaries' peculiar way of speaking Greenlandic and their foreign concepts, and the Europeans' speech habits influenced the subsequent development of the language (R. Petersen 1976). In his diary, Hans Egede's son Niels tells us that already twenty years after Egede's landing there were indeed two pidgin languages in the Nuuk area in addition to proper Greenlandic:

> On the fifth [of August 1741], I went hunting to the Nuuk Fiord area. I met some women gathering berries; they had come from Gothaab and had pitched their tents beneath the mountain. They asked me to accompany them to their tents and tell them something, then they would tell me something too. When I entered their tents, their Greenlandic was poor and rotten as they asked about several passages in the Scripture, Romans in particular. I asked them to speak proper Greenlandic since I understood it better. They answered that they had contracted the habit of speaking wrongly and gesticulating since they could not speak in other ways in Gothaab ... they said: "You speak Greenlandic like a native speaker." ... They had learned several things, but I could barely understand them before I became acquainted with them. Therefore I drew the conclusion that they must be rather unversed in the language in Gothaab; I asked whether the Moravians whom they call Nortlit, that is, the ones living on the spit, were more able to talk to them, and they said yes. (N. Egede 1744, 57–58; my trans.)

The women visited by Niels Egede apparently spoke to him in the Moravians' German-Greenlandic pidgin language ("poor and rotten Greenlandic"), and they told him that it was difficult for them to make themselves understood among the Danes and the converts living at Gothaab who spoke Danish-Greenlandic ("the language in Gothaab").[31] Accordingly, the two pidgin languages were not mutually understandable. They were spoken as foreign languages by the converts among the Danish and Mora-

---

31. Modern parlance has preserved reminiscences of the pidgin language that was spoken earlier at the Danish settlements. In Greenlandic literature it has become known as "kitchen Greenlandic"; see Jacobsen 2010, 122–23.

vian parishioners, respectively. In Niels Egede's day, the population in the Nuuk area had become multicultural; no less than five languages were represented: Greenlandic, Danish, German, and two pidgin languages.

Hans Egede's Anthology of Greenlandic Texts from 1725

Even though most of the early missionaries' manuscripts have been lost—most notably Hans Egede's son Poul's translation of substantial parts of the Pentateuch produced while Poul Egede himself was a missionary in the Disco Bay area from 1736 to 1740[32]—a number of Hans Egede's very early texts have been preserved. Earliest among these Greenlandic writings is the above-mentioned word list from 1722 (cf. n. 28). From the following years, 1723 and 1724, two catechisms survive. They have long since been published (Bobé 1925, 72–74, 132–40).

Unpublished, however, is an important manuscript completed on June 9, 1725. It is written in Hans Egede's characteristic handwriting and consists of 170 pages provided with the long-winded title, *Ten or Eleven Chapters from the Book of Creation: Translated into the Language of the Greenlanders in Order to Indicate the Advance of Our Understanding of the Language and What Progress Is Needed in Order to Be Able to Completely Explain Faith and the True Knowledge of God to Them* (H. Egede 1725b). The title does not reflect the texts included in their entirety since they rather constitute an anthology of various texts composed during the mission's first four years: biblical texts from the Old and the New Testaments (7–63), a catechism (65–85), a prayer book (86–93), a small Greenlandic dictionary (97–121), a collection of admonitory speeches (123–53), and a rudimentary Greenlandic grammar (155–72).

Hans Egede sent the manuscript to the Government Department for the Dissemination of the Gospel in Copenhagen through the Bergen Company with a dedication to the Danish crown prince written in the characteristic turgid style of his day. From the cover letter, it appears that the manuscript was intended for the use of future missionaries bound for

---

32. He began to translate Genesis in January 1737 (P. Egede 1741, 44; 1788, 68). By July 1739 he had finished Genesis, Exodus, and Leviticus when he realized, in hindsight, that his time could have been used better (P. Egede 1788, 112). On request of his father and Marcus Wöldike (1699–1750), professor of theology at the University of Copenhagen and a member of the Government Department for the Dissemination of the Gospel, he began to translate the NT instead (P. Egede 1741, 113).

Greenland (printed in Bobé 1936, 128). However, Count Johan Ludvig Holstein (1694–1763), a member of the said government department and Denmark's prime minister from 1735 to his death, incorporated the anthology in his very comprehensive collection of books and manuscripts in his palace Ledreborg outside Copenhagen and passed it on to his heirs. In 1926 the collection came to the Royal Danish Library in Copenhagen (Grønbæk 2001, 49; C. Petersen 1943, 38–39).

A note in Egede's diary shows that the primeval history (Gen 1:1–11:9) had been translated before November 6, 1724. On this day, he told a well-disposed audience about the creation and the flood, and he wrote that he had recently translated these parts of the Bible with the help of his then sixteen-year-old son Poul, who had grown much more fluent in the Greenlandic language than his father. He knew that the translation was defective. He regretted that it had not always been possible to render the words and the Hebrew phrases adequately, but he had had to settle for an approximate representation of the meaning. This not-really-satisfying approximation was due to the translator's obviously imperfect knowledge of the language, but not least to imperfections in the language itself. Even so, Hans Egede announced in his diary that he intended "to translate one of the Gospel stories and to draw up in their language what else can be useful for their edification as far as circumstances permit" (H. Egede 1725a, 150; my trans.).

Not only one, but a whole collection of "Gospel stories" follow the primeval history in Egede's compilation of texts. The aforementioned note in his diary shows that they were translated between November 6, 1724, and June 9, 1725. They are organized according to their use during the ecclesiastical year in the Danish Lutheran Church of the time: the annunciation (Luke 1:26–38); the birth of Jesus (Matt 1:18–25); the shepherds and the angelic song, and the circumcision and naming of Jesus (Luke 2:1–40); the magi (called "The Very Sensible"); the flight to Egypt, the slaughter of the innocents, and the return from Egypt with references to Old Testament prophecies (Matt 2); the sensible twelve-year-old Jesus in the temple (Luke 2:42–52); the activities of John the Baptist (paraphrasing Luke 3:1–2; Mark 1:2–3; Matt 3:5–6; Luke 3:15–16); the latter's testimony about himself (John 1:19–28); the baptism of Jesus and the voice from heaven (Matt 3:13–17); the devil's frightening Jesus in the desert (as the story is reproduced; Matt 4:1–11); and a small collection of stories from the Gospel of John: John the Baptist's pointing out Jesus (1:29), Jesus' first followers (1:35–37), the wedding at Cana making the disciples believe (2:1-11), the cleansing of the temple (2:12-25), and the story about Nicodemus emphasizing that a person should not go to the devil but to heaven where nobody ever dies (3:1-15). In view of the obvious catechetical purpose of the texts, it is worth noting that they do not include the passion or the resurrection; Jesus is introduced as sage and teacher rather than savior.

The primeval history is laid out like a real Bible, with chapter and verse divisions, whereas the Gospel texts are organized as pericopes in a prayer book, with captions in Latin indicating the relevant Sunday or church festival for each pericope. The selection of New Testament texts emphasizes Jesus' coming to the world and encourages faith, imitation, and obedience. This biblical part of the manuscript forms a whole with its own epilogue:

> This is what circumstances and abilities have permitted us to interpret and translate. It is not as perfect and accurate as it should be, which is due to imperfect knowledge of the language of the Greenlanders on our side and lack of suitable words in the language of the Greenlanders on their side, since, being a people without religion and worship, their language does not possess words that are applicable to our religion and worship, for all their aims and purposes only relate to the trade and subsistence of this life. They know nothing about higher things that do not concern them. This will be no little hindrance and delay to their education and conversion. In order for the secret of the kingdom of God to be clearly demonstrated to them, it is necessary to borrow words from our own language and naturalize them in theirs, even though it will take time to inculcate such things in them. (H. Egede 1725b, 62-63; my trans.)

The biblical part of the manuscript is followed by a section consisting of a catechism and a prayer book with Danish and Greenlandic texts. The catechism is made up by thirty-three questions and answers intended to be learned by heart, the Ten Commandments, and another eight questions and answers that look like a baptismal creed. The Lord's Prayer opens the collection of prayers: morning and evening prayers, a grace, a pair of catechetic prayers reviewing important parts of Christian faith, and a "prayer explaining to the Greenlanders their senselessness" (my trans.). The catechism and the prayer book are texts that Egede had been working on since the beginning of his tenure in Greenland. The earliest draft of a catechism that has been preserved was made already in 1723 in a very crude language (printed in Bobé 1925, 72-74). From the following year, we possess an early version of the prayer book and an expanded version of the catechism in a language that is markedly improved (Bobé 1925, 132–40).

A list containing almost nine hundred Greenlandic words and expressions with Danish equivalents and a collection of eighteen admonitory speeches constitute a section of their own. Egede tells his readers that the speeches have been delivered to the Greenlanders in order "to convince them of their senselessness and blameworthy dispositions" (H. Egede 1725b, 123; my trans.). They are new when compared to the kind of texts that Egede had sent to Bergen the preceding years.

Concluded by a rudimentary Greenlandic grammar, the manuscript may be characterized as an anthology of texts produced by the Greenlandic mission during its first four years. Hans Egede is the author and translator, but he was assisted by his son Poul and his colleague Albert Topp (1697–1742), a Norwegian priest who came to Greenland in 1723 and left the country four years later (Bergsland and Rischel 1986, 13–20). Some of the texts were meant to be learned by heart by the Greenlanders, some texts were to be used at religious ceremonies, and there were texts for the use of future missionaries as material for teaching converts as well as for their own learning of the difficult Greenlandic language. The arrangement of texts, locating the compilation of speeches next to the word list, makes this section look like a small phrase book for missionaries.

It is the word list and Egede's seminal attempt at writing a Greenlandic grammar that has aroused the interest of posterity. In 1986 those two parts of the manuscript were published in a book containing other early word lists and a more comprehensive grammar by Albert Topp from 1727, the year he left Greenland (Bergsland and Rischel 1986). However, the manuscript contains much material that should be of interest not only to linguists but to students of theology and religion too. Nevertheless, the rest of this extensive manuscript has never been printed save for a few quotations in Johann Anderson's description of Greenland issued in 1746 ("Anhang," 285–328). This book shows that Egede's manuscript circulated for some time. A lot of errors in Anderson's printed quotations of Egede's Greenlandic call for an explanation, but it is hard to give one: are they simply misprints, was it difficult for Anderson to read Egede's handwriting, or did he use an inferior transcript of the text? A Danish version of Anderson's German book appeared in 1748, but the publisher abstained from printing the Greenlandic texts "because the Greenlandic quoted in the German original has been found to be very mistaken, and, moreover, something better and more complete is expected shortly from a more able man" (276, my trans.). The better work expected may be Poul Egede's Greenlandic-Danish-Latin dictionary that appeared in 1750, the first printed dictionary in any Eskaleut language. With Anderson's quotations, Hans Egede's manuscript disappeared from literary history. The first detailed description of it may be found in a Norwegian missionary periodical (Bloch-Hoell 1960).

Circumstances forced Hans Egede to become the founder of the Greenlandic humanistic sciences. He became Greenland's first linguist and ethnographer. Influenced by the Lutheran orthodoxy of his day, he insisted on a certain amount of knowledge before his converts were allowed to be baptized. This attitude forced the missionary to procure educational material for the catechumens and invent the earliest Greenlandic literary language, and thereby become the founder of Greenlandic literature.

The Bible and Oral Tradition in Greenland

The biblical stories became part of oral tradition very early. Already in 1722, a local told the missionary about the Greenlanders' first parents, who created heaven and earth. Egede corrected this "erroneous" version of creation, but also realized that this was not an autochthonous piece of oral tradition, but his own teaching in disguise (H. Egede 1723, 51–52). His son Poul, the first missionary in the Disco Bay area, had a similiar experience in 1738. When he told one of the local sages about the resurrection of the dead, the sage, in return, gave the missionary his version:

> When ... all humankind is dead, a great river will inundate the earth and cleanse the blood of the dead; and when mountains, earth, and stones have disintegrated and are completely segregated and everything has been washed down, a wind will blow on it, and everything will assume a lovely shape. The high rocks and mountains will be smooth and level with many reindeer. The seal pups will revive and the one up there (pointing at the sky) will blow upon the dead people, twice at men, once at women, and everybody will revive. (P. Egede 1788, 92; my trans.)

Poul Egede goes on to say that he has not heard this singular account from anybody else. It may be a peculiar combination of autochthonous and biblical stories, or perhaps it is the sage's personal way of paraphrasing Christian doctrines and passages from the Bible that he has heard, such as the flood (Gen 6–8), God's spirit hovering over the waters before creation (Gen 1:2), the valleys that will be lifted up and the mountains that will be made low in the book of Isaiah (40:4), and the New Testament idea of the resurrection (1 Thess 4:16; 1 Cor 15:52). Be that as it may, the sage's story seems to be a remarkable example of the way the new biblical stories entered and changed local oral traditions. When told about the end of the world, another man was able to confirm the missionary's tale since a shaman had told his audience that the pillar of heaven was cracking, and should heaven fall down, it would crush all people (P. Egede 1788, 62). Such confrontations between traditional thinking and Christianity certainly call for further investigation.[33]

When the missionaries' linguistic abilities increased, and when Greenlandic converts learned to read and write their literary language, the locals assisted the missionaries with the translation of the Bible. In the Disco Bay area, Poul Egede, then a twenty-eight-year-old bachelor, was fascinated by the acuteness of a young woman convert, Arnarsaq. She and another young convert did not find the Old Testament texts suitable for the young Greenlandic church because of Cain's and the patriarchs' immoral behavior (P. Egede 1788, 88). They asked him to leave out the stories about the patriarchs' polygamy and posed critical questions regarding God's problematic conduct in the translation of the pentateuchal books that he was at work on (112). Poul Egede's ceaseless attempts at improving his translations of biblical and catechetical texts in keeping with his growing familiarity with the Greenlandic language aroused Arnarsaq's protests, as she asked whether it was really permissible to change God's words so often and whether he might not be angered by it. "What has been written before is understandable and sufficiently correct," she said.[34] Very early, an indigenous theological tradition began to evolve for the missionaries to take into consideration.

---

33. Cf. Sonne 1986, 216: "The above instances of Eskimos attempting to incorporate the white man's culture and ideology into their own way of thinking point to a fascinating field of investigation and certainly to a factor that should never be ignored."

34. P. Egede 1741, 125 (my trans.); Gad 1973, 241–42. Arnarsaq accompanied Poul Egede to Copenhagen in 1740 and spent a year helping him to improve his translation of the NT. Then she returned to Greenland and became an important supporter of the mission. Arnarsaq and Poul Egede never met again, and as far as we know, she never married, which was highly unusual in Greenland of the day. A short biography is provided by Lidegaard 1967.

Hans Egede's Choice and Use of Biblical Texts

Hans Egede's selection of texts begins with the creation of the world and the dispersion of the peoples throughout the world. Most fundamental, of course, is the idea that the missionaries' God created the world of the Inuit and that humans were created in the likeness of this God. The creation myths served to portray the missionaries' God as the one who provided the quarry of the Inuit's hunting economy. But a new world was also introduced with the primeval history and its exotic names of individuals, countries, cities, and rivers belonging to the biblical geography and all the precious stones and metals present in distant climes. Hans Egede took great pains to reproduce it all, including the fabulous numbers in the genealogical table of Gen 5 that were difficult to convey because the highest possible numeral of the language of the day was twenty-one. In order to understand what is going on in this strange collection of stories, lists, and numbers, education would be needed. Accordingly, we can safely say that the modern Greenlandic educational system was actually founded by this Norwegian missionary.

In this collection of biblical texts, concepts that were difficult to translate into the language of a remote oral culture of the Arctic include both important religious ideas belonging to the biblical and the missionaries' picture of the world such as God, devil, good and evil, and more general foreign phenomena such as the Mediterranean agricultural world with plants and animals that do not exist in the Arctic. The emperors Augustus and Tiberius, King Herod, Governor Quirinius, Pontius Pilate, and other biblical notables were introduced during the early years of Christian presence among the Inuit, and so were the names of Old Testament prophets quoted in the Gospels.

Among the religious concepts in Hans Egede's selection of texts, God, God's Spirit, the Savior, and the devil are among the most prominent, and they were difficult to translate. Today, Greenlanders often maintain that no religion existed in their land before Christianity arrived. This is not true; the pre-Christian Greenlandic religion may be characterized as shamanistic.[35] Behind the visible world, there was an unseen one that could be approached by the shamans, the so-called *angakkut*. Everything visible

---

35. A recent introduction to shamanism in general is DuBois 2009. An introduction to Inuit shamanism is Kleivan and Sonne 1985; Haase (1987) has a full description.

had its own spirit, *inua*. This word is the same as *inuk*, "person" or "owner," inflected in the possessed singular, literally speaking "its owner." Important *inui* (possessed plural) were the Man in the Moon, Sila (the unpredictable *inua* of the weather), and the Woman of the Sea. But none of them was supreme or the leader of a pantheon, so it was not possible for the missionaries to find an equivalent to the Christian God among the religious phenomena they encountered. Instead, they simply used the Danish word *Gud*, which today is part of the standard Greenlandic language, though partly Greenlandized (*Guuti*); and, of course, once the word *God* became part of the Greenlandic language, it was not difficult to create the phrase "Son of God." But it goes without saying that education is needed in order to understand what is meant by such loanwords and new concepts. This Son of God is, in Egede's rendering, a "protector"; but in the printed Bibles he became the "rescuer," which is more appropriate from both a linguistic and theological point of view.

In the pre-Christian religion, the shamans and their helping spirits mediated between the perceptible and the unseen world. Every shaman had his (or, rarely, her) own personal helping spirits, *toornat*. The most important one among them the shaman called his *toornaarsuk*, which probably means "the special helping spirit."[36] Helping spirits were important and necessary figures in the mind of the Greenlanders in the old society. They were potentially dangerous figures but not downright hostile (Kleivan 1979, 180). To *angakkut* and their audience they were indispensable. However, already in his earliest catechism Egede used *toornaarsuk* as the Greenlandic word for "devil" (H. Egede 1723, 72).

Every *angakkoq* (*angakkut* in the singular) had his own *toornaarsuk*, and their audiences also had different opinions regarding the appearance of this spirit if anyone asked (Sonne 1986).[37] The identification of this *toornaarsuk* with the devil that haunted the contemporary Christian world

---

36. *Toornaarsuk* is a noun derived from *toornaq*, "helping spirit," with a derivational affix *-arsuk*. In Old Greenlandic this affix meant "special" or "unusual" (Fabricius 1801, 21). In today's language the affix is mostly used pejoratively.

37. H. Egede 1741, 184–85: "even the angekuts themselves are divided in the whimsical ideas they have formed of this being; some saying he is without any form or shape; others giving him that of a bear, others again pretending he has a large body and but one arm; and some make him as little as a finger. There are those who hold he is immortal, and others, that a puff of wind can kill him. They assign him his abode in the lower regions of the Earth, where they tell you there is constantly fine sunshiny weather, good water, deer, and fowls in abundance. They also say he lives in the water."

of ideas may be seen already in a Greenlandic glossary printed in 1673 and used by Egede (Bartholin 1673, 76; cf. H. Egede 1722b, 39).[38] Accordingly, Egede brought this identification to Greenland, and it caused severe misunderstandings in the theological discussions that the missionary had with his Greenlandic neighbors. It is no wonder that the locals did not appreciate the myth of *toornaarsuk* as a fallen, disobedient angel. They tried to make him comprehend that *toornaarsuk* "was not evil and did not harm anyone but disclosed to their *angakkut* what would happen to them. If they took action accordingly, nothing evil would befall them" (H. Egede 1738, 158; my trans.). It is no wonder, either, that Egede was not convinced. It was probably unavoidable that the missionaries conceived Inuit's *toornaarsuk* as a supreme being or their God, which is how the spirit was referred to in the first printed dictionary (P. Egede 1750, 189): "The Greenlanders consider him to be originator of much evil. He is hideous and ugly, but he may to some extent be called their God even though he has no cult, since they attribute several divine qualities to him such as omnipotence [and] omniscience. He is rarely seen by others than *angakkut* to whom he speaks in his own language that only they understand. Therefore they must be his interpreter for their compatriots" (my trans.). In this way, *toornaarsuk* became the antithesis of the Christian God. However, Hans Egede and his colleagues and successors did not believe that *angakkut* really acted in collusion with the devil. To the missionaries, the *angakkut* were skillful cheaters who deceived their credulous audience, who for their part did not question that the spirits and their prince were real.[39]

This demonization of traditional beliefs made the story of Jesus being tempted by the devil (Matt 4) very complicated in Hans Egede's translation, and new meaning was added to it unintentionally. Egede had no Greenlandic word for "temptation," so instead he wrote that Jesus was frightened by *toornaarsuk*. To the Greenlandic audience of the day this

---

38. This being so, the description in Sonne 1986, 200—though reflecting a widespread opinion among students of Inuit-European relations (another example is Gad 1973, 76)—is not accurate: "he [Hans Egede] identified the first Greenlandic spirit he ever encountered with the Devil." He did not make this identification himself; he brought it with him from the little that was "known" about Greenland in Europe in his day.

39. Egede 1741, 194: "I am loth [sic] to believe, that, in these spells and conjurings, there is any real commerce with the devil; for to me it clearly appears, that there is nothing in it but mere fibs, juggling tricks, and impostures, made use of by these crafty fellows for the sake of filthy lucre, for they are well paid for their pains."

rendering must have conveyed the impression that Jesus was a shaman-to-be who had left his village and gone into the wilderness to meet his helping spirit. Such confrontations between *angakkut*-to-be and helping spirits were terrifying (Kleivan and Sonne 1985, 25); only the person able to endure such harrowing experiences would become an *angakkoq*. Hence new meaning is added to the story when Jesus turns down his *toornaarsuk*'s proposals. To the contemporary Greenlandic mind, this must have meant that Jesus refused to be a shaman and receive the help of a special helping spirit. Instead, he was served by angels, and it must have been difficult to explain the difference between the helping spirits, *toornat*, of the traditional Inuit society and the angels of the Christian world. Illustrative of the missionary's feeling that they were fundamentally different characters is that he rejected the Greenlandic *toornaq* and borrowed the Danish word *engel* in his Bible translation. The word is still in use, though fully greenlandized: *inngili*.

Regarding the spirit of God, Egede found no word that he wanted to use among the traditional religious ideas. From the verb *anersaarpoq*, "breathe," he probably formed the word *Anarsáh* (*anersaaq*) himself. In his translation of Gen 1:2, he inserted a note explaining that "Gudib Anarsáh" (*Guutip anersaava*) means "God's breath ... I can find no other word in the language suitable for articulating the idea of a spiritual being" (Egede 1725b, 7; my trans.). In a glossary written in 1727, Albert Topp has the word *Anernek* (*anerneq*), meaning "breath" (Bergsland and Rischel 1986, 145, no. 742), which is still a word in common use. The Moravian Brethren preferred this word in the sense "(God's) spirit," and so did Samuel Kleinschmidt, himself the son of a Moravian missionary and Bible translator, and he excluded Egede's word *anersaaq* from his own Bible translation and also from his epoch-making dictionary.[40] In the nineteenth century, passions ran high in Greenland regarding the choice between the two alternatives (Wilhjelm 1997, 211–13), and in today's language Egede's word *anersaaq* means "spirit" whereas *anerneq* means "breath."

"Holy" and "bless" were words that Egede borrowed from Danish and furnished with Greenlandic derivational and inflectional affixes. These words demanded extensive explanations, and in the course of time proper Greenlandic equivalents were developed. Regarding "bless," the result

---

40. Kleinschmidt 1871. This remarkable Greenlandic-Danish dictionary, though archaic in some respects, is still the best one in existence.

became *pilluaqquaa*, "to congratulate someone." Among other important religious ideas in Egede's selection of biblical texts are the concepts of good and evil (Gen 2:9) for which Egede, to his surprise, found no indigenous words (H. Egede 1725b, 11). His solution, "useful things and useless things," is still used today in the sense "good and evil." In this way, new thinking was introduced and a substantial transformation of both society and language initiated.

Other ideas were common to missionaries and Greenlanders. When God makes the man a living being in Gen 2:7, the usual rendering in the European Bibles of the day was that the man became a "living soul." Regarding this "soul," Egede and his helpers found a suitable Greenlandic expression, *tarneq*, since the idea of an immortal soul was part of the then Greenlandic world of religious ideas. In Egede's early rendering of Gen 2:7, the man receives his soul when God blows life upon him. This idea remained in the printed versions to come. Only in the latest versions did the man become a "living being," without mention of a soul.

More complicated is the Christian idea of sin, for which Egede simply chose the Danish word *synd* with various Greenlandic derivative and inflectional affixes. In today's language, this loanword has been replaced by an indigenous one, *ajorti*, meaning "making useless." In the story of Cain and Abel, Egede has Cain regret that he is sinful (Gen 4:13), which is equated with being useless. A peculiar definition is suggested in Matt 1:21, when it is said that Jesus is to save his people from their sins. In his attempt at rendering this expression, Egede combines the Danish word *synd* and a Greenlandic verb, *erippaa*, meaning "to pluck hairs or feathers out of it." The expression must have been impossible to understand without careful instruction. In the same biblical passage, Egede adds a clarifying comment that Jesus is to accompany his people away from *toornaarsuk*. Sin is, accordingly, equal to the traditional beliefs of the pre-Christian Greenlandic society.

In the rendering of Jesus' conversation with Nicodemus (John 3), the Greenlandic audience is presented with a clear alternative: either they can go to *toornaarsuk*, or they can go to heaven. As a consequence of this line of thinking, the biblical parts of Egede's manuscript conclude with this conversation and its Johannine discussion of light and darkness that obviously reflects the mission and its light in contradistinction to the darkness of heathen senselessness and superstition. And in the story of the flood, it is telling that the people extirpated in Noah's days, in Egede's rendering, are characterized as inefficient and senseless (Gen 6:5), for "senseless" is also the expression used by Egede when he characterizes the non-Christian Greenlanders. As mentioned above, his manuscript contains a "prayer explaining to the Greenlanders their senselessness" (H. Egede 1725b, 91) and a number of sermons. Their aim is to convince the Greenlanders of "their senselessness and reprehensible inclinations" (H. Egede 1725b, 123).

It is in line with this alleged senselessness of the nonbelievers that the word *sensibility* is important in Egede's very early attempts at translating biblical texts. The twelve-year-old Jesus is the "sensible child" (Luke 2:47), the visiting magi are "The Very Sensible Men" (Matt 2:1), and the scribes consulted by King Herod (Matt 2:4) and the teachers conversing with young Jesus in the temple (Luke 2:46) are "sensible." All are meant to serve as models for the new Greenlandic Christianity.

One of the first Danish words that spread in the old Greenlandic society after the arrival of Christianity was the missionary's designation of himself, "priest." Accordingly, Egede could safely use this word in his translation of biblical texts, and it is still part of the modern language, though both spelling and pronunciation have been fully greenlandized (*palasi*, from Norwegian *prest*). In Egede's version of the Bible, the priests are given a prominent position, for when John the Baptist is asked who he is, the answer given in an expanded version of John 1:23 is that he is a priest who speaks to the people about the Son of God. This version of John the Baptist's character reflects the role of the missionaries, who thus inscribed themselves in the Bible.

Hans Egede was well aware of the imperfections of his Greenlandic, and a close reading of his texts shows that his early translations and paraphrases of the Bible must have been difficult for the uneducated, monolingual audience to understand since he has only a very rudimentary understanding of the language's most basic syntax. This is only logical because no comprehensive dictionaries or written grammars existed when Egede settled in Greenland, and he did his linguistic work parallel to his daily chores as missionary and leader of a group of settlers, perhaps a hundred people, in a rough Arctic environment. As said above, however, before Egede's arrival the Greenlanders had a centuries-old tradition of bartering and communicating with visiting Europeans. In spite of all imperfections, Egede's and his colleagues' insistence that the gospel should be preached in the vernacular and his own attempts at translating biblical, catechetical, and liturgical texts initiated a development of the Greenlandic language that has saved it for posterity, contrary to so many other languages in the

American hemisphere; and today it is the official language of an autonomous nation within the Danish national community. No other aboriginal language in the American hemisphere has a comparable position.

Regarding the changes of Greenlandic culture and society, the consequences of the mission were, of course, profound. The plot line in Egede's selection of texts was simple: God created the world of the Greenlanders, and they should follow God's Son away from *toornaarsuk* in order to go to heaven, listen to the Christian priests, and become sensible. The Christian mission inscribed both themselves and the Greenlandic people in the biblical narrative, and the indigenous people embraced Christianity and its rites and pictures (K. Kjærgaard 2010). In the course of time, a proud Greenlandic nation was built and a Christian community established.

Configuring the Language to Convert the People: Translating the Bible in Greenland

Christina Petterson

> Any translation is a struggle with the material dimensions of language, and the intermedial translation especially—because it concerns itself primarily with the physical medium—makes the reader more aware of the materiality of the text. Changing from one medium to another, perhaps even more than translation proper (within a single medium) from one language to another, is always a matter of violence, disruption, and distortion. (Aichele 2001, 63)

Introduction

The landscape of western Greenland is strikingly rocky. No trees, only shrubs of varying kinds. From October to April the ground is covered in snow—a bit further in from the coast the land is covered in ice all year.[1] In 1721 the primary food was seal, whose skins, intestines, and fur served multiple purposes. Reindeer and walrus, as well as different kinds of birds, whales, and fish were also main ingredients in the diet. These were the conditions that met the Danish missionaries when they first arrived in Greenland in 1721. So how would you translate Matt 7:16: "Are grapes gathered from thorns, or figs from thistles," into Greenlandic? And how would you go about translating Rev 5:5–6, where the lion of Judah is the Lamb? What about camels or doves? And what about the really important words, such as *king* or *God*, *spirit* and *sin*? These issues in translation are not limited to translating the Bible in Greenland alone. They are issues that

---

1. This was written in 2006, when this was still the case. In 2012 the climate in West Greenland has become considerably milder.

have confronted Bible translators in many parts of the world, where the limits and limitations of language come to the fore and radically test the flexibility of the message and the creativity of its bearer.

Translating the Bible into Greenlandic meant more than finding adequate words to fix the meaning of the biblical text. It was, as was the case in so many other colonial contexts, a later step in a process of conversion and control. *Preceding* the actual translation was what Aichele above calls an "intermedial translation" of the Greenlandic language, namely converting it to the medium of writing, in its particular Western linear and alphabetized inflection. While the institutionalization of Greenlandic writing did not take place until the mid-nineteenth century, what is taking place already here is, to paraphrase David Scott, the reshaping of the conceptual conditions of possibility of social action (2004, 119). The Bible translation and its medium set the coordinates within which resistance was possible, and established new parameters for truth. *Following* the translation, then, are the social and cultural upheavals of this intrusion of writing, in terms of class formations and constructions of gender resulting from the education and labor politics of the colonial administration.

In this article, I address the practice of translation of the Bible and other religious texts into Greenlandic and its cultural implications. First, I will focus on the politics of language, that is, the hierarchical relationship between Danish and Greenlandic and the cultural implications inherent in this difference. The second issue is that of Greenlandic religious practice. What happens to this cultural aspect when it meets a dominating monotheistic worldview and religious practice, and what are the cultural implications?

The Politics of Language

The cultural particularity of language has through the centuries presented missionaries with a number of conundrums in translating the Bible and other religious texts into the various vernaculars of the colonial contexts, of which Greenland was but one. Language as an important feature of postcolonial identity formations, class alliances, and cultural practices is illustrated by the discussion between Chinua Achebe and Ngugi wa' Thiong'o and their disagreements over whether to write in English or Kikuyu. Also in contemporary Greenlandic societies, issues concerning the cross-sections between language, communication, and domination are raised again and again (see discussion and relevant literature in Langgård 2003). Germane to the problematic of language, colonialism, and power is the issue of translation, which has received considerable attention in literary and postcolonial circles (Bassnett and Trivedi 1999; Thisted 2005; Niranjana 1992; Thiong'o 1986). These analyses and discussions have—with few exceptions—focused on translations from the colonized language into the colonizer's language. Interestingly, all of these studies mention missionaries and/or the Bible, but only to leave them behind without further elaboration. However, as studies by Vicente Rafael, Homi Bhabha, and Roland Boer show, the missionaries' translations of religious texts into various vernaculars, as well as their reception in the local cultures, are equally important for assessing ambivalence, domination, and subversive practice in a colonial context (Bhabha 2004; Boer 2008; Rafael 1993). My focus in this article is less on subversion and more on the colonial *practice*, following the analyses of Jean and John Comaroff and Musa W. Dube (and again Rafael), which argue that the practice of translating into vernaculars also provides the missionaries with valuable and powerful tools of denigration and subjugation of the indigenous culture and elevation of the colonizer's culture (Comaroff and Comaroff 1991, 1997; Dube 1999; Rafael 1993).

Vicente Rafael's highly acclaimed study *Contracting Colonialism* (1993) is a detailed study of how the Spanish missionaries attempted to convert and control the native Tagalog population, and how the Tagalog people negotiated this process. Rafael uses translation in a narrow linguistic sense, as well as in a broad, cultural sense, where also one's thoughts and actions are reshaped to describe and conceptualize the resignification of Tagalog culture and Spanish Catholicism that took place in the colonial encounter. Rafael's linguistic analyses are developed on the basis of a Roman-Catholic economy of signification, which rests on a presupposed hierarchy of languages, with Latin being closest to God. This explains the desire to construct Tagalog grammar through the grid of Latin, the implementation of Latin script to express Tagalog, as well as the understanding of Castilian and its Latin pedigree as being closer to the source of all meaning than Tagalog. The broader "ethnohistorical" analyses explore conversion, confession, and reciprocity through the lens of translation and signification. Because of the unstable signification and translation process, the Spanish colonial onslaught could never be complete, and thus provided the Tagalog people with loopholes and ways of circumventing, or at least displacing, the totalizing demands of Christianity and colonialism.

Applying Rafael's insights to the situation under scrutiny in this present analysis is not without problems, which I shall return to in a moment.

The temptation to contemplate such a venture at all arises from the time span, the scope, and the geographical setting of the study. Much of the detailed postcolonial work has been carried out within the boundaries of the British Empire, which locks these analyses within the development of capitalism, social Darwinism, and relatively developed class structures (McClintock 1995; Comaroff and Comaroff 1991; 1997; Nandy 1983). In contrast, the time span Rafael covers is from the late sixteenth to the early eighteenth century, and the geographical location is the Philippines. This brings us closer to the economic stage in which the Danish exploration and subsequent colonization of Greenland took place. Furthermore, the Danish language was regarded as being of divine origin, albeit in a somewhat fallen state (Henriksen 1997, 112). There is, however, the small matter of the confessional contexts of Rafael's study and this present one. While the Spanish mission to the Philippines was Catholic, the Danish mission to Greenland was Protestant. This difference is quite important. Rafael shows that the Catholic missionaries were open to incorporating indigenous elements. On the other hand, the Protestant missionaries in Greenland eyed anything smacking of ritual as idolatrous and preferred to reject everything indigenous as belonging to the pagan past.

While the issue of translation is the central issue in Rafael's study, postcolonialism and the Bible are the central features of Roland Boer's *Last Stop before Antarctica: The Bible and Postcolonialism in Australia* (2008). The chapter dealing with Bible translation, "Dreaming the Logos," takes as its point of departure the principle of dynamic equivalence[2] and proceeds to address "meaning" and the semantic overflows, which occur in the translation process in engagement with Homi Bhabha, Walter Benjamin, and Rafael. The example is, as the title of the chapter might suggest, the translation of *logos* (which means primarily "word," but also "parable," "gospel," etc.) with the Pitjantjatjara word *tjukurpa*, which apart from "word" and "message" also means "dreaming" (as well as "story," "law," and "birthmark"; Boer 2008, 155). Thus one key religious term is used to translate another key religious concept, which undermines the presumed intentions of the translators to unequivocally signify "logos" or "gospel," and no longer carry its former determinations (158). But this intention

---

2. A translation principle that advocates the translation of the text's meaning rather than insisting on translation of its linguistic form. The principle, which entails a structuralist approach to language and meaning, is associated with the Summer Institute of Linguistics and is widely used in biblical translation.

also pertains to the results of the translations. If the intention of the Bible translators was to transmit the gospel in indigenous languages, the results moved far beyond this target, in that the translations in effect created new languages and conceptualized different ways of thinking, both of which were compatible with the colonial rule that was part and parcel of the mission (146–47, 159). I return to this toward the end of the article.

The Danish missionaries in Greenland encountered a different conceptual world than what they were accustomed to from home. The power structures among the Greenlanders were different and the spiritual world another matter. The translation of the Bible proved to be a difficult task. Poul Egede was the first to produce a translation of the New Testament into Greenlandic and recalls his troubles in the introduction to the translation completed in 1766. He stated that his difficulties were due to the "importance of the matter, the high thoughts, the unusual ways of speech, examples, and parables, and the imperfection of the Greenlandic language, which stems from the fact that they have no religion, no moral code, no authorities, and no science" (Egede 1766, n.p.; my trans.). And it then follows that there are no words or concepts to describe these matters. To this, Egede has two solutions. One is, where applicable, to create new words, because the Greenlandic language with its many details and nuances is formidable in this capacity. Where this has not been possible, he has retained the Danish word. From the list I began with above, Egede held on to "grapes," "thorns," "figs," "thistles," "lion," "dove," "king," and "God" in Danish. In the following revisions and editions of Greenlandic Bible translations, valiant attempts were made to actually translate these words—and the many others that he had kept in Danish ("tax," "gold," "crown," and "toll") (Kleivan 1979, 179–80). Thus "thorns" and "thistles" found a Greenlandic counterpart—kind of[3]—while the words signifying "grapes," "figs," "lion," "dove," "king," and "God" still are Danish loanwords.[4]

---

3. The suffix *-naq* (similar to the English *-ish*) and *-ussaq* (that which looks like) are both used to transform the odd vegetation of the Bible into something less unfamiliar (Kleivan 1979, 179 and 182).

4. Kleivan (1979) goes through a number of examples of how the missionaries translated the various objects. Otto Fabricius, who revised Egede's translation, changed the Danish loanword for "thorns" into *kakkidlarnekotaursænnit*, which means "from some which look like juniper bushes," along with a footnote explaining "sharp trees, which don't have that kind of fruit," to explain the parable; similarly with "thistles," which becomes *kênariksunnit* "from the sharp ones," which is expounded in the footnote as "from plants who don't have berries" (Kleivan 1979, 179–80).

This circumstance that some words are so important, or for that matter culturally specific, that they cannot be translated is not new within missionary histories. Rafael has shown that the missionaries among the Tagalogs also avoided translating certain concepts such as "God," "virgin," "Holy Spirit," and "crucifix." The result was not quite what had been intended, because retaining the Spanish words meant that undecipherable words intruded into the Tagalog vernacular. While from the Spanish point of view this was meant to protect the orthodoxy, it had the effect that these words presented themselves to the Tagalog ears as "opaque signifiers with no prior signifieds in Tagalog" (Rafael 1993, 117). So when the word *Dios* was pronounced, it was left to the hearers to associate and give meaning to this foreign element, a meaning that perhaps was not quite that obvious heaven-rendering truth that the missionaries had in mind. As Rafael puts it, "the very untranslatability of Christian signs could be reread in different ways by native converts. Rather than making indisputably apparent the authority of God's sign and that of the priest, such terms presented the possibility of dodging the full weight of the missionary's intent" (Rafael 1993, 117).

The intention, namely, that the word *Dios* should unambiguously convey God in all his glory and majesty, and that no adequate word could be found for this in Tagalog, reveals an implied or presupposed hierarchical notion of language and culture. Going back to the Greenlandic context, one could ask which divine and sacred qualities the Danish language possesses that are absent from Greenlandic, since Poul Egede felt that only the word *Gud*[5] was adequate to signify that particular god. It gives the impression that the Danish language is better than Greenlandic at expressing the *content* of the concept of God and thus that the Danish language is closer to the divine being than the Greenlandic. However, the hierarchy of languages that Rafael has detected in several Castilian documents is not systematically articulated within the Danish context. In his discussion of the untranslatability of central doctrinal terms, Rafael mentions that the praxis was moved by a desire to standardize Catholic discourse over against the threat of Protestantism (Rafael 1993, 29 n. 12).

That God should be called *Gud* in Greenland is put forth as a divine necessity rather than human convention, and so God and the king and

---

5. The Danish word for "god," itself derived from the Germanic *guða*, which means "the invoked" (*Politikens Nudansk Ordbog med etymologi*).

other unprecedented concepts are introduced as Danish words into the Greenlandic vernacular. But this is also the logic of mission, because, if God the signified could be expressed with a Greenlandic signifier, then mission would be superfluous and conversion impossible. It is precisely the difference between Danish and Greenlandic language, religion, and culture that makes *God* untranslatable and conversion possible. According to Egyptologist Jan Assmann, conversion and translatability exclude each other.

> As long as there is the possibility of translation there is no need of conversion. If all religions basically worship the same gods there is no need to give up one religion to enter another one. This possibility only occurs if there is one religion claiming knowledge of a superior truth. It is precisely this claim that excludes translatability. If one religion is wrong and the other is right, there can be no question of translating the gods of one into those of the other. Obviously they are about different gods. (Assmann 1996, 31)

God's untranslatability is fixed within a presupposition that Danish culture is different, superior, and closer to "the truth" than Greenlandic culture. This is what is expressed in Poul Egede's complaints about the Greenlanders not having any religion, moral code, authorities, or science. Because, as the various diaries of the missionaries show, there *were* religion, moral codes, authorities, and science, but these practices were regarded as folly, superstition, and local custom in comparison to the elevated Danish culture. The terms in which Greenlandic shamanic practice and its spiritual world were expressed could not and more importantly *should not* in any way articulate the Christian or Danish God, and so Danish words must be imported to designate this aspect. This import of central concepts in Danish in turn conferred an authoritative status to the Danish language and, by extension, Danish theology and their ability to express truth. This measure of authenticity still haunts Greenlandic (and Danish) theology today.

The Greenlandic Religious Practice after Christ

There was a way, however, that the Greenlandic religious words could signify theological terms within this hierarchy of language and culture. From the very beginning, the relationship between the missionaries and the local religious elite was at best antagonistic. The missionaries immediately attacked the practices of the shamans, who played a significant role in the societal structure. Hans Egede aggressively incorporated the world of the shamans into the Christian worldview by using the term for the central guiding spirit of the shaman, the *toornaarsuk*, to translate "the devil" (Lynge 2006; Dickmeiss 2002; Kleivan 1979). The shamans were known as "witch masters" (*hexe-mestre*) within the Egede terminology. In the preface to his New Testament translation, Poul Egede mentions that if Christ had been born in Greenland, his opponents would not have been Pharisees and Sadducees, but *hexe-mestre*. Finally, one of the central figures of the Greenlandic worldview, the Mother (or Woman) of the Sea, was dubbed "the devil's grandmother."[6] Thus the Egede missionaries recast the struggles between themselves and the shamans into a cosmic tale of good and evil, with the Greenlandic cosmology placed on line with the devil, and printed in the Bible. This is also reinforced through the use of the word *sin*, which to begin with was not translated, but the Danish word (*synd*) was used and understood as disobedience toward the missionaries (Kleivan 1979, 177). This disobedience is connected to the two competing belief systems, so that the sin becomes firmly connected to the previous religious practice of the Greenlanders. Within colonial discourse this is not an unknown procedure. Turning to the African continent, biblical scholar Musa Dube, as well as the anthropologists John and Jean Comaroff, has shown that the same practice occurred in Moffatt's translation of the Bible into Setswana (1857), some eighty-nine years later than Poul Egede's translation. Moffatt translated the demons from Matthew into *Badimo*, which means "ancestors," but as the Comaroffs note, signify "an entire cultural order in which the dead had and still have, a hallowed place" (Comaroff and Comaroff 1991, 218). Dube, herself a Botswanian scholar, goes more in depth and explains that

> the institution of *Badimo* serves as the centre of social memories or history of the society. For an oral people, the role of *Badimo* as an institution of social memories cannot be overemphasized. *Badimo* are the thread which connects the present society and families with their past and directs them to the future, for here the people of the past are kept

---

6. The Mother of the Sea lives at the bottom of the sea and sends out the animals and fish for people to catch and eat. With every transgression of taboos, her hair becomes dirtier, and finally she will refuse to send out any game. The *angakok* then has to travel down to her, and untangle her hair, and she will again release the game.

alive and actively involved in the events of contemporary society. (Dube 1999, 39)

Through an analysis of other central Setswana cultural concepts in the Bible translation and in the accompanying dictionaries, Dube concludes that through the translations and dictionaries, the English language is purged of any knowledge of evil, which then instead is pushed on to Setswana culture (1999, 48) as a means of alienating the people from their own culture. A similar point may be made in the Greenlandic context, where the demonic figures in the New Testament are represented by figures known from the Greenlandic spiritual world, and the divine figures are represented by the Danish language. I have already mentioned "God," but "angel" is also a Danish loanword.

I would like briefly to stay with the dictionaries that Dube has mentioned. A comprehensive grammar of the Greenlandic language was also compiled in Greenland dictionaries. The first to engage in this enterprise was again Poul Egede, which means that there was a high degree of compatibility between the language presented in the Bible, the grammar, and the dictionary. This structuring of the so-called disorderly language is also a common denominator in mission history and may be termed in the words of the Comaroffs as making the language into an "instrument of empirical knowledge" (1991, 311).[7] The Comaroffs note that the deepest impact of the mission on Tswana consciousness is by the means of literacy and learning. Reading the Setswana Bible, the Tswana people would have been confronted with "a form of cultural translation in which vernacular poetics were re-presented to them as a thin *sekgoa* narrative—and their language itself reduced to an instrument of empirical knowledge, Christian prayer, and just-so stories" (Comaroff and Comaroff 1991, 311).

Also, Rafael mentions the estrangement or actual alienation of the Tagalog language carried out by the missionaries, who refashioned "the vernacular ... into an object to be classified and dissected" (1993, 38). After giving it a grammar and a lexicon, they hand it back to the people in forms of prayers, sermons, and confessionals. Boer makes the same point in reference to Australian Aboriginal languages (2008, 148–49). The social impact may be explained in that the Bible translations and their grammatical accessories transformed the oral languages of Setswana and

---

7. Dube has altered the citation and made it an instrument of *imperial* knowledge.

Greenlandic into written languages. These written forms were meant to serve colonial centers such as churches, schools, and trade, which were in competition with local institutions (Dube 1999, 45).

It is, I think, important to emphasize the objectification process that takes place in the incorporation of indigenous cultural practice in the biblical text. An engagement with Christian discourse in Greenland meant being subjected to an image of Greenlanders and Greenlandic culture as being in line with the devil and thus compelled toward participating in a particularly European understanding of Greenlandic culture and custom.

Such a process is never complete. Indeed, Dube finishes her article by pointing to the subversive practice of the African independent churches in interpreting the Bible, using it as a divining set, and thus bypassing the desired suppressing and colonizing effects. Subversive practices in Greenland could entail the use of Bible pages as amulets as was done in the early twentieth century or the various prophetic movements throughout the years, which freely bring together elements from the two different traditions but are efficiently dissolved and dispersed.

A more consistent use of the former master's tools may be found in another chapter of Boer's *Last Stop before Antarctica*, where he discusses the problematic medium of language:

> those who speak within/to/from—that is, with some sort of prepositional relation to—postcolonial situations find that their ability to speak or write is always (over)determined by a range of conflicting factors, derivative mostly from the former colonial contexts themselves. For example, the very ability to be heard outside one's own context is paradoxically enabled (and then limited) by the language and connections bequeathed by the former colonial masters—an ambiguity embodied in the famous "What have the Romans done for us?" sequence in *The Life of Brian*. (Boer 2008, 109–10)

During colonization and mission, the Bible translations invaded, so to speak, the oral languages and transformed them into writing—written languages that indigenous writers (such as Thiong'o) now can express themselves in as a medium of resistance. In Greenland the written language can function as a mode of expression, resistance, and community beyond the initial intentions of the colonizers. As expression, it has resulted in an exquisite and extensive literary tradition in Greenlandic, a language that is still way beyond the grasp of most Danes and thus also functions as resistance toward Danish linguistic hegemony.[8] Finally, written Greenlandic proved to be of great value in Greenland with its fifty thousand people spread over two million square kilometers and thus lay the foundations of a Greenlandic imagined community in the late nineteenth century (see Thuesen 1988), fostering a nationalism that would eventually take the colonial power by surprise. However, this development went hand in hand with a stratification of the Greenlandic society through the class politics of the Danish colonial administration. These politics generated an educated, lettered upper class, which would produce this literary tradition as well as the imagined community.[9]

CONCLUSION

In her study on translation, history, and colonialism, Tejaswini Niranjana bemoans the lack of awareness of "the constructed nature of cultural translations" in that "translation is always *producing* rather than merely reflecting or imitating an 'original'" (Niranjana 1992, 81; emphasis original). Niranjana's discussions pertain primarily to translations into English, but her point is worth exploring in the present context.

On the one hand, we have the text itself, in this case the Bible, which is produced in a different context, far away from its point of origin, whatever that might be. It is produced through the Greenlandic language, with Greenlandic, culturally specific terms to convey its message. On the other hand, we have the Greenlandic language, which not only is written down and shaped to conform to the message it is intended to convey, but it is also introduced to new words and concepts, which, to bring back Rafael's point, initially would present themselves as "opaque signifiers with no prior signifieds in Tagalog" (Rafael 1993, 117).

The first transformation—that of the Bible—is largely the focus of studies that seek to emphasize the indigenous appropriation of the Bible

---

8. This issue, namely for whom to write, seems to be the germ of the argument between Chinua Achebe and Ngugi wa Thiong'o that thus takes on a class distinction expressed in a linguistic decision. With his decision to write only in Gikuyu and Kiswahili in the statement that prefaces *Decolonising the Mind* (1986, xvi), Thiong'o thus addresses his fellow Africans outside the English-speaking bourgeois classes in their own languages (Thiong'o 1986, 72).

9. This is the topic of my forthcoming book, *The Missionary, the Catechist and the Hunter*.

and Christianity and the subversive potential of such an appropriation. The second transformation—that of the language—is, conversely, an indication of the extent of colonial violence and intrusion into the very means of communication and social coherence. As mentioned above, Greenlanders made good use of the written language and the new means of communication and abstraction this offered. Yet the translations and their grasp (in every sense of the word) of the language provided means of reaching into the everyday lives of indigenous people. Luther's aim with vernacular Bible translations was precisely to use the language of everyday people, or, as he put it, the language spoken by the man in the field and the woman in the kitchen, and thus to penetrate into all levels of society. Thus the *means* of communication are reconstructed according to European standards of communication, a process that generates a social disruption, and, following David Scott, resets the parameters of Greenlandic social action.

Translations of the Bible are never carried out in an ideological vacuum, but have an explicit agenda, which may at one level be seen as edifying, but nevertheless serve social and political purposes.[10] Therefore, Bible translations should not be exempt from their historical and political contexts.

---

10. *The New Deal*, the Danish equivalent to *Good News Bible* (although only NT), was released in 2007 by the Danish Bible Society, whose explicit ideal was to use the language of everyday people. One could argue that this move served to mobilize an ideological unity against the growing Danish Muslim population.

"A GIFT FOR THE JEWISH PEOPLE": EINSPRUCH'S *DER BRIS KHADOSHE* AS MISSIONARY TRANSLATION AND YIDDISH LITERATURE

Naomi Seidman

The earliest known Yiddish translation of the New Testament, by the convert Paul Helic, appeared in Kraków in 1540, less than two decades after Luther's 1522 German version and closely following its formulations. Yiddish translations of the New Testament and other publications designed for missionary work among Yiddish-speaking Jews continued to appear through the seventeenth and, especially, eighteenth centuries, along with other material designed to help Christians understand Europe's Jews through the medium of their language.[1]

But the most sustained efforts to proselytize Jews through New Testament translations occurred in the context of the much broader phenomenon of the nineteenth- and twentieth-century project of disseminating the Bible first to the poor, in inexpensive editions, and then throughout the world, an outgrowth of the late-eighteenth-century evangelical revival. In the two centuries since 1804, when the British and Foreign Bible Society was founded, the Bible in whole or part was translated under the auspices of an international range of Bible societies into more than a thousand languages. Among these were a significant number in Jewish languages, including Hebrew, Yiddish, Judeo-German, Ladino, Judeo-Arabic, and Judeo-Persian; the Bible societies also published a number of parallel editions specifically directed at Jews, with a Hebrew New Testament on the right and German, French, Hungarian, Italian, Russian, Polish, Turkish,

---

1. For Protestant missionary publications directed toward the Jews and the phenomenon of "Christian Yiddishism," see Elyada 2009.

English, Romanian, Yiddish, or Judeo-German on the left-facing page.[2] The Jewish-language translations are similar to the other Bibles produced by these societies in a variety of ways: they were sponsored, printed, and distributed by Bible societies and the missionary groups they worked with; and—on principle and to avoid doctrinal controversy—they were published without notes or commentary.[3] In Jewish as in other translations, though, editors and publishers sometimes found ways of circumventing these restrictions to communicate with their readers. As with other translations, initial efforts were often deemed insufficient (the term *missionary Yiddish* for mangled and incorrect missionary tracts and translations was a familiar one), and revisions were undertaken—typically by converts who were native speakers; the early twentieth century saw a wave of such revisions in Jewish as in other languages.

Finally, Bible societies disseminated sentimental stories of the powerful effect of the New Testament on Jews as on other prospective converts. Missionaries reported that potential Jewish converts described the Yiddish New Testament in reverent terms, as having "brought peace to my troubled soul," or as "heavenly words, which are so comforting to a widow's heart."[4] One missionary described Jewish immigrants who were

---

2. By the middle of the century, Judeo-Spanish, Judeo-German, Judeo-Arabic, and Judeo-Persian versions are listed in a "Summary of Versions of the Scriptures Printed by the Society," dated 1851. For later figures see "The Bible for the Jews," *The Monthly Reporter of the British and Foreign Bible Society* (1882), 77. Both sources are quoted in Greenspoon (1998, 293). Among the earlier Yiddish NT translations associated with the Bible societies are: M. Sh. Bergman [Mortkhe Shmuel Bergmann], *Dos Naye Testament Oyf's Nay Aroysgegeben in Yudish* (London: London Missionary Society, 1887; rev. ed. 1908; other eds. 1912, 1913, 1917, 1928); Binyomin Nachmiye Solomon, *Dos Naye Testament Fun dem Meshiekh* (London: London Society for Promoting Christianity amongst the Jews, 1820; other eds. 1840, 1852, 1866, 1869); Yankev A. Adler, *Dos Naye Testament* (London: Society for the Distribution of Hebrew Scriptures, 1891; repr. 1896).

3. Leslie Howsam summarizes the principle in this way: "The 'fundamental principle' of [the British and Foreign Bible Society] was the distribution of the scriptures, *without note or comment*, a rule which the founders hoped would avoid doctrinal disputes by organizing Christians around their common acceptance of the canonical books of the Bible. Prefaces and explanatory notes, interpreting the text according to doctrines of particular creeds or of individual theologians, were explicitly forbidden" (1991, 6; emphasis original).

4. "The Power of the New Testament amongst the Jews," *The Monthly Reporter of the BFBS* (December, 1886), 207–209; quoted in Greenspoon (1998, 297).

approached on board ships bound for America as eager to hear the Christian message: "They sometimes fight for a NT in Yiddish."[5] These stories, as Homi Bhabha has suggested in his reading of the intersections between the missionary and colonialism projects, evince not only the triumphant and wondrous bestowal of the holy book, but also the deferrals and anxieties of its colonial reception, "in which it is repeated, translated, misread, displaced" (Bhaba 1994, 102).

For all the congruence between the broader project of global evangelism and the mission to the Jews, the translations produced for Jews inevitably had some unique characteristics, given the relationship of Judaism to Christianity. Jews were particularly prized converts, as evidenced by references in Bible society literature to the "ministry of special importance" that addressed "the needs of this community" (Roe 1965, 90–91). Jewish-born converts were also particularly valued as informants and language experts, not only in the target languages of missionary publications, but also in the sources to be translated, a role with deep roots in the historical Christian reliance on Jewish experts and sources for biblical knowledge. Jews were thus much more likely than other converts to rise in the ranks of these Bible societies as interpreters of the Bible and theological and strategic advisers—the most prominent example is probably Christian David Ginsburg (1836–1914), a Hebrew Bible scholar active in the Liverpool chapter of the London Mission to the Jews who worked on both revising the English Old Testament and, with Isaac Edward Salkinson (1822–1883), another Russian-born convert, producing a Hebrew New Testament that is still in general circulation.

The unique and charged relationship between Christians and Jews reflected itself, as well, on the linguistic level. Translations into Jewish languages, perhaps especially Hebrew, inevitably expressed the closeness of the religions. Christianity was more familiar to the Jews than it was to, say, the New Caledonians or the Thai: Jews had long lived among Christians and shared a major sacred text and many more religious concepts with them, which constituted a kind of shared religious grammar. Unlike Mongolian, for instance, which lacked words not only for Sabbath but also for palm tree and pomegranate, Jewish languages of any variety abundantly possessed a rich vocabulary from which a New Testament translator

---

5. British and Foreign Bible Society. Vol. 8 of Editorial Subcommittee Minute Cards: Yiddish (including Judaeo-German); quoted in Greenspoon 1998, 295. For a general overview of the Jewish mission, with a focus on America, see Ariel 2000.

could draw (Tatar 2002, 150). In the case of Hebrew, translators sometimes reported that their experiences were less of finding equivalents for a source language in a target language than of uncovering a lost precursor text. Robert Lindsey, working on a Hebrew translation of the Gospel of Mark in the 1960s, wrote that his work gave him the "frightening feeling that I was as much in the process of 'restoring' an original Hebrew work as in that of creating a new one," and spoke of "the tantalizing possibility" that he was discovering "the exact words of Jesus himself."[6] For Matthew, the Gospel richest in Hebraisms and sometimes believed to be a Greek translation of an original Hebrew text, this effect was even more apparent. For example, 1:21 ("And she shall bring forth a son, and thou shalt call his name JESUS: for he shall save his people from their sins," KJV) makes sense *only* in Hebrew translation, where the etymology of the child's name becomes clear.[7]

But other Jewish languages, via their Hebrew components, could also provide such a sense of recovery, as translators willing to leave behind the familiar and canonical language of Luther's Bible (and the resulting "missionary Yiddish") and mobilize a more correct and "Jewish" Yiddish would eventually discover.[8] Such an embrace of the Hebrew component of Yiddish was not fully realized until the mid-twentieth century, with the 1941 publication of *Der Bris Khadoshe* by Henry (Chayim) Einspruch in Baltimore. Einspruch's translation, unlike earlier versions, left German behind, taking not Luther or his Judeo-German and Yiddish revisers as his model, but rather the norms of literary Yiddish and, more specifically, the great modernist translation of the Hebrew Bible by Yehoash (Solomon Blumgarten), which appeared in 1926. As I will argue, internal developments in the sociology of Jewish conversion to Christianity also played a part in his linguistic choices. By contrast, M. Sh. Bergman's widely circulated and much revised *Dos Neye Testament* (1887) generally

---

6. Robert L. Lindsey, *A Hebrew Translation of the Gospel of Mark: Greek-Hebrew Diglot* (Jerusalem: Dugith, 1969), 9; quoted in Lapide 1984, 3, 203.

7. Eusebius cites Iranaeus on the lost original Hebrew Matthew, and the theory has had many expressions since then. For more on this history, see Lapide 1984, 1–3 and throughout.

8. Elyada makes clear, as well, that Christian Yiddishists only partially embraced Yiddish or Judeo-German as a medium, sharing in a broad Jewish as well as Christian distaste for the language as a "jargon." Thus early modern translators were encouraged to produce as "German" a translation as possible, even without the additional pressures of Luther's canonical precedent.

hewed closely to German usage: Bergman's disciples address Jesus as *lerer* in John 8:4 (Greek *didaskale*) and elsewhere (Luther has "*Meister*"), and his title for the Acts of the Apostles (Greek *prakseis apostololōn*), following Luther, is *Di Apostolgeshikhte*. Einspruch, on the other hand, has the disciples call Jesus *rebe* (Rabbi) in John 8:4, 11:8, and elsewhere, and calls the book of Acts *Di maysim fun di shlikhim*, using Yiddish's Hebrew component, with its stronger Jewish resonances.

In these and other decisions, Bible translators for Jews, and not only in Hebrew, were compelled to reflect not only on the ubiquitous translational issues of linguistic equivalence and biblical interpretation, but ultimately also on the relationship between Jews and Christians, Judaism and Christianity. These problems may be built into the very sources with which translators were working. As Willis Barnstone has argued, the rarity of the Greek term *rabbi* in the New Testament (in contrast with the ubiquity of such terms as *kyrie*, *epistata*, and *didaskale*) suggests an early attempt to distance Jesus from his Jewish context: "Clearly, to address Jesus as 'Rabbi' identifies him as a religious teacher of the Jews. To call him 'Master' [*kyrie*] averts this unpleasant designation" (1993, 71–72). If Barnstone is correct, the Greek "original" deviates from Hebrew or Aramaic (oral?) sources in which Jesus was typically addressed as rabbi. Barnstone's own translation, *The New Covenant* (2002), as well as Einspruch's earlier Yiddish one, can thus be described as retroversions (or pseudo-retroversions), recovering a lost original—and righting a historical misunderstanding—rather than rewriting an original in a foreign "target" language—although neither Barnstone's nor Einspruch's translation is Hebrew or Aramaic. Such a model of translation unsettles accepted notions of which text constitutes the original and which the translation, complicating our sense of what translation is and does. Because Judaism and Christianity are implicated in this relationship between original and translation, the destabilization of this relationship has complex religiopolitical, as well as textual, implications.

Despite what could be called the textual "sympathies" between the New Testament and Jewish languages, on the level of actual readers no such sympathies could be assumed. It was well known on both sides of the missionary enterprise that the Jews felt for Christianity a visceral distrust that was undoubtedly harder to overcome than the simple ignorance missionaries encountered in other contexts. The missionary report about Jews fighting for a New Testament onboard ships bound for America concluded with a lament about the rabbis present who forbade Jews from reading this estimable text.⁹ Einspruch was unable to find an American Yiddish press willing to print his translation and was compelled to find support in the missionary community for purchasing his own press (the press, paid for by the convert Harriet Lederer, was donated to the National Yiddish Book Center in the 1980s; Ariel 2000, 89, 92). It is this simultaneous affinity and aversion that translators had to mobilize and overcome. And they had to do so without the aid of prefaces or commentaries, given the strategic foundational choice of Bible societies "to avoid doctrinal disputes by organizing Christians around their common acceptance of the canonical books of the Bible" (Howsam 1991, 6).¹⁰

While keeping to the letter of this law, translators managed to convey a great deal of theologically charged material to their Jewish readers through epigraphs, illustrations, book covers, and other paratexts, along with their internal translation choices. Thus, while missionaries generally focused their efforts on distributing the New Testament to Jews, the translations they circulated managed to telegraph the *connection* between the Hebrew Bible and the New Testament; both *Dos Neye Testament* and *Der Bris Khadoshe* open with a well-chosen epigraph from Jer 31:30, promising in Hebrew and Yiddish translation that God will establish with the house of Israel and Judah "a new covenant" (*berit hadasha*, or, in Yehoash's version, *a neyem bund*). The phrase appears at least five times in the New Testament itself, but by choosing an epigraph from the Hebrew Bible, Bergman and Einspruch establish the provenance of their own source in a sacred text deemed holy by Jews. Making a theological and psychological claim on potential Jewish readers, these tactics let them know that the book they were holding had in fact been promised to *them*, in *their* Holy Scriptures, however new and dangerous Jewish culture traditionally deemed it.

The significance of these translations is often dismissed with a reference to the paltry number of converts that resulted from missionary efforts. Stories circulated in the communities targeted by missionaries about Yiddish New Testaments discarded or used to wrap fish. Levi Eshkol, attempting to quiet public anxiety about missionary activities in the State of Israel

---

9. "The Power of the New Testament among Jews," *The Monthly Reporter of the BFBS* (December, 1886), 209; quoted in Greenspoon (1998, 298).

10. As Howsam shows, such agreement was overstated, and the British and Foreign Bible Society was quickly propelled into denominational and doctrinal differences on the boundaries of the canon, particularly the status of the Apocrypha. See Howsam 1991, 13–34.

in a 1964 Knesset address, reminded the gathering that only about 201 Jews had converted to either Christianity or Islam since 1948, a period in which many thousands had converted to Judaism.[11] But Jews often failed to understand that what counted as success in the Jewish mission was not necessarily a high number of converts. As Yaakov Ariel has argued, the missionary enterprise was at least as much a coherent expression of evangelical (particularly premillennialist) identity as a "business plan" with projected results based on a cost-benefit analysis; moreover, rates of Jewish conversion did compare favorably with those of other non-Christian populations, which were also often small (Lapide 1984, 181).[12]

If missionaries considered their work an "aim in and of itself," some translators saw the exegetical and literary exercises at the basis of their work as motivation enough, even as they continued to hope that the uncanny effect of a Hebrew Matthew would not be lost on Jewish readers. And for the translators who were also converts, the act of translation constituted its own reward by establishing their usefulness to their new communities and symbolically expressing the fantasy of Jewish-Christian reconciliation that underlay the missionary project.[13] The translation was thus a kind of performance, functioning not only as a strategic tool to achieve Jewish conversion, but also and primarily as the *embodiment* of certain theological principles concerning the relations between Jesus and Judaism, the Old and New Testaments, the Hebraic substratum underlying the Greek of the Gospels, and so on. Missionary translations, ostensibly the most target-oriented of all translation efforts, could thus achieve many of their aims in the absence of successfully reaching this target, since the texts themselves acted, in some sense, as already-achieved Jewish-Christian conversions in their textual conflation of the Jewish and the Christian. This was particularly true of Judaizing New Testament translations, that is,

---

11. Lapide (1984, 181) quotes a government press release issued in Jerusalem on March 1, 1964.

12. The missionary work, according to Ariel, "was an aim in and of itself and derived from their premillennialist theology." Nor did missionaries expect to win huge numbers of converts, contenting themselves with spreading their message. See Ariel 2000, 74–75.

13. These converts to modern evangelical Christianity were not expected to renounce their Jewish names, affiliations, or even their Zionism, which they shared with their new Christian friends. On the contrary, by choosing Christian belief these converts were merely becoming truer to their Jewish selves. See Ariel 2000, 46–47.

of the Hebrew *Haberit hahadasha* in its many versions or of Einspruch's *Der Bris Khadoshe* (as opposed to *Dos Neye Testament*, for instance).

It is no coincidence, then, that Judaizing translation trends coincide with shifts in notions of conversion in the twentieth century, as Jewish converts felt freer to view Christianity not as apostasy but rather as a more profound realization of their Jewishness, keeping their Jewish names proudly and forming separate Jewish Christian congregations and societies.[14] Strikingly, these twin trends in notions of Jewish conversion and translation have parallels in modern secular Yiddish culture, which for reasons of its own was simultaneously moving away from a germanized Yiddish and appropriating a Jesus "revised and corrected" toward Jewishness. Perhaps it is also no coincidence that the phenomena I am tracing here coincided as well with a larger Jewish and indeed international modernist movement toward "foreignizing" translation, as evidenced by Buber and Rosenzweig's archaizing, hebraizing Bible translation on the one hand (1930), and Walter Benjamin's radical pronouncements on translation on the other (1968).

The notion of Jewish New Testament translations as performative rather than instrumental might illuminate another of their common features. Translation is usually understood as a procedure to bring source texts that readers cannot understand into a target language that they can. But New Testament translations directed to Jews often have manifestly different goals in mind: The Society for Distributing Hebrew Scriptures (founded in London in 1940; hereafter SDHS) continues to print and provide New Testaments not only in English, but also in Hebrew and Yiddish, and in Hebrew/English, Hebrew/French, Hebrew/Spanish, Hebrew/Dutch, Hebrew/Portugese, Hebrew/Arabic, Hebrew/Russian, Hebrew/Romanian, Hebrew/German, Hebrew/Yiddish, and Hebrew/Hungarian parallel editions. According to their website, the mission of the society is to "provide the bilingual Holy Scriptures to every Jewish home throughout the world and without cost to the recipient" (non-Jews, however, are asked to pay $10, $12, or $15, depending on the edition).[15] The Hebrew/English version presently provided by the SDHS is a slightly revised version of the 1885 Salkinson-Ginsburg New Testament (printed alongside the KJV), which Pinchas Lapide describes as characterized by a "remarkable combi-

---

14. For these developments see Ariel 2000, 47–50.
15. The society operates under a number of local and national groupings. See, e.g., www.sdhs.com; or, for California, www.lightforisrael.org.

nation of hyperbiblicism and poetical license" (Lapide 1984, 93). Salkinson himself described his decisions as shaped by his target audience:

> My plan is to take a good share of liberty in regard to the words and phrases … but we must remember that our New Testament is intended chiefly for our unconverted brethren. Therefore it may be of some service to have it in a style which the Jews have not yet forgotten to appreciate, that is, the biblical Hebrew.[16]

In keeping with Salkinson's attempts to align his New Testament with the Hebrew Bible, Matt 1:22 reads, "*Veyikets Yosef mishnato vayaʾas kaʾasher tsivah oto malʾakh YHWH*," language palpably closer to Biblical Hebrew (the formulation occurs with Noah, Jacob, Pharaoh, and Samson) than to the Hebrew current in the first century c.e. The language of the Salkinson-Ginsburg *Haberit hahadasha*, then, is the idiom of neither Modern Hebrew speakers nor the American Jews, who are the largest target for the distribution of texts; Lapide argues, as well, that it is inappropriate as a scholarly reading of what might have constituted a Hebraic substratum of the Greek source (1984, 92–94). American Jews can certainly access the New Testament more easily through the Gideon Bible in their hotel rooms than in the exotic bilingual text provided by the SDHS. Evidence that the Hebrew text is not meant to communicate content, in the usual translational sense, is apparent as well from the *English* letter of advertisement on the inside cover of their Hebrew/English volume (a similar letter also appears on the society website):

> Dear Sir or Madam,
> The Holy Scriptures, both Old and New Testaments, were given to the world through the Jewish people.
> The world therefore owes them a very great debt; wherever these Scriptures have come they have brought blessings of light, joy and peace.
> Is it not sad to find in this twentieth century so few Jews are familiar with their own Book—the greatest contribution to the welfare of humanity?
> Out of gratitude to the Jewish people for their gift of the Bible

---

16. Letter to Franz Delitzsch (June 11, 1877); cited in Lapide 1984, 93.

to us, and in partial repayment of our debt, we desire to present to every Jewish home a copy of the New Testament.[17]

The letter strategically presents the book as a gift rather than a threat, and then also notes that the gift is indeed not from Christians to Jews but rather the reverse. But the very language of the letter makes abundantly clear that the Hebrew of this New Testament, as well as the Hebrew bilingual versions with Russian, Hungarian, and other parallel translation, is not a medium of communication but the message itself. Hebrew functions as a bridge between the readers, who trust the Jewishness of the Hebrew alphabet (even if they cannot understand it) and recognize the biblicisms (even if they can barely follow them). The translator, although he is obviously a believing Christian (if born a Jew), affiliates himself with Hebrew in all its associations—with Jewishness, sacredness, canonicity, and familiarity. By placing the Hebrew text on the right-hand page, and the title page where it would be in a Hebrew book, the translators and editors also signal that the Hebrew functions as an original, and the English, Yiddish, Hungarian, and so on as a translation—although *both*, of course, are translations, with the 1885 Salkinson-Ginsburg translation considerably postdating the 1611 KJV.

Such techniques and the resulting effects are available not only to the Hebrew translator, but also to the Yiddish and even English one. David H. Stern's *Complete Jewish Bible*, a 1998 messianic Jewish translation of both the New Testament and the Hebrew Bible, is in English, but he uses a variety of techniques to replace Christian with Jewish and in some cases "neutral" associations: "cross" thus becomes "execution stake"; Jesus' hem or fringe (Greek *kraspidon*) appropriately reads "tsitsit"; in keeping with the transliteration rather than translation of proper nouns Pharisees are transliterated as "P'rushim"; and Rom 10:4 has the Messiah "as the goal at which the Torah aims" (a translation with considerable theological import) rather than the KJV's potentially confusing "the end of the law."[18] Some of Stern's choices are more remarkable, in particular

---

17. I am quoting from the front flap of the third edition of the 1886 Salkinson-Ginsburg *Hebrew New Testament* (ed. Eric Gabe; Hertfordshire: Society for Distributing Hebrew Scriptures, 2000), which has been distributed free to Jews beginning in 1940, when the SDHS was founded.

18. The Salkinson-Ginsburg translation has a similar intervention in mind in translating the phrase as *"takhlit hatorah."*

his sprinkling of Yiddishisms to reinforce the point that the characters of the New Testament are authentic Jews. In Luke 10:4, for instance, the apostles are warned: "Don't carry a money-belt or a pack, and don't stop to *shmoose* with people on the road," and in John 10: 19 some of the Judeans call Jesus "*meshugga*." Stern explains in his introduction that he decided to use "Jewish English" more liberally in the New Testament than in the Hebrew Bible because "I don't need to stress the *Tanakh*'s Jewishness" (1998, xxxix).[19] Stern is surely not implying that the disciples—or *talmidim*—spoke Yiddish or Yinglish; but by rendering their discourse in familiar American-Jewish idioms, he is trying to bridge the gap between these late antique *shlikhim* and present-day denizens of New York and Miami Beach. For Stern's, as for other Jewish Christian translations, the usual dichotomy of target versus source orientation, domesticating versus foreignizing translation, is hard to uphold, since one masquerades as the other, with target-group ethnicity translating itself into source-oriented pseudo-philology. That the SDHS continues to reprint and distribute Einspruch's Yiddish New Testament to this day, in the absence of a wide Yiddish-reading public, suggests that it views Yiddish in the same way, as *performing* the New Testament's Jewishness through Yiddish as much as translating the New Testament into this language.

Retroversion or pseudo-retroversion, the most coveted effect of New Testament translation into Jewish languages, is both a strategy, since retroversive effects work to establish the Jewish credentials of the New Testament as they obscure its long Christian associations, as well as a performance, since the results, a conflation of Jewishness and Christianness, embody their own argument. Art designers, too, participated in this double project, fashioning New Testaments designed to look at home on a traditional Jewish bookshelf. The beautiful second edition of Einspruch's *Bris Khadoshe*, for example, features a Star of David on the cover and is lavishly illustrated by artwork taken, without attribution, from the instantly recognizable work of the Jewish artist and illustrator Ephraim Moses Lilien (1874–1925). As is typical of Jewish Christian translations, the cover gives no sign of any non-Jewish content, unless one reads suspiciously and sees a cross hidden in the design, in the intersection between the two letters, *bet* and *ḥet*, framed by a Star of David, which together refer to the title,

---

19. For an analysis of Stern's method (which Metzger includes in a section called "Jewish Translations"), see Metzger 2001, 146–48; and Stern 1998.

Der Bris Khadoshe. This cross, if it is indeed not a product of a suspicious hermeneutics, is achieved through purely Jewish means, though an overlap between two Hebrew letters. Strategies for minimizing the radical or dangerous content of new translations are not, of course, missionary inventions. Abigail Gillman has shown that the Mendelssohn translation and commentary (*Bi'ur*) on the Pentateuch cleverly mimicked the layout of the *Miqra'ot Gedolot*, or Rabbinic Bible, in an attempt by Mendelssohn "to mitigate the innovative nature of his work through a variety of traditional strategies," suggesting "the hope that the reader's immediate visual experience of the Bible would contain no surprises" (Gillman 2002, 105).

The illustrations in the edition are used not only to conceal the Christian nature of the translated work; they also serve, as Einspruch's language does, to conflate Jewish and Christian ideas or images. A wine goblet engraved with the phrase, taken from the Havdalah ceremony, *kos yeshuot esa*, somewhat puzzlingly serves as the closing image for the book of John and thus the Gospels in their entirety. The relevance to John only becomes apparent by recognizing the name *yeshua* embedded in the blessing, here referring not only to the redemption referred to in the ceremony, but also, of course, to Yeshua the Redeemer. The message may indeed be more powerful for being concealed: the Jewish roots of Christianity extend not only to recognizing the Jewishness of Jesus; they may manifest themselves in the reverse direction, by discovering Christian associations in such emblematically Jewish ritual objects as a Havdalah goblet.

Lilien's oeuvre includes a range of Jewish images, from representations of biblical scenes to modern images and—most famously—Zionist iconography. But the publishers of the second edition drew far less from images that might evoke Jewish life in first-century Palestine than from Lilien's representations of traditional Jewish iconography, and more particularly, images of traditional Eastern European Jews. Thus *Di besure loyt Matya* opens with a rendering of a pious old Jewish man wearing a yarmulke and wrapped in a tallis reading a *sefer* (a traditional or sacred book) by candlelight, providing a visual echo of the word *sefer* in the first line. As Yaakov Ariel puts it, "The scene clearly suggests that the New Testament is an old Jewish book that should be read and studied like a sacred Jewish text" (2000, 90). By contrast, *Dos Neye Testament* begins with the phrase *Dos bukh*, the Yiddish term that lacks the sacred connotations of the Hebrew-derived *sefer*. Significantly, this is one of the instances in which Einspruch does not follow Yehoash, who consistently translates *sefer* as *bukh*: in Adam's genealogy, which is the closest intertext to Matthew's, Yehoash has *Dos is dos bukh fun di geburtn fun odemn* (Gen 5:1). Einspruch's translation choice and the illustration together signify that this is a *sefer*, and not a *bukh*, much less the *treyf posl* (heretical or forbidden book) that traditional Jewish culture generally considered the New Testament to be. The image that opens Einspruch's New Testament, then, is an illustration not of the text it accompanies but rather of its ideal reception, imagining and in some sense supplying the traditional Jewish reader who will fulfill Einspruch's eschatological and authorial hope that the New Testament would be accepted among Jews as part of their heritage.[20]

The first line of Matthew is worth closer examination, since it frames the entire book. The most striking translation choice is the word *yikhes* to translate the Greek *geneseōs*, which the KJV renders as "generations" and the NIV as "genealogy" (LSJ 343 gives the primary definition as "origin"). The first verse of Matthew has a host of readily available intertextual connections in the genealogies of Genesis and Chronicles, from which translational equivalents could be sought. (There were reasons, moreover, to avoid using the term *yikhes* for Jesus' genealogy, in fact, since it appears in a possibly anti-Christian context in the mishnaic text in *Yebamot* 4:13, which describes a *megilat yohasin* [genealogical book] found in Jerusalem claiming that "so-and-so" was the product of an illicit union, a text sometimes taken as indirectly and pejoratively referring to Jesus.) The Hebraism that stands behind Matthew's Greek is clearly *toldot*, or more expansively, *ve'eleh toldot*, a phrase Yehoash renders as *geburtn* in the Adamic genealogy and as *geshikhte* in the different Noahic context of *Ve'eleh toldot noyekh* (Gen 6:9). But while Einspruch often follows Yehoash, and indeed quotes his translation of Jeremiah in the epigraph that introduces his translation, in Matt 1:1 he chooses to use the term *yikhes*, borrowing an earlier translation from Bergman and others. *Yikhes* is not totally inappropriate, and Harkavy does give the first meaning as "genealogy." The term *yikhes-briv*, in Yiddish as in the Mishnaic Hebrew *megilat yohasin*, can also means something like a family tree, but I would guess that the more immediately recognizable signification of *yikhes*, for Einspruch's average if not ideal Yiddish reader, is pedigree or what could be called high-status lineage, and among its most salient cultural associations are the negotiations by which marriages are arranged. As is well known, Matthew's main

---

20. Indeed, Ariel describes Orthodox Jews as "more open to the evangelical message than other Jews," since there was "common ground for discussion and persuasion as both groups viewed the Bible as the revealed word of God" (2000, 15).

interest was in establishing a Davidic lineage for Jesus. But Einspruch, by suggesting that he is providing not only Jesus' Davidic genealogy but also his exalted Jewish pedigree, shifts the discourse into an altogether different register, one in which he himself plays the role of *shadkhan* (matchmaker)—hoping to match Judaism and Christianity by granting Jesus, or Rabbi Yeshua, a *yikhes-briv* fully meaningful in a Jewish context.[21]

The question of how Einspruch's translation was actually received in the Yiddish world—as opposed to how its reception was imagined and framed—is a surprisingly complex one, bearing on the larger polysystem of Yiddish literature of the period. Gideon Toury, whose work brings together translation studies and polysystem theory, suggests that translations are properly studied as part of the target culture, which not only "invites" translations as a means to fill in literary and cultural gaps, but is also transformed by each newly introduced text. In Toury's formulation, translation is most fruitfully studied as a cultural *fact* in the target culture in which it circulates:

> Semiotically, then, translation is as good as *initiated* by the target culture. In other words, the starting point is always one of a certain deficiency in the latter, even if sometimes—e.g., in a "colonial" situation—an alleged gap may be factually pointed out for it by a patron of sorts who also purports to "know better" how that gap may best be filled. (Toury 1995, 27)

Einspruch's translation provides an interesting test case for Toury's theories, since many elements of his target culture (the Yiddish-reading public) would have vociferously argued against the notion that they had initiated this translation, or that their culture lacked and needed a Yiddish New Testament. Toury's suggestion that some "gaps" may be less "real" than perceived by "a patron of sorts" would certainly apply to missionary perspectives, which have widely been linked in postcolonial criticism with the very colonial situation Toury mentions. But such an analysis does not account for another aspect of Einspruch's reception, the strongly favorable response he found not among the readers he seemed to be addressing, that

---

21. Ariel (2003) comes to a similar conclusion: "Often used in match-making to point to the high value of potential brides and grooms, *yikhes* means 'pedigree'; it relates to honored ancestors and boosts the credentials of the '*yakhsan*'—the individual claiming the pedigree. Jesus, it is implied, has excellent credentials by virtue of his '*yikhes*.'"

is, potential converts to Christianity, but from the Yiddish poet Melekh Ravitsh, whose review of the translation appeared in the Mexico City Yiddish periodical *Der veg* shortly after the publication of *Der Bris Khadoshe*. Einspruch was a believer in the dispensational millennialist variety of the Lutheran Evangelical creed, a Christian Zionist (as well as a Jewish one, who had spent time in the *yishuv* and written for the Left Po'alei Tsiyon before his return to Poland and conversion to Christianity), and a missionary hoping to bring more Jews into the fold; Ravitsh, on the other hand, was a secular Yiddish modernist, a champion of Spinoza and critic of both Zionism and traditional Judaism, who was committed to a worldly, cosmopolitan Jewish nationalism. Nevertheless, Ravitsh's review makes no mention at all of Einspruch's Christianity or association with missionary efforts. On the contrary, he speaks of the relationship between Einspruch's project and that of Yehoash, and in very similar terms: "The present translation of the NT into Yiddish … by Dr. Chayim Einspruch … is unquestionably beautiful. One feels that the translator is familiar with modern Yiddish, and that he is master of the finest nuances of the language" (1967, 15). Ravitsh delicately continues:

> For well known reasons the NT has remained for many of us Jews a book sealed with seven seals. And that is truly a pity, for to some 700 million people it is a sacred work. A cultured person should know such a work; I myself have read it and recommend it to every intelligent Jew. (1967, 17)

This new translation, in Ravitsh's view, was a welcome contribution to Yiddish literature, truly the gift to the Jewish people the Bible societies claimed to be making.

Ravitsh's review, and the relative silence in the Yiddish press on Einspruch's translation, can be contrasted with the outcry that had greeted the publication, the year before, of the English translation of *The Nazarene*, Sholem Asch's novel (1939) that explored the Jewishness of Jesus. Among other sins, Asch had been accused of apostasy and having written *a shtik shmad-propaganda* (a piece of proselytizing propaganda)—precisely points that were true of Einspruch's project.[22] These attacks were not universal: Melekh Ravitsh, for instance, was among Asch's defenders (Norich 2004, 261). Anita Norich (2004, 252) and Hannah Berliner Fischthal (2004, 275) have suggested that the fervor of the attacks had less to do with the sub-

---

22. Ephraim Kaplan in the *Morgen zhurnal*; quoted in Berliner Fischthal 2004, 269.

ject matter—Yiddish literature had a well-established interest in the Jewish Jesus—or even with the timing of the publication, at a moment when Europe's Jews were under attack by European Christians; what accounted for the dimensions of the scandal was that *The Nazarene* had appeared first in English translation, with the Yiddish text not appearing until 1943. Where Einspruch had been compelled to purchase his own printing press after the Yiddish publishing world put obstacles in his path, Asch had turned to English translation when Abraham Cahan refused to publish a serialized Yiddish version of *Der man fun natseres*. In Norich's words, his Yiddish readers felt that Asch "had somehow betrayed his primary Yiddish audience" (2004, 264). Einspruch, by implicit contrast, despite being the apostate and proselytizer that Asch was not, was making a true contribution to Yiddish literature. For the beleaguered Yiddish literary culture of the period, first publication in English rather than any subscription to Christian dogma was the true betrayal.

Toury's view of translation as filling gaps in literary polysystems is especially germane to Yiddish literature, which deliberately undertook translation as a means of enriching its repertoire. I. L. Peretz, in his famous speech at the 1908 Czernowitz Convention, had called for "the translation of all Jewish cultural treasures of our past, especially the Bible," inaugurating Yehoash's great translation project and setting the stage for a concerted effort to bring not only the Bible but other high-status literary works into Yiddish (1994, 323). The twentieth century brought literary translations of Byron, Dostoyevsky, Goethe, Gogol, Hugo, Kipling, Lao-Tzu, Shakespeare, Shaw, Twain, Oscar Wilde, Zola, and many others. Aside from his Hebrew Bible translation, Yehoash also produced Yiddish versions of *Hiawatha* and *The Rubaiyat of Omar Khayyam* (from Edward Fitzgerald's English version) and parts of the Qur'an. As Jeffrey Shandler writes of Yehoash's and others' work, "This profusion of literary translations exemplifies modern Yiddish vernacularity at its zenith, evincing a culture that strove to offer comprehensive access to the wealth of world cultures through Yiddish" (2006, 99).

Einspruch's positive reception in the Yiddish press is less surprising, then, than it first might appear. At least certain Yiddish literary circles aspired to a cosmopolitanism that included the world's cultural treasures. Einspruch's own ambitions were not exhausted by his missionary activities: he aspired to be taken seriously as a Yiddish writer and stylist; and in fact Ravitsh's review, according to Ariel, gave Einspruch "an entry into Yiddish literary circles" (2000, 91). From the other perspective, Ravitsh had a particular interest in Christianity, one that should not be distinguished from his central role in the development of Yiddish poetry. Ravitsh, one of the expressionist "gang" *Khaliyastra*, used Christian imagery in both his modernist manifestoes and his poetry: in the inaugural issue of *Albatros*, Ravitsh concluded his call for a naked poetry by directly alluding to and subverting John's equation of Jesus with the Logos: "nakit hengt ofn kreyts dos vort" (naked hangs the word on the cross; 1922, 16). As Matthew Hoffman describes Ravitsh's daring manifesto, the crucified and naked Jesus "becomes a metaphor for modernist Yiddish poetry itself!" (2007, 146).

As Hoffman has shown, the Yiddish literary "reclamation of Jesus" had a range of significations: marking the Jewish entry into the European literary tradition, the appropriation of a central figure of European Christendom for Jewish purposes, a statement of Jewish literary universalism, a wry commentary on Christian persecution of Jews, a critique of Jewish prejudices against other religions, an embrace of Jesus' ethical principles, a rebellion against Jewish parochialism, the closeness of the two religions, and the suffering of the "crucified" modern artist. The Jewish reclamation of Jesus was often bitterly contested in modern literary circles; Hoffman points, for instance, to *di tseylem frage* (the "cross question")—fought between Zhitlowsky and Ansky—in the Yiddish world, and to the similar debate between Ahad Ha'am and Brenner in the Hebrew world (2007, 61–116). But what the Jewish use of Christian images and symbols did not mean was Jewish apostasy, even if some critics accused writers like Asch of encouraging it. The writers who mobilized the figure of Jesus and Christian tropes were, nearly without exception, secularists, if not openly atheist. Nevertheless, the interests of a missionary translator like Einspruch and a cultural critic and expressionist like Ravitsh converged in Einspruch's Yiddish New Testament, even as others in the Jewish world put obstacles in Einspruch's way (as they did in Asch's). Shandler writes that Ravitsh

> argued for expanding Jewish cultural boundaries while flouting the [missionary] publisher's expectations that reading the New Testament in Yiddish would promote the abandonment of Judaism. In a deft act of subversion, Ravitsh transformed the emblematic meaning of this translation from a challenge to Jewish religious convictions into a validation of the capacity of secular Yiddish literary art. (Shandler 2006, 102)

The convergence Shandler notes between missionary and secular Yiddish interests extends beyond the value of a Yiddish New Testament. Modern revisers of older New Testament translations shared with Yiddish writers an appreciation for a literary Yiddish freed from its dependence on and subjugation to German and an interest in a more Jewish Jesus, values that coincided with trends in Jewish literary modernism despite radical differences in the religious and political cultures involved.[23] The rapprochement envisioned by the converted translators on Jewish-Christian religious grounds gave way to a different, more secular, and unexpected commonality on the rich cosmopolitan ground of modern Yiddish culture: The Spinozist critic and Jewish Christian missionary spoke in a single voice about what modern Yiddish literature needed—if only for the briefest cultural moment.

---

23. Chana Kronfeld has traced a similarly unexpected overlap in "the aesthetic demands of the external modernist affiliation and the particular needs of the newly revived Hebraic tradition," describing how poets of the 1920s "employed neologisms both as a vehicle for modernist (futurist-inspired) poetics and as part of the push toward lexical innovation that was necessary for the revival of the Hebrew language" (1996, 81–82).

Masculinidad en la traducción de la Biblia en Latinoamérica*

Esteban Voth

ABSTRACT: The practice of translation is never a neutral enterprise. This maxim applies to biblical translation as well. The present article addresses the issues of Bible translation and masculinity in translations of the Bible used in Latin America. Six Spanish Bible translations are analyzed. These come from different religious traditions and represent different theories of translation. It is no secret that males have dominated the practice of Bible translation, and male ideology is certainly present in all of the translations studied. This study also presents a case study based on the most recent Bible translation published in Latin America. Cultural realities are very present in these Bible translations. Based on the findings, the study makes a plea for all translations to be revised bearing in mind the presence of what might be called a "masculine hegemonic influence" in Bible translation. It is my contention that translations of the Bible can be improved and thus be made more "gender friendly."

¡Toda traducción es traición! Así lo ha definido un famoso dicho italiano que dice *traduttore traditore*: "El traductor es un traidor." Si esto es cierto para la práctica de la traducción en general, cuánto más cierto es para la traducción de la Biblia, siendo que este es un documento tan antiguo y proviene de una cultura tan diferente a la occidental. Es bien sabido que ninguna traducción es objetiva ni neutra. Esta afirmación es igualmente cierta respecto de las traducciones de la Biblia. Durante muchos años la iglesia cristiana vivió bajo una especie de ilusión de que el texto que leía estaba libre de prejuicios, ideologías e interpretaciones. Hoy podemos

---

* A version of this paper will be published in an in-house publication of Sociedades Bíblicas Unidas as part of a monograph created in honor of Dr. William Mitchell.

decir con confianza que, cuando menos, toda traducción es "interpretación." Y es así porque traducir no es meramente trasponer un texto de un sistema lingüístico a otro; también es como mínimo, reescribirlo en otro sistema literario, en el contexto de la lengua de destino (Waisman 2005, 8). Eugene Nida nos ha enseñado a tomar en cuenta tres principios básicos de correspondencia semántica que deben sostener todo análisis semántico adecuado: (1) ningún vocablo (o unidad semántica) tiene exactamente el mismo significado en dos diferentes unidades de habla o emisión; (2) no existen sinónimos completos dentro de un mismo idioma; y (3) no hay correspondencias exactas entre palabras relacionadas en diferentes idiomas. En otras palabras, la comunicación perfecta es imposible, y toda comunicación es parcial (Nida 1958, 281).

Es por demás claro que esta comunicación parcial es en parte producto del hecho de que el traductor inevitablemente hace su trabajo de traducción desde su contexto cultural y socio histórico. Si bien intenta despojarse lo más posible de influencias subjetivas, una objetividad completa es imposible. Esto se hace muy evidente en la traducción de la Biblia. Cada traducción de los textos hebreos, arameos y griegos se lleva a cabo en un contexto particular y un momento particular que son marcadamente diferentes a los contextos originales del texto bíblico. Esto significa que varios factores juegan un papel importante en todo ejercicio de traducción. Entre estos factores, sugiero que los más importantes son las realidades de raza, clase, género, historias personales, posturas teológicas, alianzas políticas, características culturales y, por último, y de mucho peso, cuestiones de mercadeo. Todos estos factores específicos contribuyen a conformar la "ideología" y la "cosmovisión" del traductor o traductores. Puede sostenerse con toda confianza que toda traducción del texto bíblico exhibe una "ideología" definida, ya sea consciente o inconscientemente. Es decir, no existe tal cosa como una traducción "inmaculada" del texto bíblico. Tal como lo expresa Stanley Porter, "La historia de la traducción de la Biblia está cargada de cuestiones ideológicas" (1999, 18). Por lo tanto:

> Al enfrentarnos con una traducción debemos tener en cuenta el contexto del original, el del texto de destino y, más importante aún, la distancia entre los dos. Es en esta distancia –en una Babel de desplazamientos lingüísticos, temporales y espaciales—donde ocurre todo: donde se transmiten o se pierden, se renegocian, reexaminan y reinventan textos y culturas. (Waisman 2005, 9)

Es en este perder, renegociar, reexaminar y reinventar que es necesario colocar este estudio. El propósito del mismo es hacer un análisis somero de algunas traducciones de la Biblia al castellano que consideramos representativas con el objetivo de discernir la influencia de género en dichas traducciones. Particularmente buscamos dilucidar la influencia de la masculinidad en la manera de traducir la Biblia. Es bien sabido que la mayoría, sino todas las traducciones de la Biblia al castellano utilizadas en Latinoamérica son obra primordialmente de hombres (varones). Por ejemplo, sabemos que en la *Nueva Versión Internacional* publicada por la Sociedad Bíblica Internacional en el 2000, participó solamente una mujer y sólo en la revisión de algunos libros del Nuevo Testamento. También podemos señalar que algunas mujeres trabajaron en la traducción de partes del Nuevo Testamento de la versión *El Libro del Pueblo de Dios*, y también en la versión recientemente publicada por las Sociedades Bíblicas Unidas llamada *Traducción en Lenguaje Actual*. Es probable que existan algunas otras excepciones, pero la inmensa mayoría de los traductores de Biblia en castellano han sido, y siguen siendo hombres.

El uso del lenguaje nunca es inocente. El lenguaje que caracteriza al género masculino inevitablemente se ha ido filtrando en la traducción de la Biblia, consciente o inconscientemente. Nuestra metodología será mirar con cierto detenimiento algunos textos bíblicos en seis versiones diferentes. Este no puede ser un estudio exhaustivo ni abarcativo. Las versiones que hemos elegido son representativas, pero no necesariamente las más importantes ni las únicas que merecen ser analizadas. Estas son *Reina Valera* (1960; *RVR60*), *El Libro del Pueblo de Dios* (1981; *LPD*), *La Nueva Biblia de Latinoamérica* (1986; *LAT*), *Dios Habla Hoy Versión de Estudio* (1995; *DHHE95*), *La Nueva Versión Internacional* (2000; *NVI*), y la *Traducción en Lenguaje Actual* (2003; *TLA*). Estas versiones representan diferentes teorías de traducción, diferentes bases textuales, diferentes confesiones cristianas, y están pensadas para públicos diferentes. Esta diversidad nos parece significativa y necesaria para el análisis que queremos hacer. Idealmente uno debería analizar todas las versiones existentes, pero eso escapa al marco permitido en esta publicación. Sugerimos que sería un buen tema para trabajar en una tesis doctoral.

Consideraciones Preliminares

En primer lugar es necesario exponer lo que entendemos en términos muy básicos por masculinidad. Coincidimos en que es imprescindible hablar de "masculinidades" y no meramente de "masculinidad." El pretender comprender esta realidad en singular, nos parece un reduccionismo equivocado. Sin duda existe un modelo de masculinidad impuesto por diferentes culturas en el mundo que está unido a ciertas cualidades asociadas con la fuerza, potencia, violencia, agresividad, racionalidad, independencia, actividad, el trabajo y el ser público. Pero ya varios han llegado a la conclusión de que el hombre varón, en general, no puede llegar a cumplir el estereotipo cultural, y por lo tanto esta visión de un modelo hegemónico es una idealización. De hecho, muchos hombres nunca logran alcanzar este modelo y por ende se sienten frustrados. Esta realidad nos lleva a plantear que es más acertado hablar de masculinidades. Esto implica que hay muchos modos de ser hombre. No obstante, a la vez nos parece necesario admitir que el modelo hegemónico ha estado presente de manera importante y que por cuestiones de sociabilidad básica el hombre ha incorporado este único modelo hasta donde ha podido. Sugerimos entonces que esto ha tenido su influencia en la manera en que los hombres han traducido la Biblia. Con esto no pretendemos eliminar la complejidad del tema. No es una cuestión que se puede enmarcar en términos de blanco y negro, ni de masculino vs. femenino. Simplemente queremos afirmar que el hecho de que propongamos que debemos pensar en masculinidades, no quita que en el imaginario social no exista un fuerte modelo hegemónico que tiene influencia y consecuencias en múltiples niveles de cualquier sociedad y cultura. La traducción de la Biblia no ha estado ni está exenta de estas realidades.

En segundo lugar, es necesario pensar en los límites que confronta la traducción bíblica. En general existe un consenso en cuanto a que la Biblia es un documento que está histórica y culturalmente delimitado. Esto significa que muchos elementos que participan en todo proceso de traducción están condicionados por el contexto histórico, social, político, económico y cultural del cual surge el texto bíblico. La Biblia no es un documento *a-histórico*, ni se creó en un vacío. Es una colección de escritos que se redactaron a lo largo de más de mil años y representa una diversidad de culturas pertenecientes al cercano Oriente Antiguo. Es un error hablar de "la" cultura bíblica, ya que los documentos que conforman la Biblia provienen de contextos geográficos y culturales muy diferentes entre sí. Si a esto le agregamos el factor tiempo, a decir, más de mil años de composición, estamos frente a un texto muy complejo.

Estos factores sin duda se ven más afectados por el hecho de que la Biblia es considerada la revelación de Dios, por muchos que la traducen.

Este hecho, combinado con todo lo anteriormente expuesto tiene ingerencia sobre la estructura del idioma, el lenguaje que se usa para referirse a Dios o dioses, y sobre la o las "cosmovisiones" presentes en el texto bíblico. Todas estas consideraciones no pueden estar ausentes a la hora de evaluar la influencia de una masculinidad en la traducción de la Biblia. Es importante reconocer que estamos tratando con un texto que aparece dentro de contextos patriarcales, donde la posición del hombre predomina en casi todos los aspectos de la vida cotidiana. Esta realidad, típica del mundo antiguo en varios contextos no se puede minimizar en función de querer ser sensible a criterios modernos. Las enseñanzas en la Biblia respecto a la mujer respiran las condiciones socio-económicas del mundo antiguo. Y en ese sentido es imposible plantear que la mayoría de los textos bíblicos abogan por una igualdad social, política, religiosa y legal de la mujer respecto al hombre. Son más los textos que proponen una subordinación de la mujer al hombre, que aquellos que plantean una situación igualitaria La subordinación de la mujer es una realidad ineludible en el mundo al cual pertenece la Biblia.

No obstante esta realidad, consideramos que hay textos en la Biblia que han sido traducidos con una neta tendencia masculina y que no necesariamente esa inclinación forma parte del "mensaje original." En este estudio queremos indagar en los contextos donde *no* es necesario privilegiar una visión masculina y que por lo tanto el mismo texto permite una traducción más equilibrada e igualitaria y no tan androcéntrica. Para demostrar esto presentaremos un muestreo breve de ciertos textos y compararemos cómo diferentes versiones los han traducido. Nos centraremos en ciertas palabras clave que a lo largo de las últimas décadas han sido objeto de mucho estudio y cuestionamiento. El auge de traducciones de la Biblia que privilegian lo que se ha dado a llamar *lenguaje inclusivo* ha generado mucha discusión y debate. En la medida de nuestras posibilidades, intentaremos no forzar el texto bíblico para que se adapte a sensibilidades modernas ni para que suene "políticamente correcto."

Traducción de Palabras Clave

En primer lugar queremos recordar lo afirmado al principio acerca de la realidad de una traducción. Este no es el lugar para profundizar en lo que puede llamarse la traductología y la filosofía de traducción. No obstante, queremos afirmar que todo traductor de la Biblia se enfrenta con dos problemas básicos. El primero es comprender el significado del texto en su contexto histórico y cultural original. En lo posible se intenta descubrir cuál era la intención del autor y de qué manera lo percibieron los primeros oyentes o lectores. El segundo problema es cómo se va entender ese mensaje o significado en el idioma receptor. En otras palabras, ¿cómo ha de percibir ese significado el oyente o lector moderno? A continuación haremos un análisis de ciertas palabras clave que presentan diferentes posibilidades de traducción.

'Adam

El vocablo hebreo *'adam* puede traducirse de diversas maneras según su contexto y su función semántica en la unidad de discurso en la cual se encuentra. Este término puede significar: (a) hombre (varón), (b) ser humano, (c) humanidad, (d) persona, (e) individuo, (f) uno, (g) gente, (h) alguien, (i) quien o el que, y hasta (j) nombre propio. Ahora bien, muchas traducciones del Antiguo Testamento en su afán de ser más literales, tradujeron este vocablo casi siempre con la palabra "hombre." Veamos los siguientes ejemplos.

En Génesis 1:26 cuando se narra la creación de *'adam*, la mayoría de las versiones traducen el vocablo hebreo con la palabra "hombre." Si bien, uno podría aceptar que se usa la palabra en términos genéricos, es mucho más preciso traducir *'adam* en este contexto por "ser humano." De las seis versiones que hemos elegido, cuatro traducen "hombre" (*RVR60*; *LAT*; *DHHE95*; *LPD*). Solamente *NVI* y *TLA* traducen con el término colectivo universal "ser humano." Estas dos versiones ayudan a que el énfasis masculino se matice y además la traducción "ser humano" es más fiel al significado original, ya que el contexto habla de la creación de toda la humanidad y no solamente de un ser masculino.

Un caso parecido se puede ver en Génesis 6:7. En este contexto Dios habla de que va a borrar de la tierra al *'adam*. Tres de las versiones traducen con "hombre" u "hombres" (*DHHE95*; *LPD*; *RVR60*), mientras que las otras tres prefieren los términos "ser humano" o "humanidad." Es obvio que la intención de Dios es destruir a todo el mundo. Por lo tanto nos parece que la traducción "humanidad" es cultural e históricamente muy precisa en el contexto bíblico y además preferible para la lengua y contextos receptores. Dios no ha de destruir solamente al hombre varón, sino que su intención es acabar con toda la humanidad. Tanto para el lector original como para el lector del siglo XXI "humanidad" o "todo el mundo" son opciones válidas.

Otro ejemplo parecido lo encontramos en Génesis 9:6 donde hay una advertencia contra matar a una persona. Una vez más vemos que la mayoría de las traducciones traducen 'adam por "hombre" (*LAT, DHHE95, LPD, RVR60*). El contexto claramente señala que la referencia es para toda persona. No es una advertencia dirigida específicamente al hombre varón, ni tiene que ver con la posible muerte de un varón. Es por eso que tanto la *NVI* como la *TLA* traducen "ser humano" y "persona," respectivamente. Estas traducciones evitan una tendencia masculina en la traducción que es absolutamente innecesaria y que no está presente en el idioma original. Esto lo podemos ver también en el contexto de sabiduría. En Proverbios 3:13 el refrán habla de lo dichosa que es la persona que halla la sabiduría. En este caso, las diferentes traducciones han luchado un poco más con la traducción de 'adam. Por ejemplo la versión *LAT* ha optado por colocar "mortal." En cambio dos versiones intentan evitar una tendencia demasiada masculina al colocar "el que" (*DHHE95, NVI*). Sin embargo, uno podría argumentar que el intento de traducir con "el que" sigue privilegiando lo masculino ya que se utiliza el vocablo "el" que es masculino. Una opción que se podría haber elegido es la palabra "quien." Aun la *TLA* que en general es la más cuidadosa en cuanto al uso de lenguaje inclusivo cuando el texto lo permite, no logra un equilibrio total ya que optó por poner "el joven." Como habría de esperarse tanto la *RVR60* como el *LPD* traducen "hombre."

Cada uno de estos ejemplos nos muestra que en general la tendencia en las traducciones es de privilegiar el uso de términos masculinos aun cuando el contexto permite y hasta exige algo mucho más genérico, abarcativo e inclusivo. De esta manera comenzamos a sugerir que el uso exagerado de la palabra "hombre" produce "significado," y este sutilmente margina a la mujer del mensaje bíblico de manera innecesaria. Los y las traductoras en el futuro deberán estar más atentos a estas posibilidades legítimas de traducción que ofrecerían un "significado" más democratizador.

'ISH

El vocablo hebreo *'ish* en términos generales se utiliza más para referirse al hombre varón. No obstante veamos las diferentes opciones que nos ofrecen los diccionarios hebreos para *'ish*: hombre, padre, marido, ser mortal, varón, individuo, uno, ser racional, alguien, alguno, quien, quienquiera, y con negativo, ninguno, nadie. Esto indica que si bien *'ish* se utiliza más específicamente para señalar al varón, también se utiliza en contextos donde se refiere al ser humano en general.

Uno de los ejemplos más sobresalientes de esta realidad lo encontramos en el Salmo 1:1, "Bienaventurado el *'ish* que no anduvo en consejo de malos." Tal como lo esperaríamos la *RVR60* traduce "varón." Asimismo, cuatro versiones traducen "hombre" (*LAT*; *LPD*; *DHHE95*; *NVI*). La única versión que rompe con la tradición tan masculina es la *TLA* que opta por la palabra más inclusiva "quien." El contexto de este salmo de sabiduría claramente indica que la palabra *'ish* no se refiere solamente a varones sino que señala a toda persona o a cualquier persona. En otras palabras lo que queremos afirmar es que la poesía declara que el ser humano que no se deja llevar por la influencia de los malos es realmente dichosa.

Otro ejemplo del uso más amplio de la palabra *'ish*, aparece en Deuteronomio 24:16. Si bien es cierto que este vocablo muchas veces se refiere solamente al varón, en este caso todas las traducciones analizadas optaron por algo más inclusivo. La *RVR60* y la *NVI* han traducido este vocablo por la frase "cada uno," que quizá para algunas esta traducción todavía tiene resabios de masculinidad. En cambio *LAT, DHHE95* y *LPD* optaron por traducir "cada cual," y la *TLA* utilizó la palabra "nadie." Es decir, "nadie debe ser castigado por un crimen que no haya cometido." Es claro que el contexto en el cual se utiliza la palabra *'ish* sugiere que esta se refiere a todo ser humano y no solamente al varón. En este caso los traductores de todas las versiones estuvieron dispuestos a flexibilizar su traducción del vocablo en cuestión, y por ende no prevalece el énfasis masculino.

Un caso interesante por el hecho de que aquí las traducciones no parecen ser coherentes está en Éxodo 32:28. En este contexto la palabra *'ish* sin duda está revestida de ambigüedad. El contexto es uno de violencia, y por lo tanto la *TLA* considera que en esta situación murieron tres mil "varones." De forma parecida la *RVR60, DHHE95* y la *LAT* dicen que cayeron tres mil "hombres." En cambio, la *NVI* traduce "israelitas," mientras que *LPD* traduce "personas." Es verdad que en un contexto de batalla, uno esperaría que *'ish* se refiriera a "varones-soldados." Pero en este caso, el contexto deja abierta la posibilidad de que los levitas hayan matado a varones, mujeres y niños.

Anthropos

En el Nuevo Testamento escrito en griego, el vocablo equivalente al hebreo *'adam* es el término *anthropos*. Los diversos diccionarios griegos ofrecen las siguientes opciones para este vocablo: hombre, ser humano, individuo, uno, persona, gente, marido.

Un ejemplo donde dos versiones tienen un énfasis innecesario en cuanto a la masculinidad de la traducción está en Mateo 5:13. En este contexto Jesús habla de que cuando la sal pierde su capacidad de servir como catalizadora de combustión, o se vuelve insípida, se echa fuera y es pisoteada por "*anthropon* (pl)." Tanto la *RVR60* como *LPD* traducen "hombres," dando a entender que sólo los hombres varones llevan a cabo esta acción. En cambio, las otras cuatro versiones optan por traducir con la palabra "gente," lo cual amplía el espectro y además no refuerza innecesariamente el énfasis masculino del contexto original y del contexto receptor.

En Mateo 12:12 tenemos un caso donde se habla del valor de un *anthropos*. En el contexto se compara el valor de una oveja con respecto al valor de un *anthropos*. Esta es una situación donde los traductores deben tener especial cuidado en su forma de traducir para no marginar a nadie. Sin embargo, cuatro versiones han optado por traducir "hombre" (*RVR60*; *DHHE95*; *LPD*; *NVI*). De alguna manera, al traducir "hombre" están diciendo que sólo el hombre vale más que una oveja, y de esta manera, la mujer y los niños quedan marginados. Consideramos que tanto la *LAT* (ser humano) como la *TLA* (persona) han sido más sensibles a esta realidad y de esta manera minimizan el predominio del lenguaje masculino en la traducción de la Biblia. En estas traducciones la persona puede comprender que todo ser humano vale más que una oveja.

Un dato significativo comienza a aparecer al notar que en varios contextos la *RVR60* es la única que traduce *anthropos* sistemáticamente por "hombre," mientras que las otras versiones han hecho el intento de darle a esta palabra una posibilidad más inclusiva. En Mateo 7:12 donde está la declaración de la ley perfecta, vemos que *RVR60* tiene un énfasis marcado en lo masculino: "Así que, todas las cosas que queráis que los hombres hagan con vosotros, así también haced vosotros con ellos; porque esto es la ley y los profetas." Notamos el uso de las palabras masculinas: hombres, vosotros, ellos. En cambio las otras versiones que estamos considerando han optado por "ustedes" y "demás," y de esta manera la "ley perfecta" incluye a todo ser humanos y no sólo a los varones. Esto mismo ocurre en el relato paralelo de Lucas 6:31.

Algo similar aparece en el famoso encuentro entre Jesús y la mujer samaritana. Más allá que en esta ocasión Jesús dignifica a la mujer en la sociedad judía de manera sorprendente y radical, vemos que la *RVR60* una vez más es la única versión que insiste en traducir *anthropon* con la palabra "hombres." En Juan 4:28, cuando la mujer samaritana vuelve al pueblo para anunciar la presencia de Jesús, *RVR60* dice que ella fue a decirle a los "hombres," mientras que todas las otras versiones dicen que la mujer le avisó a la "gente." Lo más probable es que la mujer haya anunciado su experiencia a toda persona que se le cruzaba, sea mujer, niño, niña u hombre.

El último ejemplo que daremos al respecto es el que se encuentra en Santiago 3:8. Aquí el tema en cuestión es que nadie puede dominar su lengua. La *RVR60* dice que "ningún hombre" puede hacerlo, mientras que las otras versiones no masculinizan el término *anthropos* y utilizan la palabra "nadie" o "no hemos," de esta manera incluyendo a todos por igual en este problema.

Hemos resaltado estas diferencias con respecto a la traducción de *anthropos* con especial atención a la *RVR60* debido a que ésta es la versión más leída y aceptada por el mundo evangélico-protestante en América Latina. A su vez, es la versión que más se ha utilizado para adoctrinar a los creyentes de estas iglesias. Sin duda, su énfasis en la masculinidad ha tenido y sigue teniendo una influencia importante en la manera de pensar y practicar la teología.

Aner

El vocablo griego *aner* es equivalente al término '*ish* en hebreo. Al igual que '*ish* la palabra *aner* en griego se utiliza para hablar del hombre varón y del marido. No obstante, en muchos casos aun los diccionarios dicen que *aner* se puede referir a la persona en general.

Mateo 12:41 es un caso en el Nuevo Testamento donde las diversas versiones analizadas no siguen una misma línea de pensamiento. Allí se habla de los *aner* de Nínive. Tres versiones (*RVR60*; *LAT*; *LPD*) hablan de los "hombres de Nínive." En cambio, *DHHE95* y *TLA* traducen "los de Nínive," mientras que la *NVI* traduce "los habitantes de Nínive." Estas últimas tres reflejan un intento por comprender el uso más amplio de *aner*, particularmente en un contexto donde es evidente que no se está refiriendo solamente a hombres varones.

Un caso similar se encuentra en Mateo 14:35 donde también se habla de los *aner* de un determinado lugar. Lo más probable es que se refiera a la gente o los habitantes del lugar, tal como lo han entendido las versiones *DHHE95*, *NVI* y *TLA*. En cambio, como es de esperar, tanto la *RVR60* como la *LAT* y *LPD* optan por hablar de "los hombres" del lugar. Este es un caso donde la masculinización del término es innecesaria y hasta un tanto incorrecta tanto para el contexto original como para el contexto receptor.

Sugerimos que al traducir por "habitantes" o "la gente" no se está forzando el texto griego a decir algo que no tenía intención de transmitir.

En Romanos 4:8, cuando Pablo cita el Salmo 32:1-2 (probablemente de la LXX—31:1-2) también podríamos sugerir que se está refiriendo al ser humano en general. En el texto hebreo del Salmo 32:1-2 aparece la palabra *'adam* que ya hemos analizado. A su vez en la Septuaginta (LXX) aparece la palabra *aner*. Así como en el Salmo 1 habíamos sugerido que la bienaventuranza se refería a todo ser humano, aquí entendemos lo mismo. No obstante algunas versiones como *RVR60, LAT, LPD* y *DHHE95* han preferido traducir "hombre." En cambio la *NVI* y *TLA* han optado por "aquel" o "aquellos." Estas últimas dos representan un avance, pero consideramos que se podría mejorar aún más ya que "aquel, aquellos" pueden entenderse como masculino. A la vez, reconocemos que en la poesía, por cuestiones de sonido, de ritmo y de otras consideraciones se tiene que negociar mucho más para elegir qué palabra colocar.

Otro caso similar donde está en juego una bienaventuranza lo encontramos en Santiago 1:12. Es interesante que cuatro versiones (*RVR60; LAT; LPD; DHHE95*) elijan "varón" u "hombre" para traducir *aner*, cuando el contexto claramente indica que se está hablando de todo ser humano. La *NVI* y *TLA* al traducir "el que" y "al que" tampoco alcanzan a expresar bien el uso de *aner* en este contexto. Sugerimos, junto con diversas versiones en inglés (*TEV; NRSV; CEV; NLT*) que sería mejor traducir "Dichosa/feliz es 'la persona' o 'la gente.'" Una traducción así, no viola el sentido del texto original y minimiza la presencia masculina hegemónica en la traducción del texto bíblico.

Un Caso-Estudio[1]

El análisis hecho hasta aquí muestra que la traducción llamada *Traducción en Lenguaje Actual* (*TLA*) es la que muestra una sensibilidad mayor al uso

---

1. Para esta sección quiero mencionar y agradecer el trabajo hecho por mis colegas Irene Foulkes (y su equipo), Elsa Tamez, Alfredo Tepox y Edesio Sánchez que participaron junto conmigo en este proceso. Hago mención también de un trabajo inédito escrito por Edesio Sánchez que surgió de este proceso titulado *¡No más violencia contra la mujer!* Este trabajo hace un resumen de los resultados del trabajo de relectura que se hizo particularmente del Nuevo Testamento de la *TLA*. A su vez, este proceso fue motivado por un proyecto que tiene como fin publicar una Biblia para la mujer.

del lenguaje inclusivo y busca minimizar un excesivo énfasis en lo masculino, particularmente cuando el texto fuente no lo exige de manera explícita. En esta sección presentaremos un proceso interesante que se ha dado recientemente con esta traducción. Tal como informamos más arriba, esta traducción tuvo la participación activa de mujeres en el proceso de traducción. Sin embargo, luego de su publicación, los que formamos parte del equipo editorial final de la traducción nos fuimos dando cuenta que en ciertos casos, aun la presencia de mujeres en el trabajo de traducción no evitó ciertas interpretaciones y traducciones cargadas de masculinidad. A su vez, motivados por el llamado del Consejo Mundial de Iglesias a que consideremos a esta década como "el decenio para superar la violencia," decidimos hacer una relectura de varios pasajes bíblicos que podrían estar fomentando, ayudando y generando violencia contra la mujer. Esta relectura tiene como propósito *ofrecer una Biblia que tanto en su texto como en sus ayudas para el lector sea realmente inclusiva.*

Comenzaremos citando un párrafo de un documento inédito que ya forma parte de todo este proceso en las Sociedades Bíblicas Unidas.

> Tal como se notará en los ejemplos que siguen, la inclusividad en la *TLA* no solo se restringe al uso del lenguaje, es decir, de palabras (sustantivos y pronombres) que abarcan a ambos géneros, sino también a la exégesis y a la hermenéutica. En ambos casos, estamos seguros que con la *TLA* hemos logrado un avance no alcanzado en otras versiones castellanas existentes. Esto es más alentador y esperanzador dado que esta versión ha sido preparada pensando en las nuevas generaciones de lectores y oyentes del texto bíblico: los niños y los jóvenes. De este modo, formamos parte del gran proceso pedagógico eclesiástico que busca preparar una generación menos opresora, menos exclusiva y menos violenta. (Sanchez inédito, 7)

Veamos entonces algunos ejemplos que nos ayudarán a ver de qué manera el texto de la *TLA* ha sido modificado como resultado de una exégesis más sensible al énfasis masculino en la traducción y del uso de un lenguaje más inclusivo.

Subtítulos

En primer lugar veremos algunos cambios en los subtítulos de algunas secciones del texto bíblico. Somos conscientes que los subtítulos no solamente representan una interpretación del pasaje, sino que condicionan al lector y la lectora al acercarse al texto en sí.

Josué 2

Si bien varias traducciones ponen como título "Josué y los espías" para este sección, es evidente que la protagonista principal de esta narrativa es Rahab. Por lo tanto el subtítulo para esta sección en la *TLA* es "Rahab y los espías."

Lucas 8.1

El título de la *TLA* para este párrafo era: "Algunas mujeres ayudan a Jesús." Pero este título daba la idea de una ayuda puntual y quizá circunstancial que brindaban algunas mujeres a favor de Jesús. Sin embargo, el contexto de los siguientes versículos sugiere que estas mujeres habían asumido el rol de ayudantes que acompañaban a Jesús y su grupo y que lo hacían por un tiempo prolongado. Es por esto que ahora el subtítulo es "Mujeres que ayudaban a Jesús."

Hechos 18.24

En este contexto, la mayoría de las versiones ponen en el subtítulo algo como "Apolo predica en Éfeso." Originalmente, la *TLA* también public un título similar: "Apolo anuncia la buena noticia en Éfeso." Sin embargo, son Priscila y Áquila quienes le dan las instrucciones acerca de la buena noticia de Jesús a Apolo, y este es el tema principal del párrafo. Por lo tanto ahora el subtítulo en la *TLA* es "Priscila, Áquila y Apolo."

Textos Específicos del Nuevo Testamento

Veamos a continuación una serie de textos bíblicos que han sido modificados con el propósito de ser más equilibrados en la interpretación. Cada uno de estos pasajes ha sido estudiado cuidadosamente y las sugerencias de cambio han sido analizadas y evaluadas por varios expertos en estudios bíblicos y traducción de la Biblia.

Mateo 1.3

En la *TLA* habíamos puesto la siguiente traducción: "Fares y Zérah (su madre se llamaba Tamar)." Es más que evidente que al poner "la madre se *llamaba* Tamar" le quitamos un rol preponderante como madre y además no ayudamos a evocar la memoria tan importante de estas madres (ver 1:5 también) cuyas situaciones y vivencias fueron irregulares y sin embargo aparecen en el linaje del Mesías. Por esta razón se cambió a "su madre *fue* Tamar." Con esta redacción le hacemos justicia a la memoria de estas madres que se quiere transmitir a través del texto.

Mateo 1.18

En la *TLA* habíamos puesto la siguiente traducción: "Así fue como nació Jesús, el Mesías: Una joven llamada María estaba comprometida para casarse con José, pero antes de que vivieran juntos se supo que ella estaba embarazada." Al colocar la palabra "joven" de alguna manera utilizamos una palabra que está cargada de significaciones y estereotipos patriarcales. Además, la frase que sí está en el texto griego es "su madre." Incluir esta traducción ayuda a darle continuidad a la línea de descendencia que viene de los versículos anteriores. Por lo tanto se ha cambiado este texto a: "Así fue como nació Jesús, el Mesías: *su madre*, María, estaba comprometida para casarse con José, pero antes de que vivieran juntos se supo que ella estaba embarazada."

Mateo 26.13

Para este versículo la *TLA* tenía: "*Les aseguro que esto que ella hizo se recordará en todos los lugares donde se anuncien las buenas noticias de Dios.*" Ahora se ha cambiado a la siguiente redacción: "Les aseguro que en cualquier lugar donde se anuncien las buenas noticias de Dios, se contará la historia de lo que hizo esta mujer y se guardará la memoria de ella."

De esta manera se recuperan dos elementos muy importantes: no solamente se recordará la historia de lo que la mujer hizo, sino que se "contará"; es decir, también se guardará la memoria de la mujer como persona.

Marcos 5.40–41

En este pasaje del libro de Marcos, los traductores ofrecimos la siguiente traducción: "entró en el cuarto donde estaba la niña. Lo acompañaron los *padres* y tres de sus discípulos."

Hemos sido advertidos que en este contexto el texto griego especifica algo que no es muy común, a decir, padre y madre. Por lo tanto es aconsejable no sustituir esta especificación con una expresión masculinizante que de alguna manera vuelve invisible a la mujer dentro de un término masculino plural. Por lo tanto hemos decidido cambiar a: "entró en el cuarto donde estaba la niña, junto con el *padre y la madre* de ella y tres de sus discípulos."

1 CORINTIOS 11.3

Este es un pasaje de la Biblia que se ha utilizado mucho para exigir, desde lo teológico, la dominación masculina tanto en el hogar como en la sociedad. El eje de la interpretación gira alrededor de cómo se traduce la palabra *kefalé*. Las diversas traducciones traducen esta palabra por "cabeza" o "autoridad." Originalmente la *TLA* también tradujo de esta manera: "Ahora quiero que sepan esto: Cristo tiene autoridad sobre todo hombre, el hombre tiene autoridad sobre su esposa, y Dios tiene autoridad sobre Cristo."

Sin embargo a través de una exégesis que entiende que el contexto tiene que ver con el origen de la mujer (Génesis 2:21-22) y no con alguna autoridad sobre ella, ahora la *TLA* ofrece la siguiente traducción para este texto de Corintios: "Ahora quiero que sepan esto: Cristo es el origen del varón, el varón es el origen de la mujer y Dios es el origen de Cristo."

2 CORINTIOS 6.18-7.1

El último versículo del capítulo 6 tiene la siguiente frase "ustedes serán para mí como mis hijos y mis hijas." El capítulo 7 comienza diciendo "Queridos hermanos en Cristo...." Se ha decidido cambiar nuevamente a "Queridos hermanos y hermanas en Cristo" por lo siguiente. En 6:18 Pablo hace referencia a 2 Samuel 7:14, pero le agrega algo al texto al incluir la palabra "hijas," además de "hijos." Sugerimos entonces que el contexto permite y hasta sugiere que nuestra traducción sea más inclusiva. Todo indica que el llamado cariñoso de Pablo incluye a hombres y mujeres por igual.

Filipenses 4.3

La *TLA* en este contexto había ofrecido, "Ellas me han ayudado mucho para anunciar la buena noticia." El cambio que se ha adoptado es el siguiente: "Ellas *han luchado junto conmigo por* anunciar la buena noticia."

La traducción anterior podía entenderse como que la actividad de estas mujeres se reducía a un simple apoyo de cuyas características no sabemos nada. Sin embargo el verbo en griego que utiliza el autor sugiere algo más fuerte y sustancioso. Este verbo habla de "trabajar en conjunto luchando por lograr algo." En Filipenses 1:27 este mismo verbo ha sido traducido "y que luchan unidos por anunciar la buena noticia." El cambio introducido reivindica el trabajo duro que las mujeres están realizando a la par de Pablo.

1 Timoteo 3.16

En este texto, la *TLA* tenía "Cristo vino al mundo como hombre." Si bien es verdad que según los relatos del Nuevo Testamento Jesús nació como varón, hemos considerado que es mejor ser coherente y traducir "Cristo vino al mundo como ser humano." De esta manera le damos un sabor más inclusivo al texto y de ninguna manera violamos el contexto original.

Santiago 2.15

La *TLA* comenzaba diciendo: "Si alguien no tiene ropa ni comida." Esto se ha cambiado a "Si algún hermano o hermana de la iglesia no tiene ropa ni comida." El razonamiento para este cambio es el siguiente. En primer lugar es muy interesante notar que el autor de la carta incluye el femenino de "adelfos," que es "adelfé." Nos parece importante dar cuenta de tal detalle como lo han hecho otras traducciones. Además es probable que la explicitación poco común del femenino esté allí para señalar que la pobreza entre las mujeres era más notoria que entre los hombres.

Podríamos ofrecer muchos más ejemplos de cómo una traducción como la *TLA*, que tuvo participación de mujeres en su trabajo y que intentó ser inclusiva, necesita re-trabajarse una y otra vez. Sugerimos que el trabajo no está terminado. Toda traducción de la Biblia necesita ser revisada constantemente. para descubrir contextos donde consciente o inconscientemente los traductores y traductoras han permitido un énfasis ideológico que no está en el texto o que de manera innecesaria margina a algún sector de la creación de Dios. Sugerimos que el trabajo hecho en la *TLA* representa un progreso en esta dirección. Nuestro propósito ha sido minimizar la masculinidad hegemónica que conduce muchas veces a la violencia contra la mujer. De esta manera buscamos que la traducción sea liberadora para todo ser humano.

Reflexiones Finales

A modo de conclusión quisiéramos referirnos a algunos temas puntuales. En primer lugar, reiterar el concepto de que debemos como traductoras y traductores resistir la tentación de hacer que el texto sea hecho a imagen y semejanza de nuestras sensibilidades políticas e ideológicas modernas. En otras palabras, debemos de cuidar de no hacerle decir al texto fuente (en este caso el texto bíblico) lo que no dice. No es aconsejable convertir a un texto que contiene muchos contextos exclusivos en un texto totalmente inclusivo. Esto sería violar su contexto y cosmovisión original. Quizás debamos seguir el consejo de C.R. Fontaine cuando dice que si el texto es realmente exclusivo, así debemos traducirlo y luego arrepentirnos en las notas de estudio al pie de página llamando la atención a otros textos bíblicos que presentan otras alternativas más inclusivas (2004, 275). Un ejemplo de esto es el texto que aparece en Eclesiastés 7:8 donde las traducciones no pueden evitar el énfasis exclusivo y masculino del texto: "¡todavía no he encontrado lo que busco! He encontrado un hombre bueno entre mil, pero no he encontrado una sola mujer buena" (*TLA*).

En segundo lugar, debemos evitar el otro extremo al colocar la palabra "hombres" o alguna connotación masculina cuando en el texto bíblico no está. Por ejemplo, en Apocalipsis 5:9 no hay ninguna palabra en el texto griego que exija una interpretación o traducción masculina. Sin embargo traducciones como la *LAT* y la *LPD* insertan la palabra "hombres" innecesariamente dándole al texto una masculinidad inexistente. El texto dice, en una traducción de carácter literalista: "y con tu sangre nos has redimido para Dios, de todo linaje y lengua y pueblo y nación" (*RVR60*). En cambio, la *LAT* dice: "y con tu sangre compraste para Dios / *hombres* de toda raza, lengua, pueblo y nación." Y la *LPD* dice: "y por medio de tu Sangre, / has rescatado para Dios / a *hombres* de todas las familias, / lenguas, pueblos y naciones."

La inclusión de la palabra "hombres" que no está en el texto griego es gratuita y margina sin necesidad a la mujer. En nuestra opinión esto es lo que se debe evitar. Sugerimos que ésta es una forma de opresión y de violencia contra la mujer. Tal como dice C. Martin: "experiencias de opresión, como toda experiencia humana, afecta la manera en que mujeres y hombres codifican y decodifican la realidad sagrada y la realidad secular" (2004, 42; traducción personal). La *RVR60* por ser una traducción más literal o de equivalencia formal, en este caso, resulta ser menos sexista que otras.

En tercer lugar, si bien subrayamos el hecho de que hay que evitar una masculinidad excesiva en la traducción, también sugerimos que hay que interpretar y evaluar cada caso en su contexto. No se debe tomar una decisión unilateral para todos los textos de la Biblia. Esto requerirá un esfuerzo exegético importante para no caer en traducciones a la ligera o traducciones hechas a la manera de una concordancia. Y además, en los casos donde el texto sea ambiguo, o dé lugar a la duda, sugerimos que se elija la traducción que no margine a ningún grupo humano.

Finalmente, nos queda una pregunta sin responder pero que representa un desafío para un futuro estudio de este tema tan importante. En los círculos de traducción de la Biblia, en general, uno está de acuerdo que una traducción de Biblia no puede ser una que termine siendo una *(sub)versión* de la misma. ¿O quizá, sí? Por otro lado, estamos plenamente de acuerdo en que una traducción de la Biblia puede *(sub)vertir* a otras traducciones existentes. Es en este sentido que hacemos un llamado a todo intento de traducción de la Biblia a que entre otras cosas, busque la manera de ser un agente de liberación y así subvertir una ideología hegemónica opresora.

Is There Justice in Translation?

Matt Waggoner

1

The theory and practice of translation runs thick with layers of social meaning and political myth. It necessitates attention to issues of difference and identity, host, home and the other, identity, plurality, assimilation, cultural consumption, incorporability, origin and genesis, and various kinds of cultural and political fantasies that mark the desire to speak to the other, to be spoken by the other, or to make the other speak. In other words, translation tinkers with what the Hegelians call the politics of recognition: the risky, uneven process in which self-consciousness is, not without difficulty, confirmed by seeing oneself in another, seen by another, or through the eyes of another (Gutman 1994). And it is for that reason that translation is subject to many of the same ethical dilemmas as the Hegelian narrative: To what extent is the other merely the occasion and the material for the fashioning of the self? To what extent is the other consumed in the process of self-fashioning? To what extent does translation harbor, in a life-and-death way, fear of otherness? Or, to what extent does or might translation acknowledge that otherness is constitutive of the self, something without which there can be no self? In the same way that the productive ambiguities of Hegel's narration of selfhood in relation to otherness have contributed so richly to the self-reflection of modern identity (the identity of selves, cultures, races, genders, nations, etc., but also to the identity of the modern), so too is the project of translation implicated, consciously or not, in a whole set of inquiries into, and constructions of, modern identity.

It would be misguided to think that one is simply or opportunistically borrowing from cultural and literary criticism when bringing contemporary theorizations of translation to bear on the practice of biblical translation. Particularly with postcolonial theory in mind, however, it is true that cultural and literary studies supply some of the more sophisticated, recent attempts to think through the issues, and especially the politics, of translation; what is probably more significant is that the problems represented by translation, and the role they play in the Western machine of knowledge production today (the study of other cultures, foreign languages, foreign literatures, etc.), are inexorably haunted, if you will, by biblical narratives. We might almost say that for the modern West, the problem of translation begins with biblical literature—not just because of the guilty conscience of early modern missionary histories of biblical translation, caught up as they were in colonial and imperialistic imperatives, but because biblical literature supplies a set of ancient mythemes about the origin and meaning of linguistic difference and of overcoming it through translation. If, for example, Freud could posit the universality of certain ancient Greek stories for the structure of the unconscious mind (e.g., Oedipus), can we not say that the entire question, so pressing in academic circles today, of the "ethics of translation" owes its sense of original guilt, its suspicion of cultural hubris, its questions about cross-cultural engagement, and its worries about the moral legitimacy of overcoming differences to a story like that of the tower of Babel?

The Gen 11 account of the peoples of the earth erecting a tower to reach the heavens, and then being scorned and punished by God (according to Josephus's interpretation, at least) for the hubris of trying to overcome the boundary between God and humankind by the curse of multiple languages, contains all of the ingredients for a later legacy in which the attempt to bridge this new boundary (between humans) would evoke a sense of shame and guilt. Linguistic pluralism was, in this story, associated with the sin of conflating the universal and the particular, and the work of translation, by implication, became analogous to the punishing toil to which Adam and Eve were subjected upon their banishment from the garden. Furthermore, translation bears the disgraceful mark of a repeat offense, a lingering, sinful urge to return to that prepunishment state in which the peoples of the earth could speak to one another, that is, to that state in which they were not so cursed by their particularity. Within this sort of biblical diegesis, translation is a dirty fantasy curbed only by the austerity or the asceticism of a prohibitionist caution against the sinful arrogance of making the particulars speak to one another as they once did in the days when humankind believed it could approximate God.

The moral guilt that connects this ancient story of an arrogant desire for bad universalism (conflating the particular for the universal) certainly bears important lessons for the modern situation, one in which the West, viewing itself as the embodiment of universal values and truths, and in a relation of dominance to the rest of the world, engaged in the task of translating other texts into its own language, or its own texts into other languages (or other cultures into its own narrative of cultural development, etc.), in conjunction with imperialistic practice. By now (and we owe this to postcolonial theory) we are well aware of the deeply embedded role of translation work in the day-to-day affairs of colonial and imperial subjugation.[1] We could extend this insight by noting the various ways that modern Western thought has narrativized the predicament of multiculture. We know, for example, that the early- and high-modern study of the origin of languages became the occasion for theories of Western supremacy and the invention of race-thinking. We know that a certain Platonic way of seeing the world in terms of a natural teleology persisted well into the late Enlightenment in the form of various ideas about different rates of cultural and evolutionary progress directed at some single, developmental end point of which the West was thought to have been representative. Many of these theories posited an eventual coming together of the peoples of the world by natural means, or by economic means, or by means of providence or civilization or *Geist* or proletarian consciousness or what have you. The sciences of anthropology, society, culture, and language (including the science of translation) often functioned in various ways and for a long period of time as adjuncts of this long cultural narrative of what was envisioned as the inevitable homogenization of humankind in a Babel-like state, and the ciphers for that homogenization were terms like *progress* and *civilization*. This is the story of cultural imperialism that we have come to know, and to respond to with obligatory shame whenever we participate in its academic legacies, for example, anthropology, comparative studies, and, of course, textual translation.

The point I wish to make is that there is a kind of easy moralism or liberal guilt that postcolonial theory gives leeway to, and that is not completely unfounded, but that should not go unquestioned and should not prevent serious inquiry into the practice of translation merely because of

---

1. See, e.g., the work of Mary Louise Pratt in comparative literature (1992); David Chidester in comparative religions (1996); Edward Said (1978) or Gayatri Spivak (1987, 1995, 2003).

a looming sense that we ought to feel guilty for wanting to bridge differences. In recent articulations of cultural theory, one of the signs of willingness to think anew about the value of previously and popularly stultified concepts or practices, like that of literary and cultural translation, has been the effort to rethink, at a theoretical level (but with practical implications), the meaning of and the relationship between the universal and the particular, and to do so partly within the purview of its Hegelian construction.[2] While, for example, Hegel's narration of the path to self-conscious identity seemed to privilege the moment at which, having traversed the other, the self returns home, there is room within that narration for alternative readings that emphasize the way in which "home" is never self-identical but always also traversed by the other, so that, as Kierkegaard once put it, the real art of living is not to be at home in one's home. Perhaps the tower of Babel story—to whatever extent it may inform our cultural consciousness (or, to borrow a phrase from Foucault, our cultural unconsciousness)—is susceptible to reinterpretation, so that instead of Josephus's emphasis upon language diversification as punishment for the sin of hubris (becoming like God), we see it as another kind of lesson: it was not that God punished humankind for traversing the boundary between humans and the Divine, but that God sought to install in humans another kind of boundary, an internal and constitutive boundary (multiculture), one that would require not an overcoming but an engagement as the occasion for ethical opportunity. To engage the other within, the other not as wholly other but as a kind of rupture in the self, is to know oneself not as a self-contained whole set against other self-contained wholes but as a being (or a people, or whatever) that is at once undone by the other, given over to the other, and inextricably linked to the other. The sin, in this case, was not in becoming like God, but in thinking that alterity resides on the other side of an abyss, something to consume or incorporate, when instead we might think of alterity as that which is in us that we cannot possess. However that may be (and forestalling, for the purposes of the present essay, further inquiries into Lacanian ethics), what is worthy of discussion is the way translation has become in recent writings the site of a more fruitful kind of investigation into ethical opportunities than what the lingering legacy of Western guilt has afforded us so far.

---

2. See, e.g., Judith Butler's commentaries on Hegel's "concrete universal" (Butler, Laclau, and Žižek 2000).

2

An example of such investigation is the set of essays contained in *Nation, Language, and the Ethics of Translation* (Berman and Wood 2005). The volume addresses literary and cultural translation broadly speaking, including issues of national and postnational identity, and can be viewed in terms of three main gestures. The first is its acknowledgment that the modern world compels a certain scope and intensity of translation: "Waves of migrating peoples have made the contemporary nation-state, and especially its urban centers, into global sites with multiplicities of languages and cultures. At the same time, the international trade, finance, and information technologies that support these sites both depend upon and often seek to bypass translation for economic growth within world and regional markets" (1). In other words, the volume begins with an historical materialist (Marxian) premise that contemporary globalization causes greater and greater degrees of cultural exchange, while, at the same time, doing so in ways that entail the (capitalist) supposition of the even commensurability of exchanges. The way that such commensurability glosses over real-world unevenness (discrepancies of wealth and power) is regarded as an analogue of the way commensurability in cultural translation also conceals dynamics of power. The second gesture is to explore the sites and the problems of cultural translation in the realm of text and culture, of social and political identity, and of cultural meaning and its patronage in national contexts or in the context of centers of knowledge production. Here both the ethics and the politics of translation are unpacked, illustrated, analyzed, and evaluated. There is, however, a third kind of gesture that I want to suggest is encapsulated by Gayatri Spivak's remark that "translation is the most intimate act of reading" (2005, 94). Spivak and others push the envelope of what I have described as a contemporary knee-jerk academic guilt with respect to translation and ask instead how translations of all sorts (including, for example, in the arena of a discourse of human rights) are at once necessary, problematic, and yet capable of opening us up to ethical encounters. Elsewhere Spivak has described this as the possibility to "write the self at its othermost" (2003, 91).

Although section one of this volume (on which I shall focus) purportedly takes up the question of media, it also concerns itself quite consistently with the ethical dimensions of translation. A common theme among these essays is that the ethical consists not in purifying translation through fidelity to the original or concealing the translator's work, but in making transparent the contaminating effects of translation on the host language and the work alike. Pierre Legrand writes, "the host language makes the work other-than-itself while the work offers the host language the opportunity to differ from itself" (2005, 39). Vulnerability to the prospect of being contaminated by the other in the translation process yields ethical opportunities.

In other words, contamination, as opposed to purification, is embraced throughout several of these essays as an orientation to translation work that confronts and comes to terms with how translation makes way for an ethical experience by exposing the otherness within the self, an exposure that reveals a sort of "intimacy" to which translations respond either by embracing it or disavowing it. We could explore this idea by recalling that in an issue of Forbes Magazine one finds the boldface introduction to an article on property acquisitions that originally read: "Bored of your assets in Los Angeles, Miami, and New York? Try getting yourself a piece of Asian ..." (Flannery 2006). It read "office space" here, but who does not get the point? Sex, we know, has been vital to the imperial imagination. Robert Young's *Colonial Desire* (1995) stressed the role sex played in Western race-thinking: the obsession with purity and the disavowal of hybridity, intimacy, and contact. Young suggested that this contradiction between the official rhetoric of cultural authenticity and essences on the one hand, and the disavowed realities of sexual desire and cross-cultural contact on the other hand, was critical to Western identity formation.

In addition to tropes of blood purity (linking racial and sexual discourses), imperialism also routinely invoked the trope of horticulture, yet another breeding metaphor haunted by issues of contamination. Justifications for imperial acquisition and development frequently involved some reference to the colony and its inhabitants as uncultivated, wild, chaotic, unproductive, barren, fruitless, in need of a good gardener. We find this language in the context of Zionist imperialism, as when David Ben-Gurion, speaking at the Biltmore Hotel in New York City in 1942, said that in the course of settling Palestine the Jewish people have "made the waste places to bear fruit and the desert to blossom. Their pioneering achievements in agriculture and in industry ... have written a notable page in the history of colonization" (2003, 187). We might also point to contemporary landscaping shows on television like *Curb Appeal*, channeling "sex appeal," as evidence that these themes persist in the cultural imaginary of the West. We fear and disavow the contaminations that secretly make us what we are. Overgrowth in our lawns and hybrids in our families and cultures are the offspring of an uncultivated fertility that scares us. Fidelity and purity, the integrity of cultures and their boundaries, these things reassure us by repressing the memory of desire and the messy reality of cross-contamination.

So too with translation, but translation is after all part of the work of imperialism, both in its colonial and capitalist operations: translating native subjects into colonial subjects; native cultures into civilized cultures; translating raw, barren lands and labor into commodities. There is a consistency here that makes contamination important to understanding the centrality of translation to the interactions between empires and appropriated others. But it is not as simple as saying "translation is guilty and we should avoid it." Translation is surely unavoidable; the question is "how, then, do we translate, knowledgeable of its imperial functions in the past and hopeful about some more subversive and just role for translation?" To stress contamination in translation is to do as Edward Said recommends in his contribution to this volume: to take up counterdiscourse, countermemory, and counternarrative, reviving traces of the nonidentical, those necessary, constitutive exclusions that Derrida used to speak of (2005, 28). I read this volume as something like a celebration of Stuart Hall's pronouncement that "the future belongs to the impure" (1997, 299).

3

These authors stress contamination as requisite to any consideration of the ethics of translation. When I translate, I alter the work just as it alters me. An ethics of translation means something like mutual openness to the vulnerability of this dialectic, to the fact that I never walk away from translation the same. The work I translate reconstitutes me; the "I" that translates is never secure and self-given but always given over to the work/other. However, I am not entirely sure the phrase "ethics of translation" is exactly what we mean to say; or, I am not certain this is really what a number of the authors in section one are trying to say. They seem to speak more of justice in translation than an ethics of translation. Before turning to their essays—and I am limiting myself to those by Said, Legrand, and Weber—I shall say something about the ethics-justice distinction.

Historically, this distinction invokes the antithesis between empirical and a priori claims. To Plato's insistence that right actions follow right ideas, Aristotle's ethics emphasized becoming good by doing good. Ethics, like ethos, usually implies something like "one's nature" or the natural way of oneself in the context of the community into which one is born. We talk about the ethos of a people, for instance. In the modern period, Immanuel Kant's *Grounding* (1981) and second *Critique* (1997) rescued the old a priori argument that morality has only to do with conformity to right ideas, the moral law, whereas Hegel in *Philosophy of Right* (1996) revived the Aristotelian thesis that it makes little sense to rest the whole question of the good on abstract ideas. He argued that the good occurs historically as individuals participate in the life of a community and embody its norms, habits, life-ways, and so on.

Today, we still have Kantians of various stripes who maintain that there is a universal logic and rationality and that we can come to some consensus about the norms that we should live by. But we also have virtue theorists, communitarians, and, of course, Foucaultians, who for various reasons reject the universality of norms and take up instead the position that ethics is a much less cerebral and instead a more corporeal, as well as cultural, activity. There are no transcendent norms that hold good in all times and places; there are only localized practices and techniques of self-cultivation. It is significant that Charles Taylor traced his (communitarian) ideas not just to Hegel but to Herder, the father of modern nationalism (1994), and that Foucault embraced the language that most reflects the heart of the ethical tradition when he spoke so eloquently about "cultivating" the self. On this model, an ethics of the self is like a landscaping project.

With respect to Foucault, this is to be expected, given the influence of Nietzsche on his "ethical turn"; Nietzsche redefined morality in terms of self-mastery, channeling rather than punishing one's nature. Already Nietzsche had envisioned a new ethics of the self through the language of horticultural breeding: pruning the self, caring for it, making it grow and flourish, even in some more controversial ways invoking the idea of ridding oneself and one's culture of impurities. The point is that when we speak of ethics today we tend to mean either the embodiment of cultural norms and local definitions of the good, in opposition to abstract and universal dogmas about the good, or we mean a kind of self-cultivation, a horticulture of the self.

One thing that unites all the various schools of ethics in the fashionable ethical turn today is their opposition to moral universalism. But what one finds in section one of this volume is, again, this emphasis on contamination that troubles both sexual and horticultural metaphors. Contamination as they discuss it produces something along the lines of an opportunity for justice, not because it achieves or accomplishes justice, but because it disrupts the smooth functioning systems of translation (textual, global, cultural, economic, etc.), intervening as the nonidentical in this overwhelming process of global translating systems and saying, "Some things cannot be accomplished, some things fail, some things do not compute, and some things do not translate without remainder." These authors suggest that there is something supremely just about taking the side of those remainders, those contaminants, those impurities, and turning them into reminders of the failed totality of systems, the incompletion of the smooth functioning processes of the global, and the obstinate dignity of the particular within the machinations of equivalence and exchange so characteristic of late modern society.

Speaking on the role of the writer, Said defends the idea that justice is more than a cultural construct; we may not and need not have a detailed theory of justice to go to war against injustice. Said contests the claim that when we are confronted by the evils of torture, famine, censorship, and ignorance we are resigned to localized definitions of the good and of the bad. He calls himself a foundationalist for regarding the wrongness of these things as being "as real as anything we can encounter" (2005, 28). Later in the essay he encourages writers to acknowledge through their work that some problems, some dialectical oppositions, are not reconcilable.

On one hand, Said is insisting that we must know the limits of translation, so to speak, because there are problems to which we do injustice if we present our audiences with handy solutions and syntheses. His example is the Palestinian crisis, and his point is that the work of the critic is not to resolve but to render visible the impossibility of the situation, the incompatibility between justice and available solutions. For our purposes we might say that Said's recommendation is not to overtranslate, but instead to respect the limits of translation by giving voice to the untranslatable. Justice emerges in the aporia of the untranslatable when it is not swept under the rug of easy solutions but staged as a reminder of the contradictions that characterize the world we live in. To do this is, again, to oppose a world organized by the logic of equivalence and exchange, of systemic translation or what the tradition of critical theory used to call identitarian reason.

Legrand applies literary theory to legal theory to argue that legal borrowing is a kind of translation that yields opportunity for host traditions to be undone by the traditions they borrow from: "legal borrowing does not transform an original foreign law into one the importers may call their own, but rather renders radically foreign that law they envisage as being theirs" (2005, 42). In reference to something Gayatri Spivak wrote, he mentions the need for the translator to surrender to language; that is, the translation must not look so natural within the host language that it no longer looks like a translation. Translation should not be a form of assimilation but instead one of hospitality—the work and the host language mutually respect and give themselves over to the alterity of the other rather than impose their identities on the other. Each is "deterritorialized" and vulnerable within the process, but in that vulnerability there is real hospitality.

We could pause to note the way the spirit of Kantian justice is quietly informing the conversation taking place in the volume. It was in "Toward Perpetual Peace," the famous essay on cosmopolitanism, that Kant commented on hospitality as the unrestricted right of visitation for the foreigner. And this argument was supported by Kant's conclusion (a version of the Platonic natural teleology referenced earlier) that the shape of the earth (not a cube with delineated sides, but a sphere with a continuous surface) suggested that natural design does not intend for anyone or any group to assert exclusive possession of a part of the earth's surface, a territory. Rather, natural design intends that all inhabitants of the earth equally share in the mutual possession of the earth's surface; thus the right of visitation and the duty of hospitality. This logic is wielded, surreptitiously, as it were, by Kant as both a challenge to the sovereignty of nations and as an argument for the moral obligations that follow from nature's own deterritorializing injunction (Kant 1983). In short, we are by nature, as it were, always already given over to the other, and this condition of being othered implies moral duties to respect the alterity of the other. Legrand concludes that self-displacement is key, not simply to what is ethical, but to what is just in translations "only in deferring to the non-identical can the claim to justice be redeemed" (2005, 42).

There is a fascinating link between this reference to hospitality in Legrand's essay and Samuel Weber's discussion of Walter Benjamin's "Task of the Translator." If I were to give that link a name it would be a "geometry of justice." For, in much the same way that Kant derived claims about social justice from the way we as inhabitants of the earth's surface are like points on the circumference of sphere, Benjamin derived claims about the rightness of a translation through the analogy of the tangent touching a circle. In both cases, we cannot own the center or origin; we are displaced and decentered, deterritorialized; and whether translating from one language to another or from one citizenship to another, the point is that we are always constituted primarily by what we are not, by an alterity to which we must be hospitable.

I cannot in the space I have left capture all the nuance of Weber's argument. The genius of his past works is apparent here too as he deftly weaves together the theme of touching and dispersion in the Genesis creation narrative with the theme of touching and displacement in translation in Benjamin's essay. But I believe I can summarize the main thesis of the essay. Weber's thesis seems to be that meanings do not capture the original; they *graze* them. Moreover, the original cannot be captured by translations because the origin is not a fixed object; it is a relational process, a movement, a repetition, alteration, transformation, and what have you. This was Benjamin's insight. Translations do not conquer originals like empires conquer foreign lands and assimilate them. Translations merely render visible the "differential interplay of diverse ways of signifying" (Weber 2005, 74). The task of the translator is to render this interplay visible, to serve as a stopping point in an ongoing movement. Translations do not communicate a fixed meaning but point to the movement of symbolization itself. Translations only capture an instance in the perpetual displacement of the original "as the tangent fleetingly touches the circle" (Benjamin 1968, 80).

Translations succeed when they fail, or, to put as Kant might have, when they know their limits, when they recognize the impossibility of their own endeavor. Translations succeed and do justice to the work of cultural interaction when they stage the remainders of the process itself, those unincorporable particulars that resist the generalizing movement toward abstraction, equivalence, and exchange. In the Kantian tradition, justice was spoken of in these terms, as a limit concept, a boundary of impossibility that marked the horizon of what was hoped for but unaccomplished. Justice was violated by claims to have resolved the contradiction, to have crossed the boundary and grasped the original. Justice consisted in rendering itself as that which could not be assimilated, incorporated, embodied, and contained. Justice, Legrand rightly puts it, could only be redeemed by referring to the nonidentical.

4

It would seem to me to be of crucial importance to the community of linguistic and cultural translators to recognize, first, that translation is inexorably enmeshed in a history and an overwhelming machinery of the logic and apparatuses of equivalence and exchange, of commodification and cultural imperialism. Second, it would seem important to recognize that translation is necessary and inevitable, and the question is not how to avoid it but how to do it justice. And it is in response to this second question that I see these authors making a contribution. Their contribution is to say that we do justice to translation when translation undoes itself, renders its own task impossible, gives itself over to the limits of untranslatability, to the excessive remainders that resist incorporation, the nonidentical. Translation has to view itself in these terms if it is not to simply recapitulate its historically conditioned role as an apparatus of assimilation.

In conclusion, I shall return to the theme of not being at home in one's home, an idea I earlier attributed to Kierkegaard, but which was also quoted by others, including Walter Benjamin (in the *Arcades Project*; 2002) and Theodor Adorno (in *Minima Moralia*; 1974). I cannot overlook the references to Adorno in the introduction to the volume, in Said's conclusion, in Weber's analysis of Adorno's co-collaborator and friend, Walter Benjamin, as well as the fact that Weber has been a translator of Adorno and written specifically on the task of translating Adorno. Finally, one of Adorno's signature themes seems to me to be right at the center of so much of this first section of the volume, the nonidentical.

Unlike Martin Heidegger, whose desire to recover the purity of language mirrored his unconditional commitment to German culture, for Adorno the presence of foreign words in a text has a disenchanting effect. It dispels language's illusion of perfectly reconciling words and things, demystifying and defamiliarizing the projected coherence and unity that Heidegger claimed was the result of the forgetting of Being, a forgetting that needed to be recovered by philosophy. Adorno liked that untranslatable words stand out in a text, disrupt it, confront its hidden incoherence, prevent it from passing itself off as origin and uncontaminated mediation. Adorno went so far as to attribute to them an almost messianic quality, saying of untranslatable words that what they consist in textually is "unknown in the positive sense, a language that overtakes, overshadows, and transfigures the existing one as though it were itself getting ready to be transformed into the language of the future" (Nicholsen 1997, 89).[3]

His point, and the point of these authors, is that translation is necessary, but in order not to perpetuate its complicity with an imperialist legacy, translation has to be willing to fail. It has to be hospitable to the

---

3. Further discussed in Nicholsen 1997.

alterity of what cannot translate without remainder, refusing the tendency toward ruthless and seamless assimilation. There is justice in translation when this condition of mutual undoing, common vulnerability, the condition of hospitality, is taken seriously and made visible. To Forbes's property acquisitions metaphor we might respond with Adorno's citation of Kierkegaard about home owning from *Minima Moralia*, which is also the text with which the editors chose to preface this volume. Nietzsche once said that he was fortunate never to have been a home owner (Adorno 1974). Adorno remarked that we should instead say that one must never be at home in one's home. Exilic displacement is the unsettled condition in which mutual vulnerability begets mutual hospitality. This caution is as true for making oneself at home in one's home as it is for making oneself at home in language. The question is not, or should no longer be, how not to commit the sin of translation. This sense of guilt is overdetermined by a particular legacy of the biblical tradition (owing, I have tentatively suggested, to certain readings of the tower of Babel story, among other things), and by the very clear role of translation in colonial and imperial histories. But translation is neither intrinsically unethical nor is it conceivable or even desirable that we would stop translating. The question should instead be, what, and who, is the real object of translation? How am I rightfully undone by translating myself toward the other and the other toward myself? How does and can translation expose the rupture of the other within me and, by doing so, open me to the other? We should go so far as to claim that there can be no opportunity for the ethical apart from translation.

Language, Power, and the "T-Word"

John Eipper

I was flattered—and to no small degree intimidated—by Scott Elliott's invitation to comment on the essays assembled in this volume. First, let me air the necessary disclaimers: I am a Hispanist by training and trade, and though I was reared in the United Methodist tradition, I have been a practicing agnostic (can this be called a "practice"?) since my college days. I have no Hebrew, and as for Greek—well, we know what they say about Greek. Translation, to be sure, has always been central to my work: I have grappled with the cadence and surreal metaphors of the Chilean poet Pablo Neruda, and throughout the 1990s I translated into English several scatological allegories of the late Argentinian prosaist Osvaldo Lamborghini. Lamborghini is a cult figure in his native land, but most of his work, I have found, rings too harsh on the Anglophone ear—meaning that with the exception of one short story, I cannot find a publisher!

The latest theories of second-language (L2) teaching have relegated the "T-word" (translation) to a pariah status of sorts. Rote memorization of grammar rules and vocabulary lists are out; the "communicative approach" is in, although few in my profession can agree on what this approach means other than engaging the student in the target language as much as possible. But of course, I say: who would advocate language teaching via a "noncommunicative" method? What "communicativity" seeks to accomplish is an idealized learning process where the student acquires the L2 with no outside interference. For the teacher to assign translation exercises is a no-no, akin to the mind-numbing Latin parsing drills of a nineteenth-century schoolmaster. We strive rather to connect the student with the Spanish logos in a pure, uncontaminated state—assuming, rather like prosthelytizers in the Spanish New World, that the business of translating languages and cultures is best left to the experts. The ubiquitous Rosetta Stone advertisements—check any in-flight magazine—boast that with their software you will learn language like a baby. How students are to acquire the marketable skill of translation is a question rarely breached. Perhaps through divine inspiration, like the Septuagint translators discussed by Virginia Burrus in this volume, or Joseph Smith with his golden tablets? One senses that we are placing our faith in machines as the new Angel Moroni.

Of course, in the Hispanist business, to channel Sayre (or was it Kissinger? Woodrow Wilson?), translation politics can afford to be acrimonious because the stakes are so low. But what happens when matters of translation impact religious orthodoxy, Truth, the Word of God? Who is empowered to midwife translations of the Christian Bible, and what are the real-world implications of their decisions? In short, who benefits, and who *suffers,* from biblical translation? The debate turns heated when the stakes are high, too. These are the weighty matters taken up by the contributors to this anthology.

The Spanish conquest and colonization of the Americas from the sixteenth century onward constituted probably the largest mass translation project in history. In that *annus mirabilis* 1492, the Salamanca academic Antonio de Nebrija published the first grammar of any vernacular language. In his prologue he wrote, "Siempre la lengua fue compañera del Imperio" (Language has always been the companion of Empire; 5). Writing before Columbus's voyage became the continental sensation, Nebrija prophesied language's vital role alongside the guns, germs, and steel that reduced a hemisphere to Spanish dominion. Indeed, if we accept Tsvetan Todorov's take on the New World encounter, it was the Spaniards' superior reading and manipulation of signs that sealed their triumph over the native peoples. Missionaries such as the Dominican Bartolomé de las Casas and the Franciscan Bernardino de Sahagún compiled massive tomes of native history and beliefs. A century later, the Peruvian mestizo chronicler Inca Garcilaso de la Vega would boast of his knowledge of the Quechua language, which he "drank in his mother's milk" (47) as proof of his interpretive superiority over the monolingual Spaniards in his *Royal Commentaries of the Incas*. Garcilaso's narrative privileges the Inca civilization over other pagan cultures (or, for Garcilaso, *non*cultures), drawing a comparison between the Inca capital Cuzco and pre-Christian Rome as lacking only Christ to achieve perfection. The Inca religion is even described in a grammar readily intelligible to the Christian reader—including the cross symbol, an embryonic tripartite deity, and easily recognizable quasi-Mosaic laws. As Naomi Seidman points out in her discussion of the Yiddish Bible, some non-Christians are portrayed as more capable of receiving evangelization than others—for the Yiddish translators these select are the Jews, for Garcilaso, the Peruvians.

Questions of religion and translation were in the forefront, yes, but not Bible translation. A contrary process took place, as sacred native "texts" of all sorts were rendered into Spanish to lay the groundwork for the conversion process. Pioneering works of ethnography were born, paradoxically, out of the urgency to destroy indigenous beliefs. In the early eighteenth century, the Dominican friar Francisco Ximénez oversaw the translation and bilingual transcription of the Maya-Quiché *Popul Vuh*, often termed the Bible of Mesoamerica—which it literally is, if we recognize how the text was informed by the Bible, with the native chroniclers supplying Christian-nuanced representations of the Mayan creation and destruction narratives that enabled Ximénez to posit the *Popul Vuh* as a useful preliminary step for the arrival of Christianity.

As the Counter-Reformation freed the Spanish in the New World from the problem of familiarizing the biblical strange, Jerome's Latin Vulgate continued to occupy the place of supreme authority until the post-Independence era. (The Lutheran-inspired, sixteenth-century Reyna-Valera Spanish translation that occupies a central place in Esteban Voth's essay was probably never seen in colonial Spanish America.) Indeed, it has been argued that the analogous role of the KJV (1611) for codifying the written English language was fulfilled for Spanish by Cervantes' *Don Quixote* (1605; part 2, 1615). The translation of sacred texts was too risky, offering too much space for subversion. In setting up their missions in Paraguay, the Jesuits (forebears of today's language teachers?) jealously guarded their mantle as cultural gatekeepers, and sought to protect the Guaraní people by maintaining an isolation from their Spanish and Portuguese neighbors. By doing so, they bestowed an ambiguous blessing upon the Guaranís: they codified and preserved a language that thrives to this day on an official basis, yet demanded a total obedience—an obedience predicated on *untranslatability*, I would venture—that condemned the Paraguayans to centuries of hierarchy and a patriarchal system that led to one of history's most devastating wars (1864–1870), when Paraguay was all but wiped out by the triple alliance of Brazil, Argentina, and Uruguay.

One wonders if Spanish-American history would have played out differently if Spain had experienced the Protestant Reformation, with a resultant translation of the Bible into dozens if not hundreds of indigenous languages. As I review the studies by Flemming A. J. Nielsen and

Christina Petterson on the Greenlandic Bible, I am inclined to think not. In the example of the Lutheran evangelization of the Greenlanders, we see that translation drives the same Faustian bargain played out in the Hispanic Americas: in exchange for a written language and a nascent sense of nationhood—Benedict Anderson (1996) termed it the "imagined community"—the semiotics of belief are assigned new signifieds, whether it be the christianization of the *Popul Vuh* or the rendering of the indigenous Greenlandic *toornaarsuk* (the shaman's helping spirit) as the biblical devil. Instead of making the strange familiar, these acts of translation perform the reverse.

If I read Virginia Burrus correctly, Augustine in his epistolary polemic with Jerome foreshadowed the Protestant position, when he stressed the importance of the personal interpretation of Scripture while privileging, rather contradictorily, the authority of the Septuagint translators. Language and power lead to paternalism on either side of the Protestant-Catholic divide: a clear parallel can be drawn between the illustrated children's Bibles explored in Jacqueline Du Toit's essay and the missionary theatrical productions, known as *autos sacramentales*, that were performed among the indigenous in the New World. Nebrija, with his linkage of language and empire, would find a kindred spirit in the nineteenth-century Committee for the Revision of the Authorized Version of the New Testament, the subject of Alan Cadwallader's essay, which admitted the participation of UK Nonconformists but largely ignored the input of American and Commonwealth scholars. The late Victorian period was still a time when "empire," and the hegemony of the Established Church, were ideals that required no dissimulation.

Insofar as the "T-word" boils down ultimately to questions of authority and power, can there be justice in translation, as Matt Waggoner so pointedly asks? Whenever I deliver a tongue-in-cheek "Learn Spanish in One Easy Step" lesson to my students, they learn that a workable answer to any and all questions is "*depende*": it *depends*. Foucault fans will point out that power *is* injustice, as evidenced by the inevitable resistance with which it is met. Walter Benjamin may have had some of history's more egregious missionary endeavors in mind when he famously wrote, "there is no document of civilization that is not simultaneously a document of barbarism" (1968, 256). Yet in the different translation moments explored in this volume, I am struck by a unifying thread in which biblical translators, from the Septuagint scholars to Jerome to Poul Egede to Henry Einspruch to the Sociedades Bíblicas Unidas of today, have sought justice *in* translation (i.e., the "correct" rendering of the signs themselves), but also justice *through* translation. In the most felicitous cases, such as the "recovery" of gender inclusiveness to more closely approximate the Hebrew and Greek originals, both can be accomplished at the same time. Du Toit points out that illustrated children's Bibles, with varying degrees of success, seek to match the visual imagery to the reader's cultural context—a process the software industry would term "localization."

Looking backward, it is obvious from our perspective that mistakes were made: we readily capture the injustice of calquing "God" from the Danish colonizing language, while leaving the embodiment of "devil" in the Greenlandic. The Greenlanders did not ask to be christianized, after all. But we can also picture Poul Egede's work in the bleakness of the Arctic night as no less a search for justice than twenty-first-century attempts to eliminate masculine bias in the Spanish New and Old Testaments. Even the nineteenth-century white man characterized his duty as a "burden," after all—spiritual colonization, together with economic and political, were seen as the right things to do. Is this justice? I will have to go with a single weasel-word answer: *Depende*.

Esteban Voth begins his essay with the well-known Italian refrain: *traduttore traditore*—all translation is betrayal, or, if we are to take the literalist path, the translator is a traitor. But isn't the betraying always done by someone who has plowed the textual field before us? Retranslations of the Bible—and except for novelties such as the ongoing Klingon Bible project, is there any other type?—will always engage in a dialogue with previous renderings, with the tacit assumption that justice is best served by engaging with the *traditores* of the past. The present volume delves into diverse, specific moments of rupture, all of which probably tell us less about Scripture than about the translators themselves. Vernacular Bibles will continue to be fine-tuned to reflect changing linguistic norms (a straightforward task), as well as shifting cultural values. The latter issue is more contentious, given the debates within the Christian denominations about homosexuality, gay marriage, and (for Roman Catholics) priestly celibacy. Translation will continue to be massaged to fit the message. How will the message be received? These are questions of authority, and ultimately, power. After digesting this eclectic collection of thought-provoking case studies, I am convinced that future translators will never cease to mine Hebrew and Greek ambiguities to generate meanings we are presently unable to fathom.

Works Consulted

Adorno, Theodor. 1974. *Minima Moralia: Reflections from Damaged Life*. Translated by E. F. N. Jephcott. New York: Verso.
Aglionby, Francis K. 1907. *The Life of Edward Henry Bickersteth Bishop and Poet*. London: Longmans, Green.
Aichele, George. 2001. *The Control of Biblical Meaning: Canon as Semiotic Mechanism*. Harrisburg, Pa.: Trinity Press International.
Alexander, Pat. 1991. *The Lion Children's Bible*. Oxford: Lion Hudson.
———. 2000. *My Gunsteling Kinderbybel: Die Wêreld se Wonderlikste Verhaal in Kindertaal*. Translated by Andries Cilliers and Sonja Cilliers. 2nd ed. Cape Town: Struik Christelike Boeke.
———. 2008. *Bibele ya Bana*. Bellville: Bible Society of South Africa.
Anderson, Benedict. 1996. *Imagined Communities: Reflections on the Origin and Spread of Nationalism*. Rev. ed. London: Verso.
Anderson, Johann. 1746. *Nachrichten von Island, Grönland und der Straße Davis, zum wahren Nutzen der Wissenschaften und der Handlung*. Hamburg: Georg Christian Grund.
———. 1748. *Efterretninger om Island, Grønland og Strat Davis*. Copenhagen: Gabriel Christian Rothe. [Danish version of Anderson 1746.]
Angus, Joseph, and J. Waddington. 1862. *Christian Churches*. London: Ward.
Appelt, Martin, and Hans Christian Gulløv, eds. 1999. *Late Dorset in High Arctic Greenland: Final Report on the Gateway to Greenland Project*. Danish Polar Center Publication 7. Copenhagen: Danish National Museum.
Ariel, Yaakov. 2000. *Evangelizing the Chosen People: Missions to the Jews in America (1880–2000)*. Chapel Hill: University of North Carolina Press.
———. 2003. When Missionaries Wrote in Yiddish: The Rise and Fall of Missionary Yiddish in America. *The Mendele Review* 7:1–14. Cited 17 October 2009. Online: http://yiddish.haifa.ac.il/tmr/tmr07/tmr07008.htm.
Armitage, Thomas. 1890. *A History of the Baptists*. New York: Bryan, Taylor.
Arneborg, Jette. 2005. Det europæiske landnam—nordboerne i Grønland, 985–1450 e.v.t. Pages 219–78 in *Grønlands forhistorie*. Edited by Hans Christian Gulløv. Copenhagen: Gyldendal.
Artaud, Antonin. 1976. *Selected Writings*. Edited by Susan Sontag. Translated by Helen Weaver. New York: Farrar, Strauss, Giroux.

Asch, Sholem. 1939. *The Nazarene*. Translated by Maurice Samuel. New York: Putnam's Sons.
Assmann, Jan. 1996. Translating Gods: Religion as a Factor of Cultural (Un)Translatability. Pages 25–36 in *The Translatability of Cultures: Figurations of the Space Between*. Edited by Sanford Budick and Wolfgang Iser. Stanford, Calif.: Stanford University Press.
Atuagarssuit, tássa agdlagkat iluartut tamarmiussut ... 1864. Nuuk. [The Book of Genesis in Greenlandic.]
Atuagarssuit, tássa agdlagkat ivdlernartut tamarmiussut, tastamantitorᴋamigdlo tastamantitâmigdlo agdlagkat. 1900. Copenhagen: Rosenberg. [The Bible in Greenlandic.]
Baker, Mona. 2006. *Translation and Conflict: A Narrative Account*. London: Routledge.
Bal, Mieke. 1997. *Narratology: Introduction to the Theory of Narrative*. 2nd ed. Toronto: University of Toronto Press.
Barnstone, Willis. 1993. *The Poetics of Translation: History, Theory, Practice*. New Haven: Yale University Press.
Bartholin, Caspar. 1673. Vocabula Gróenlandica. Pages 71–77 in *Acta Medica and Philosophica Hafniensia*. [Facsimile in Robert Petersen and Jørgen Rischel, "Sproglig indledning og kommentar til Resens tysk-grønlandske ordliste," *Grønland* 33 (1985): 159–62.]
Bassnett, Susan, and Harish Trivedi. 1999. *Post-colonial Translation: Theory and Practice*. London: Routledge.
Die Belangrikste Storie ooit Vertel. 2000. Translated by Rosalie van Aswegen. Vereeniging: Christelike Uitgewersmaatskappy.
Ben-Gurion, David. 2003. The Biltmore Program. Declaration Adopted by the Extraordinary Zionist Conference at the Biltmore Hotel of New York City, May 11, 1942. Pages 186–88 in *The Middle East and Islamic World Reader*. Translated by Marvin Gettleman and Stuart Schaar. New York: Grove.
Benjamin, Walter. 1968. The Task of the Translator. Pages 69–82 in *Illuminations: Essays and Reflections*. Edited by Hannah Arendt. Translated by Harry Zohn. New York: Schocken.
———. 1968. Theses on the Philosophy of History. Pages 253–64 in *Illuminations: Essays and Reflections*. Edited by Hannah Arendt. Translated by Harry Zohn. New York: Schocken.
———. 2002. *The Arcades Project*. 1999. Repr. Cambridge: Harvard University Press.
Bergsland, Knut, and Jørgen Rischel, eds. 1986. *Pioneers of Eskimo Grammar*. Travaux du cercle linguistique de Copenhague 21. Copenhagen: Linguistic Circle, Reitzel.
Berliner Fischthal, Hannah. 2004. Reactions of the Yiddish Press to *The Nazarene*. Pages 266–78 in *Sholem Asch Reconsidered*. Edited by Nanette Stahl. New Haven: Beineke Library.
Berman, Sandra, and Michael Wood, eds. 2005. *Nation, Language, and the Ethics of Translation*. Princeton: Princeton University Press.
Bhaba, Homi K. 2004. Signs Taken for Wonders: Questions of Ambivalence and Authority under a Tree outside Delhi, May 1817. Pages 102–22 in *The Location of Culture*. 1994. Repr. London: Routledge.

The Bible and Culture Collective. 1995. *The Postmodern Bible*. New Haven: Yale University Press.
The Bible for Little Ones. 2007. Wellington: LuxVerbi.
Biibili. 2000. Copenhagen: Det Danske Bibelselskab. [The Bible in Greenlandic.]
Bloch-Hoell, Nils Egede. 1960. Et Egede-manuskript fra 1725. *Norsk Tidsskrift for Misjon* 14:98–113.
Bobé, Louis, ed. 1925. *Hans Egede: Relationer fra Grønland 1721–36 og Det gamle Grønlands ny Perlustration 1741*. Meddelelser om Grønland 54. Copenhagen: Reitzel.
———. 1936. *Diplomatarium Groenlandicum 1492–1814*. Meddelelser om Grønland 55. Copenhagen: Reitzel.
———. 1952. *Hans Egede: Colonizer and Missionary of Greenland*. Copenhagen: Rosenkilde and Bagger.
Bodmer, George. 2003. Arthur Hughes, Walter Crane, and Maurice Sendak: The Picture as Literary Fairy Tale. *Marvels and Tales* 17:120–37.
Boer, Roland. 2008. *Last Stop before Antarctica: The Bible and Postcolonialism in Australia*. 2nd. ed. Semeia Studies 64. Atlanta: Society of Biblical Literature.
———. 2009. *Political Grace: The Revolutionary Theology of John Calvin*. Louisville: Westminster John Knox.
———. Forthcoming. *In the Vale of Tears: On Marxism and Theology V*. Leiden: Brill.
Bottigheimer, Ruth B. 1996. *The Bible for Children: From the Age of Gutenberg to the Present*. New Haven: Yale University Press.
Bruno, Bonnie, and Carol Reinsma. 2007. *Read Together Bible for Young Readers*. Illustrated by Jenifer Schneider. Vereeniging: Christian Art.
Buber, Martin, and Franz Rosenzweig. 1930. *Die fünf Bücher der Weisung*. Berlin: Lambert Schneider.
Burgon, John W. 1871. *The Last Twelve Verses of the Gospel according to S. Mark Vindicated against Recent Critical Objectors*. Oxford: J. Parker.
Burnett, Fred W. 2000. Historiography. Pages 106–12 in *Handbook of Postmodern Biblical Interpretation*. Edited by A. K. M. Adam. St. Louis: Chalice.
Butler, Judith, Ernesto Laclau, and Slavoj Žižek. 2000. *Contingency, Hegemony, Universality: Contemporary Dialogues on the Left*. New York: Verso.
Cadwallader, Alan H. 2007. The Politics of Translation of the Revised Version: Evidence from the Newly Discovered Notebooks of Brooke Foss Westcott. *Journal of Theological Studies* 58:415–39.
———. 2013. *The Politics of the Revised Version*. Sheffield: Sheffield Phoenix.
Carey, William. 1817. Dr. Carey to Dr. Baldwin, Calcutta, July 23, 1816. *The American Baptist Magazine, and Missionary Intelligencer* 2:64–65. Courtesy of the Center for Study of the Life and Work of William Carey, D.D. (1761–1834), William Carey University, Hattiesburg, Miss. Online: http://www.wmcarey.edu/carey/bibles/translation.htm.
Chatman, Seymour. 1978. *Story and Discourse: Narrative Structure in Fiction and Film*. Ithaca: Cornell University Press.

Chidester, David. 1996. *Savage Systems: Colonialism and Comparative Religion in Southern Africa*. Charlottesville: University Press of Virginia.
Ciglia, Francesco Paolo. 2004. Auf der Spur Augustins: *Confessiones* und *De civitate Dei* als Quellen des *Stern der Erlösung*. Pages 223–44 in *Rosenzweig als Leser: Kontextuelle Komentare zum "Stern der Erlösung."* Edited by Martin Brasser. Tübingen: Niemeyer.
Clark, Elizabeth A. 2004. *History, Theory, Text: Historians and the Linguistic Turn*. Cambridge: Harvard University Press.
Cobley, Paul. 2001. *Narrative*. London: Routledge.
Comaroff, Jean, and John Comaroff. 1991. *Of Revelation and Revolution*. Vol 1. *Christianity, Colonialism, and Consciousness in South Africa*. Chicago: University of Chicago Press.
———. 1997. *Of Revelation and Revolution*. Vol 2. *The Dialectics of Modernity on a South African Frontier*. Chicago: University of Chicago Press.
Currie, Mark. 1998. *Postmodern Narrative Theory*. New York: Palgrave.
Derrida, Jacques. 1976. *Of Grammatology*. Translated by Gayatri Chakravorty Spivak. Baltimore: Johns Hopkins University Press.
Dessain, C. S., and T. Gornall. 1973. *The Vatican Council, January 1870 to December 1871*. Vol. 25 of *The Letters and Diaries of John Henry Newman*. Oxford: Clarendon.
DeVries, Catherine. 2007. *The Beginner's Bible. Book of Devotions: My Time with God*. Illustrated by Kelly Pulley. Grand Rapids: Zonderkidz.
Dickmeiss, Eskil. 2002. Giv os i dag vor daglige sæl'—et essay om sprog, kultur og teologi. *Grønlandsk kultur og samfundsforskning* 00/01:23–37.
Dietrich, Walter, and Ulrich Luz. 2002. *The Bible in a World Context: An Experiment in Contextual Hermeneutics*. Grand Rapids: Eerdmans.
Docherty, Thomas. 1993. Postmodernism: An Introduction. Pages 1–31 in *Postmodernism: A Reader*. Edited by Thomas Docherty. New York: Columbia University Press.
Dollerup, Cay. 1999. *The Grimm Tales from Pan-Germanic Narratives to Shared International Fairytales*. Amsterdam: John Benjamins.
Dorais, Louis-Jacques. 1993. *From Magic Words to Word Processing: A History of the Inuit Language*. Iqaluit: Arctic College.
———. 2010. *The Language of the Inuit: Syntax, Semantics, and Society in the Arctic*. Montreal: McGill-Queen's University Press.
Dube, Musa W. 1999. Consuming a Colonial Cultural Bomb: Translating *Badimo* into "Demons" in the Setswana Bible (Matthew 8.28–34; 15.22; 10.8). *JSNT* 73:33–58.
———. 2000. *Postcolonial Feminist Interpretation of the Bible*. St. Louis: Chalice.
———. 2001a. Introduction. Pages 1–19 in Dube 2001b.
———, ed. 2001b. *Other Ways of Reading: African Women and the Bible*. Global Perspectives on Biblical Scholarship 2. Atlanta: Society of Biblical Literature.
DuBois, Thomas A. 2009. *An Introduction to Shamanism*. Cambridge: Cambridge University Press.
du Toit, Jaqueline S. 2011. "Translated and Improved": Retelling the Bible for Children. Pages 379–91 in *Retelling the Bible: Literary, Historical, and Social Contexts*. Edited by Lucie Doležalová and Tamás Visi. Frankfurt am Main: Peter Lang.

du Toit, Jaqueline S., and Luna Beard. 2007. The Publication of Children's Bibles in Indigenous South African Languages: An Investigation into the Current State of Affairs. *Journal for Semitics* 16:297-311.

Eadie, John. 1876. *The English Bible: An External and Critical History of the Various English Translations of Scripture.* 2 vols. London: Macmillan.

Eco, Umberto. 1979. *The Role of the Reader.* Bloomington, Ind.: Indiana University Press.

———. 2003. *Mouse or Rat? Translation as Negotiation.* London: Phoenix.

———. 2008. *Experiences in Translation.* Translated by Alastair McEwen. 2001. Repr. Toronto: University of Toronto Press.

Egede, Hans. 1722a. Relation angaaende dend Dessein med dend Grønlandske Mission. Pages 1-29 in *Hans Egede: Relationer fra Grønland 1721-36 og Det gamle Grønlands ny Perlustration 1741.* Edited by Louis Bobé. Meddelelser om Grønland 54. Copenhagen: Reitzel, 1925.

———. 1722b. Kort Relation om Grønland og dets Indbyggeris Beskaffenhed saa vitt vi endnu til Datum kand hafve Opliusning om. Pages 30-40 in *Hans Egede: Relationer fra Grønland 1721-36 og Det gamle Grønlands ny Perlustration 1741.* Edited by Louis Bobé. Meddelelser om Grønland 54. Copenhagen: Reitzel, 1925.

———. 1723. Continuation af dend Journal Relation angaaende dend nye anfangne GrønLandske Mission fra dend 21. Junij 1722 indtil Ultimo Julij 1723. Pages 45-88 in *Hans Egede: Relationer fra Grønland 1721-36 og Det gamle Grønlands ny Perlustration 1741.* Edited by Louis Bobé. Meddelelser om Grønland 54. Copenhagen: Reitzel, 1925.

———. 1725a. Dend Fierde Continuation udaf Journal-Relationen Betreffende det Grønlandske-Missions-Verch fra d. 30. Julij 1724 indtil d. 31. Maij Indeværende 1725. Pages 141-66 in *Hans Egede: Relationer fra Grønland 1721-36 og Det gamle Grønlands ny Perlustration 1741.* Edited by Louis Bobé. Meddelelser om Grønland 54. Copenhagen: Reitzel, 1925.

———. 1725b. *Ti till Ellefve Capitler udaf Skabelsens-Bog: Ofversatt udj Grønlændernis Sprog for at viise hvor vitt Mand er avangerit udj Sproget, og hvad endnu fattis, førend Mand fuldkommeligen kand forestille dem Troen og dend Sande Guds Kundskab.* Unpublished manuscript: Ledreborg 339 4°, The Royal Danish Library, Copenhagen, Manuscript Department.

———. 1738. *Omstændelig og udførlig Relation, angaaende den Grønlandske Missions Begyndelse og Fortsættelse.* Repr. Copenhagen: Rosenkilde og Bagger, 1971.

———. 1741. *Det gamle Grønlands nye Perlustration, eller Naturel-Historie.* English translation: *A Description of Greenland.* 2nd ed. London: Allman, 1818. Repr. New York: Kraus Reprint, 1973.

Egede, Niels. 1744. *Tredje Continuation Af Relationerne Betreffende Den Grønlandske Missions Tilstand Og Beskaffenhed.* Repr. Copenhagen: Rosenkilde og Bagger, 1971.

Egede, Poul. 1741. *Continuation af Relationerne Betreffende Den Grønlandske Missions Tilstand Og Beskaffenhed, forfattet i Form af en Journal fra Anno 1734 til 1740.* Repr. Copenhagen: Rosenkilde og Bagger, 1971.

———. 1744. *Evangelium Okausek tussarnersok Gub Niarnarmik Innungortornik okausianiglo, Usornarluleniglo, tokomello umarmello, Killaliarmello, Innuin annauniartlugit, aggerromartomiglo, tokorsut tomasa umartitsartortlugit. Karalit okausiet attuartlugo aglekpaka.* Copenhagen.

———. 1750. *Dictionarium Grönlandico-Danico-Latinum.* Copenhagen.

———. 1766. *Testamente Nutak eller Det Nye Testamente oversat i det Grønlandske sprog, med Forklaringer, Paralleler og udförlige Summarier.* Copenhagen: Trykt paa Missionens bekostning af Gerhard Giese Salikath.

———. 1788. *Efterretninger om Grønland uddragne af en journal holden fra 1721 til 1788.* Paraphrased in modern Danish and annotated by Mads Lidegaard. Det Grønlandske Selskabs Skrifter 29. Copenhagen: Det grønlandske Selskab, 1988.

Ellicott, Charles J. 1881. Preface. Pages v–xxii. *The New Testament of Our Lord and Saviour Jesus Christ Translated out of the Greek: Being the Version Set Forth A.D. 1611 ... and Revised A.D. 1881.* Oxford: Oxford University Press.

Ellicott, Charles J., and Edwin Palmer. 1882. *The Revisers and the Greek Text of the New Testament by Two Members of the New Testament Company.* London: Macmillan.

Elyada, Aya. Protestant Scholars and Yiddish Studies in Early Modern Europe. *Past and Present* 203 (2009): 69–98.

Fabricius, Otto. 1801. *Forsøg til en forbedret Grønlandsk Grammatica.* Copenhagen: Schubart.

Fabricius, Otto, and Niels Gjessing Wolf. 1822. *Testamentitokamit Mosesim aglegéj siurdleet.* Copenhagen: Schubart.

Fanon, Frantz. 1967. *Black Skin, White Masks.* New York: Grove.

Flannery, Russell. 2006. Asia's REIT Push. *Forbes Magazine.* October 16, 2006. Online: http://www.forbes.com/forbes/2006/1016/085.html.

Fontaine, C. R. 2004. The NRSV and the REB: A Feminist Critique. *Theology Today* 47:273–80.

Fortescue, Michael D. 1980. Affix Ordering in West Greenlandic Derivational Processes. *International Journal of American Linguistics* 46:259–78.

———. 1998. *Language Relations across Bering Strait: Reappraising the Archaeological and Linguistic Evidence.* London: Cassell.

Fortescue, Michael D., Steven Jacobson, and Lawrence Kaplan. 2010. *Comparative Eskimo Dictionary: With Aleut Cognates.* 2nd ed. Alaska Native Language Center Research Paper 9. Fairbanks: Alaska Native Language Center, University of Alaska Fairbanks.

Frank, David B. 2004. Cultural Dimensions of Translation into Creole Languages. Paper presented at the Conference on Bible Translation. Cave Hill, Barbados. Online: http://linguafranka.net/saintluciancreole/workpapers/cultural_dimensions.htm.

Fürst, Alfons. 1999. *Augustins Briefwechsel mit Hieronymus.* Jahrbuch für Antike und Christentum Ergänzungs Band. Münster: Aschendorffsche Verlagsbuchhandlung.

Gad, Finn. 1970. *Earliest Times to 1700.* Vol. 1 of *The History of Greenland.* London: Hurst.

———. 1973. *1700 to 1782.* Vol. 2 of *The History of Greenland.* London: Hurst.

———. 1982. *1782–1808*. Vol. 3 of *The History of Greenland*. Copenhagen: Nyt Nordisk.
Galli, Barbara Ellen. 1995. *Franz Rosenzweig and Jehuda Halevi: Translating, Translations, and Translators*. Montreal: McGill-Queen's University Press.
Garcilaso de la Vega, El Inca. 1609. *Comentarios reales de los Incas*.
Gentzler, Edwin. 2008. *Translation and Identity in the Americas: New Direction in Translation Theory*. London: Routledge.
Gillman, Abigail E. 2002. Between Religion and Culture: Mendelssohn, Buber, Rosenzweig and the Enterprise of Biblical Translation. Pages 93–114 in *Biblical Translation in Context*. Edited by Frederick W. Knobloch. Bethesda: University Press of Maryland.
Goffman, Erving. 1963. *Stigma: Notes on the Management of Spoiled Identity*. Harmondsworth: Penguin.
———. 1972. *Encounters*. Harmondsworth: Penguin.
Goulburn, Edward M. 1892. *John William Burgon: Late Dean of Chichcester*. 2 vols. London: John Murray.
Greenspoon, Leonard Jay. 1998. Bringing Home the Bible: Yiddish Bibles, Bible Societies, and the Jews. Pages 291–304 in *Yiddish Language and Culture, Then and Now*. Edited by Leonard Jay Greenspoon. Vol. 9 of *Studies in Jewish Civilization*. Edited by Leonard Jay Greenspoon. Omaha: Creighton University Press.
Grønbæk, Jakob H. 2001. Gehejmestatsministerens bibliotek på Ledreborg: Om et 1700-tals herregårdsbibliotek. *Fund og Forskning* 40:49–80. Online: http://img.kb.dk/tidsskriftdk/pdf/ffo/ffo_2001_40-PDF/ffo_2001_40_101168.pdf.
Grudem, Wayne. 2005. Are Only *Some* Words of Scripture Breathed Out by God? Why Plenary Inspiration Favors "Essentially Literal" Bible Translation. Pages 19–56 in *Translating Truth: The Case for Essentially Literal Bible Translation*. Edited by Wayne Grudem et al. Wheaton, Ill.: Crossway.
Gulløv, Hans Christian. 2005a. Nunarput, Vort Land—Thulekulturen 1200–1900 e.v.t. Pages 283–343 in *Grønlands forhistorie*. Edited by Hans Christian Gulløv. Copenhagen: Gyldendal.
———. 2005b. Arktiske hvalfangere. Pages 201–10 in *Grønlands forhistorie*. Edited by Hans Christian Gulløv. Copenhagen: Gyldendal.
———. 2005c. Kulturmøder i nord. Pages 211–17 in *Grønlands forhistorie*. Edited by Hans Christian Gulløv. Copenhagen: Gyldendal.
———. 2011. Prehistory. Pages 24–64 in *Cultural Encounters at Cape Farewell*. Edited by Einar Lund Jensen, Kristine Raahauge, and Hans Christian Gulløv. Monographs on Greenland 348; Man and Society 38. Copenhagen: Museum Tusculanum.
Gulløv, Hans Christian, ed. 2005. *Grønlands forhistorie*. Copenhagen: Gyldendal.
Gutman, Amy, ed. 1994. *Multiculturalism: Examining the Politics of Recognition*. Princeton: Princeton University Press.
Haase, Evelin. 1987. *Der Schamanismus der Eskimos*. Acta culturologica 3. Aachen: Edition Herodot, Rader.
Hall, Stewart. 1997. Subjects in History: Making Diasporic Identities. Pages 289–99 in *The House That Race Built*. Edited by Wahneema Lubiano. New York: Pantheon.

Hallamaa, Panu. 1997. Unangam Tunuu and Sugtestun: A Struggle for Continued Life. *Senri Ethnological Studies* 44:187–223. Online: http://ir.minpaku.ac.jp/dspace/bitstream/10502/808/1/SES44_012.pdf.

Halldórsson, Ólafur. 1985. *Eiríks saga rauða: Texti Skálholtsbókar AM 557 4to*. Reykjavik: Hið Íslenska Fornritafélag.

Ham, Ken. 2006. *My Creation Bible*. Illustrated by Jonathan Taylor. Green Forest, Ariz.: Master Books.

Hansard, House of Commons Debates. 1870. Vol. 202. Online: http://hansard.millbanksystems.com/commons/1870/jun/14/motion-for-an-address.

Hegel, G. W. F. 1996. *Philosophy of Right*. Translated by S. W. Dyde. New York: Prometheus.

Hennings, Ralph. 1994. *Der Briefwechsel zwischen Augustinus und Hieronymus und ihr Streit um den Kanon des Alten Testaments und die Auslegung von Gal. 2,11–14*. Supplements to Vigiliae Christianae. Leiden: Brill.

Henriksen, Carol. 1997. Sprogets natur. Om sprogsynet hos 1700-tallets danske grammatikere. Pages 105–18 in *Digternes paryk: Studier i 1700-tallet: Festskrift til Thomas Bredsdorff*. Edited by M. Alenius. Copenhagen: Museum Tusculanum Press.

Hens-Piazza, Gina. 2000. Lyotard. Pages 160–66 in *Handbook of Postmodern Biblical Interpretation*. Edited by A. K. M. Adam. St. Louis: Chalice.

Herman, David, ed. 2003. *Narrative Theory and the Cognitive Sciences*. Stanford, Calif.: CSLI.

Hodgson, Robert. 2008. Translation Studies: An Introduction. Unpublished paper courtesy of the Nida Institute for Biblical Scholarship, n.p. Online: http://www.nidainstitute.org/TheNidaSchool/NidaSchool2008.dsp.

Hoffman, Matthew. 2007. *From Rebel to Rabbi: Reclaiming Jesus and the Making of Modern Jewish Culture*. Stanford, Calif.: Stanford University Press, 2007.

Holtved, Erik. 1964. Samuel Kleinschmidt. *Arctic* 17:142–44. Online: http://pubs.aina.ucalgary.ca/arctic/Arctic17-2-142b.pdf.

Holy Bible for Little Hearts and Hands: New Living Translation. 2007. 2nd ed. Carol Stream, Ill.: Tyndale House.

Hope, Nicholas. 1995. *German and Scandinavian Protestantism 1700 to 1918*. Oxford History of the Christian Church. Oxford: Clarendon.

Howsam, Leslie. 1991. *Cheap Bibles: Nineteenth-Century Publishing and the British and Foreign Bible Society*. Cambridge: Cambridge University Press.

Indaba Ebalulekile Kunazo Zonke Ezake Zaxoxwa. 1999. Translated by Manie van den Heever. Vereeniging: Christelike Uitgewersmaatskappy.

Israel, Hephzibah. 2009. Translating the Bible in Nineteenth-Century India: Protestant Missionary Translation and the Standard Tamil Version. Pages 209–29 in vol. 4 of *Translation Studies*. Edited by Mona Baker. 4 vols. Critical Concepts in Linguistics. London: Routledge.

Jacobs, Andrew S. 2004. *Remains of the Jews: The Holy Land and Christian Empire in Late Antiquity*. Divinations: Rereading Late Ancient Religion. Stanford, Calif.: Stanford University Press.

Jacobsen, Birgitte. 2010. Greenland Chat: Language Encounter in Cyberspace. Pages 115–32 in *Cultural and Social Research in Greenland: Selected Essays 1992–2010*. Edited by Karen Langgaard et al. Nuuk: Ilisimatusarfik/Atuagkat.
Jacobson, Steven A. 1995. *A Practical Grammar of the Central Alaskan Yup'ik Eskimo Language*. Fairbanks: Alaska Native Language Center and Program, University of Alaska.
Jakobson, Roman. 1987. *Language in Literature*. Edited by Krystyna Pomorska and Stephen Rudy. Cambridge: Belknap Press.
Jespersen, Knud J. V. 2004. *A History of Denmark*. Palgrave Essential Histories. Basingstoke: Palgrave MacMillan.
Kant, Immanuel. 1981. *Grounding for the Metaphysics of Morals*. Translated by James W. Ellington .Indianapolis: Hackett.
———. 1983. Toward Perpetual Peace. Pages 107–43 in *Perpetual Peace and Other Essays*. Translated by Ted Humphrey. Indianapolis: Hackett.
———. 1997. *Critique of Practical Reason*. Edited and translated by Mary Gregor. Cambridge: Cambridge University Press.
Kilham, C. A. 1991. *Translation Time: An Introductory Course in Translation*. Darwin: Summer Insitute of Linguistics.
Kinane e e Gaisang Tsothle: The Most Important Story Ever Told. 2002. Translated by Johannes Kelber. Vereeniging: Christelike Uitgewersmaatskappy.
Kjærgaard, Kathrine. 2010. Grønland som del af den bibelske fortælling—en 1700-tals studie. *Kirkehistoriske Samlinger* 51–130.
Kjærgaard, Kathrine, and Thorkild Kjærgaard. 2008. Prints and Pictures in Greenland 1721–1900. Pages 269–83 in *Commercio delle stampe e diffusione delle immagini nei secoli XVIII e XIX*. Edited by Alberto Milano. Rovereto: ViaDellaTerra.
Kjærgaard, Thorkild. 2010. An Unnoticed Example of How the Black Death Altered the Course of History: Why America Was Discovered from Spain and Not from Scandinavia. Pages 273–81 in *Le interazioni fra economia e ambiente biologico nell'Europa preindustriale secc. XIII–XVIII*. Atti delle Settimane di Studi e altri Convegni 41. Edited by Simonetta Cavaciocchi. Florence: Florence University Press.
———. 2011. Genesis in the Longhouse: Religious Reading in Greenland in the Eighteenth Century. Pages 133–58 in *Religious Reading in the Lutheran North: Studies in Early Modern Scandinavian Book Culture*. Edited by Charlotte Appel and Morten Fink-Jensen. Newcastle upon Tyne: Cambridge Scholars.
Kleinschmidt, Samuel. 1851. *Grammatik der Grönländischen Sprache*. Berlin: de Gruyter.
———. 1871. *Den Grønlandske Ordbog*. Copenhagen: Louis Klein.
Kleivan, Inge. 1979. Studies in the Vocabulary of Greenlandic Translations of the Bible. Pages 175–89 in *Eskimo Languages: Their Present-Day Conditions. Majority Language Influence on Eskimo Minority Languages*. Edited by Bjarne Basse and Kirsten Jensen. Aarhus: Arkona.
Kleivan, Inge, and Birgitte Sonne. 1985. *Eskimos, Greenland and Canada*. Iconography of Religions 8/2. Leiden: Brill.

Kragh, Peter. 1829. *Testamentitokab makpérsægèjsa illàngoeet, Profetit Mingnerit Danieliblo Aglegèit* [The Books of the Twelve Prophets and Daniel in Greenlandic]. Copenhagen: Fabritius de Tengnagel.

———. 1832. *Testamentitokab makpérsegejsa illangoeet, Mosesim aglegèjsa ardlejt tedlimejdlo, Jobib, Esrab, Nehemiab, Esterib Rutiblo aglegejt* [The Books of Exodus, Deuteronomy, Job, Ezra, Nehemiah, Ester, and Ruth in Greenlandic]. Copenhagen: Fabritius de Tengnagel.

———. 1836. *Testamentitokab makpérsægèjsa illangoeet, Josvab er' kartoursirsudlo aglegèjt, Samuelim aglegèj siúrdleet ardlèjdlo, aglékkæt Konginnik siúrdleet ardlèjdlo* [The Books of Joshua, Judges, Samuel, and Kings in Greenlandic]. Copenhagen: Fabritius de Tengnagel.

Kress, Gunther, and Theo van Leeuwen. 1996. *Reading Images: The Grammar of Visual Design*. London: Routledge.

Kronfeld, Chana. 1996. *On the Margins of Modernism: Decentering Literary Dynamics*. Berkeley and Los Angeles: University of California Press.

Krupnik, Igor. 1991. Extinction of the Sirenikski Eskimo language: 1895–1960. *Études/Inuit/Studies* 15:3–22.

Lane, Leena, and Gillian Chapman. 2005a. *My Eerste Bybel*. Translated by Hester Fourie. Wellington: Lux Verbi.

———. 2005b. *My First Bible*. Berkhamsted: AD.

Langgård, Karen. 2002. Inderivation in Greenlandic. Pages 67–119 in *Complex Predicates and Incorporation: A Functional Perspective*. Travaux du cercle linguistique de Copenhague 32. Edited by Ole Nedergaard Thomsen and Michael Herslund. Copenhagen: Reitzel.

———. 2003. Magt og demokrati—og sprog. Pages 215–35 in *Demokrati og magt i Grønland*. Edited by G. Winther. Aarhus: Aarhus Universitetsforlag.

Lapide, Pinchas. 1984. *Hebrew in the Church: The Foundations of Jewish-Christian Dialogue*. Translated by Erroll F. Rhodes. Grand Rapids: Eerdmans.

Lathey, Gillian. 2010. *The Role of Translators in Children's Literature: Invisible Storytellers*. Children's Literature and Culture. London: Routledge.

Legrand, Pierre. 2005. Issues in the Translatability of Law. Pages 30–50 in *Nation, Language, and the Ethics of Translation*. Edited by Sandra Berman and Michael Wood. Princeton: Princeton University Press.

Lewis, David. 2001. *Reading Contemporary Picturebooks: Picturing Text*. London: Routledge.

Lévi-Strauss, Claude. 1970. *Tristes Tropiques*. New York: Atheneum.

Lidegaard, Mads. 1967. Grønlandske portrætter: Arnarsaĸ. *Grønland* 16:157–65.

Lightfoot, Joseph B. 1871. *On a Fresh Revision of the English New Testament*. London: Macmillan.

Lincoln, Bruce. 1989. *Discourse and the Construction of Society: Comparative Studies of Myth, Ritual, and Classification*. New York: Oxford University Press.

Louw, Johannes P., and Eugene A. Nida. 1989. *Greek-English Lexicon of the New Testament: Based on Semantic Domains*. 2nd ed. 2 vols. New York: United Bible Societies.

Lukens, Rebecca J. 2007. *A Critical Handbook of Children's Literature*. 8th ed. Boston: Pearson.
Lynge, Finn. 2006. Tro og udsyn. Pages 95–116 in *Grønland i verdenssamfundet*. Edited by H. Petersen. Nuuk: Atuagkat.
Lyotard, Jean-François. 1984. *The Postmodern Condition: A Report on Knowledge*. Translated by Geoff Bennington and Brian Massumi. Theory and History of Literature 10. Minneapolis: University of Minnesota Press.
Ma, H. J. 2003. *A Study of Nida's Translation Theory*. Beijing: Teaching and Research Press.
Macaulay, Thomas Babington. 1952. Indian Education: Minute of the 2nd of February, 1835. Pages 719–30 in *Macaulay, Prose and Poetry*. Selected by G. M. Young. Cambridge: Harvard University Press.
Magnusson, Magnus, and Hermann Palsson. 1966. *The Vinland Sagas: The Norse Discovery of America*. New York: New York University Press.
Malbon, Elizabeth Struthers. 2008. Narrative Criticism: How Does the Story Mean? Pages 29–57 in *Mark and Method: New Approaches in Biblical Studies*. Edited by Janice Capel Anderson and Stephen D. Moore. 2nd ed. Minneapolis: Fortress.
Markham, Albert Hastings, ed. 1880. *The Voyages and Works of John Davis the Navigator*. 2 vols. in 1. London: Hakluyt Society.
Marquardt, Ole. 2002. Greenland's Demography, 1700–2000: The Interplay of Economic Activities and Religion. *Études Inuit/Inuit Studies* 26:47–69.
———. 2004. The Importation of European Diseases to Greenland and the Great Smallpox Epidemic in the Nuuk Region in 1733–34. Pages 131–44 in *Dynamics and Shifting Perspectives: Arctic Societies and Research. Proceedings of the First IPSSAS Seminar, Nuuk 2002*. Edited by Michèle Therrien. Nuuk: Ilisimatusarfik.
Martin, C.J. 1990. Womanist Interpretations of the New Testament: The Quest for Holisitic and Inclusive Translation and Interpretation. *Journal of Feminist Studies in Religion* 6:14–61.
Matthew, H. Colin G., ed. 1982. *January 1869–June 1871*. Vol. 7 of *The Gladstone Diaries*. Oxford: Clarendon.
———. 1990. *January 1881–June 1883*. Vol. 10 of *The Gladstone Diaries*. Oxford: Clarendon.
Mbuwayesango, Dora R. 2000. How Local Divine Powers Were Suppressed: A Case of Mwari of the Shona. Pages 63–77 in *Other Ways of Reading: African Women and the Bible*. Edited by Musa W. Dube. Atlanta: Society of Biblical Literature.
McClintock, Anne. 1995. *Imperial Leather: Race, Gender and Sexuality in the Colonial Conquest*. New York: Routledge.
Members of the American Revision Committee. 1879. *Anglo-American Bible Revision: Its Necessity and Purpose*. Philadelphia: American Sunday-School Union.
Merivale, Judith A. 1898. *Autobiography and Letters of Charles Merivale*. Oxford: Horace Hart.
Meschonnic, Henri. 1970–1978. *Pour la poétique*. 5 vols. in 6. Paris: Gallimard.
Metzger, Bruce. 2001. *The Bible in Translation: Ancient and English Versions*. Grand Rapids: Baker Academic.

Møller, J. Kisbye. 1985. Resens Grønlandsbeskrivelse 1687. En uudgivet tysk-grønlandsk ordliste. *Grønland* 33:149–51.
Moon, George W. 1882. *The Revisers' English*. London: Hatchards.
Moore, Stephen D. 1994. *Poststructuralism and the New Testament: Derrida and Foucault at the Foot of the Cross*. Minneapolis: Fortress.
———. 2007. A Modest Manifesto for New Testament Literary Criticism: How to Interface with a Literary Studies Field That Is Post-Literary, Post-Theoretical, and Post-Methodological. *BibInt* 15:1–25.
Moravians in Greenland. 2008. *This Month in Moravian History* 27. Online: www.moravianchurcharchives.org/thismonth/08%20jan%20greenland.pdf.
The Most Important Story Ever Told. 2000. Vereeniging: Christelike Uitgewersmaatskappy.
Nandy, Ashis. 1983. *The Intimate Enemy: Loss and Recovery of Self under Colonialism*. Oxford: Oxford University Press.
Nebrija, Antonio de. 1492. *Gramática de la lengua castellana*.
Nicholsen, Shierry Weber. 1997. *Exact Imagination, Late Work: On Adorno's Aesthetics*. Cambridge: MIT Press.
Nida, Eugene A. 1947a. *Bible Translating: An Analysis of Principles and Procedures, with Special Reference to Aboriginal Languages*. New York: American Bible Society.
———. 1947b. *A Translator's Commentary on Selected Passages*. Glendale, Calif.: Summer Institute of Linguistics.
———. 1949. *Morphology: The Descriptive Analysis of Words*. 2nd ed. Ann Arbor: University of Michigan Press.
———. 1951. *An Outline of Descriptive Syntax*. Glendale, Calif.: Summer Institute of Linguistics.
———. 1952. *God's Word in Man's Language*. New York: Harper & Bros.
———. 1954. *Customs and Cultures: Anthropology for Christian Missions*. New York: Harper & Bros.
———. 1957. *Learning a Foreign Language: A Handbook Prepared Especially for Missionaries*. 2nd ed. New York: Friendship Press for the Committee on Missionary Personnel, Division of Foreign Missions, National Council of the Churches of Christ in the U.S.A.
———. 1958. Analysis of Meaning and Dictionary Meaning. *International Journal of American Linguistics* 24:279–92.
———. 1964. *Toward a Science of Translating, with Special Reference to Principles and Procedures Involved in Bible Translation*. Leiden: Brill.
———. 1966. *A Synopsis of English Syntax*. 2nd ed. The Hague: Mouton.
———. 1975a. *Componential Analysis of Meaning: An Introduction to Semantic Structures*. The Hague: Mouton.
———. 1975b. *Exploring Semantic Structures*. Munich: Fink.
———. 2000. Principles of Correspondence. Pages 153–79 in *The Translation Studies Reader*. Edited by Lawrence Venuti. London: Routledge.
———. 2003. *Fascinated by Languages*. Amsterdam: John Benjamins.

Nida, Eugene A., and Johannes P. Louw. 1992. *Lexical Semantics of the Greek New Testament*. Society of Biblical Literature Resources for Biblical Study 25. Atlanta: Scholars Press.

Nida, Eugene A., and C. R. Taber. 1969. *The Theory and Practice of Translation*. Leiden: Brill.

Niranjana, Tejaswini. 1992. *Siting Translation: History, Post-Structuralism, and the Colonial Context*. Berkeley, Calif.: University of California Press.

Nodelman, Perry. 1988. *Words about Pictures: The Narrative Art of Children's Picture Books*. Athens: University of Georgia Press.

Norich, Anita. 2004. Sholem Asch and the Christian Question. Pages 251-65 in *Sholem Asch Reconsidered*. Edited by Nanette Stahl. New Haven: Beineke Library.

Norton, David. 1993. *From 1700 to the Present Day*. Vol. 2 of *A History of the Bible as Literature*. Cambridge: Cambridge University Press.

Noss, Philip A., ed. 2007. *A History of Bible Translation*. Eugene A. Nida Institute for Biblical Scholarship. Rome: Edizioni de Storia e Letteratura.

Nowak, Elke. 1987. *Samuel Kleinschmidts "Grammatik der Grönländischen Sprache."* Studien zur Sprachwissenschaft 4. Hildesheim: Olms.

Nünning, Ansgar. 2004. Where Historiographic Metafiction and Narratology Meet: Towards an Applied Cultural Narratology. *Style* 38:352-75, 399, 403.

Oittinen, Riitta. 2003. Where the Wild Things Are: Translating Picture Books. *META* 48, nos. 1-2:128-41.

———. 2006. The Verbal and the Visual: On the Carnivalism and Dialogics of Translating for Children. Pages 84-97 in *The Translation of Children's Literature: A Reader*. Edited by Gillian Lathey. Topics in Translation 31. Clevedon: Multilingual Matters.

Oldendow, Knud. 1957. *Bogtrykkerkunsten i Grønland og mændene bag den: En boghistorisk oversigt*. Copenhagen: Bording.

Olearius, Adam. 1656. *Vermehrte Newe Beschreibung der Muscowitischen vnd persischen Reyse*. Schleßwig: Fürstl. Druckerey.

O'Neill, Patrick. 1994. *Fictions of Discourse: Reading Narrative Theory*. Toronto: University of Toronto Press.

Page, Ruth. 2007. Gender. Pages 189-202 in *The Cambridge Companion to Narrative*. Edited by David Herman. Cambridge: Cambridge University Press.

Patte, Daniel, ed. 2004. *Global Bible Commentary*. Nashville: Abingdon.

Payne, Ernest A. 1942. The Development of Nonconformist Theological Education in the Nineteenth Century, with Special Reference to Regent's Park College. Pages 229-40 in *Studies in History and Religion, Presented to Dr. H. Wheeler Robinson, M.A., on His Seventieth Birthday*. Edited by Ernest A. Payne. London: Lutterworth.

Peretz, I. L. 1996. Speech at the 1908 Czernowitz Language Conference. Pages 323-25 in *Selected Works of I. L. Peretz*. Edited by Marvin Zuckerman and Marion Herbst. Malibu, Calif.: Joseph Simon/Pangloss Press, 1996.

Petersen, Carl S. 1943. *Det Kongelige Biblioteks Haandskriftsamling*. Copenhagen: Munksgaard. Online: http://www.kb.dk/permalink/2006/manus/693/dan/.

Petersen, Robert. 1975. Om grønlandsk—og om den nye grønlandske retskrivning. *Sprog i Norden: Årsskrift for de nordiske sprognævn* 57–66.

———. 1976. Nogle træk i udviklingen af det grønlandske sprog efter kontakten med den danske kultur og det danske sprog. *Grønland* 24:165–208.

———. 2009. Erik Holtved. Pages 333–50 in *Grønland—en refleksiv udfordring: Mission, kolonisation og udforskning*. Edited by Ole Høiris. Aarhus: Aarhus Universitetsforlag.

Petersen, Robert, and Jørgen Rischel, eds. 1985a. Sproglig indledning og kommentar til Resens tysk-grønlandske ordliste. *Grønland* 33:156–71.

———. 1985b. Resens tysk-grønlandske ordliste. *Grønland* 33:172–92.

Peterson, Eugene H. 2007. *My First Message: A Devotional Bible for Kids*. Illustrated by Rob Corley and Tom Bancroft. Vereeniging: Christian Art.

Petterson, Christina. In press. *The Missionary, the Catechist and the Hunter: Foucault, Protestantism and Colonialism*. Studies in Critical Research on Religion. Leiden: Brill.

Pfaff, C. G. F., and P. Lauridsen. 1890. *Bibliographia Groenlandica*. Meddelelser om Grønland 13. Copenhagen: Reitzel.

Phy, Allene Stuart. 1985. The Bible as Literature for American Children. Pages 165–91 in *The Bible and Popular Culture in America*. Edited by Allene Stuart Phy. Bible in American Culture 2. Philadelphia: Fortress.

Pike, Kenneth R. 1964. *Language in Relation to a Unified Theory of the Structure of Human Behavior*. The Hague: Mouton.

———. 1982. *Linguistic Concepts: An Introduction to Tagmemics*. Lincoln: University of Nebraska Press.

Plank, Frans. 1990. Greenlandic in Comparison: Marcus Wöldike's "Meletema" (1746). *Historiographia Linguistica* 17:309–38.

Porter, Stanley E. 1999. The Contemporary English Version and the Ideology of Translation. Pages 18–45 in *Translating the Bible: Problems and Prospects*. Edited by Stanley E. Porter and Richard S. Hess. Journal for the Study of the New Testament: Supplement Series 173. Sheffield: Sheffield Academic Press.

Powell, Mark Allan. 1992. *What Is Narrative Criticism?* Guides to Biblical Scholarship. Minneapolis: Fortress.

Pratt, Mary Louise. 1992. *Imperial Eyes: Travel Writing and Transculturation*. New York: Routledge.

Pym, Anthony. 2000. *Negotiating the Frontier: Translators and Intercultures in Hispanic History*. Manchester: St. Jerome.

———. 2007. Translation Technology as Rupture in the Philosophy of Dialogue. Pages 1–9 in *Translation Technologies and Culture*. Edited by Ian Kemble. Portsmouth: University of Portsmouth.

Quine, Willard Van Orman. 1960. *Word and Object*. Cambridge: MIT Press.

Rafael, Vicente L. 1993. *Contracting Colonialism: Translation and Christian Conversion in Tagalog Society under Early Spanish Rule*. 1988. Repr. Durham: Duke University Press.

Räisänen, Heikki, et al. 2000. *Reading the Bible in the Global Village: Helsinki*. Global Perspectives on Biblical Scholarship 1. Atlanta: Society of Biblical Literature.

Rajak, Tessa. 2009. *Translation and Survival: The Greek Bible of the Ancient Jewish Diaspora*. Oxford: Oxford University Press.
Ravitsh, Melekh. 1922. Di naye, di nakete dikhtung: zibn tesizen. *Albatross* 1:15–16.
———. 1967. A Most Important Book. Pages 15–17 in *Raisins and Almonds*. Edited and translated by Henry and Marie Einspruch. Baltimore: The Lewis and Harriet Lederer Foundation.
Rensburg, Ewald van. 2006. *God's Storybook: Adventures through the Bible*. Wellington: Lux Verbi.
Resseguie, James L. 2005. *Narrative Criticism of the New Testament: An Introduction*. Grand Rapids: Baker Academic.
Rhoads, David. 1982. Narrative Criticism and the Gospel of Mark. *Journal of the American Academy of Religion* 50, no. 3:411–34.
Ricci, Nino. 2002. *Testament: A Novel*. Boston: Houghton Mifflin.
Rice, Anne. 2005. *Christ the Lord: Out of Egypt*. New York: Knopf.
———. 2008. *Christ the Lord: The Road to Cana*. New York: Knopf.
Rimmon-Kenan, Shlomith. 2002. *Narrative Fiction: Contemporary Poetics*. 2nd ed. London: Routledge.
Roe, James Moulton. 1965. *A History of the British and Foreign Bible Society: 1905–1954*. London: British and Foreign Bible Society.
Rosenzweig, Franz. 1979. *Briefe und Tagebücher*. Edited by Rachel Rosenzweig, Edith Rosenzweig-Scheinmann, and Bernhard Casper. 2 vols. Franz Rosenzweig: Gesammelte Schriften. Berlin: Springer.
———. 1995. Afterword. Pages 169–84 in Barbara Ellen Galli, *Franz Rosenzweig and Jehuda Halevi: Translating, Translations, and Translators*. Montreal: McGill-Queen's University Press.
———. 2005. *The Star of Redemption*. Translated by Barbara Galli. Madison: University of Wisconsin Press.
Ross, Steve. 2005. *Marked*. New York: Seabury.
———. 2008. *Blinded: The Story of Paul the Apostle*. New York: Seabury.
Rousseau, Philip. 2007. Introduction: From Binding to Burning. Pages 1–9 in *The Early Christian Book*. Edited by William E. Klingshirn and Linda Safran. Washington, D.C.: The Catholic University of America Press.
Said, Edward. 1978. *Orientalism*. New York: Vintage.
———. 2005. The Public Role of Writers and Intellectuals. Pages 15–29 in *Nation, Language, and the Ethics of Translation*. Edited by Sandra Berman and Michael Wood. Princeton: Princeton University Press.
Sánchez, Edesio. Unpublished. *No Más Violencia Contra la Mujer*. Páginas 1–12.
Schaff, Philip. 1882. *The History of Creeds*. Vol. 1 of *Creeds of Christendom, with a History and Critical Notes*. New York: Harper.
Schleiermacher, Friedrich, 1982 [1813]. On the Different Methods of Translation. Translated by André Lefevere. Pages 1–30 in *German Romantic Criticism*. Edited by A. Leslie Willson. New York: Continuum.
Schultz-Lorentzen, Christian Wilhelm. 1930. Forklaring til de grønlandske Ord i Teksten. Pages 90–94 in John Davis: *Tre Rejser til Grønland i Aarene 1585–87*. Det Grønlandske Selskabs Skrifter 7. Copenhagen: Gad.

Scott, David. 2004. *Conscripts of Modernity*. Durham, N.C.: Duke University Press.
Scrivener, Frederick H. A. 1883. *A Plain Introduction to the Criticism of the New Testament*. 3rd ed. Cambridge: Deighton, Bell.
Seaver, Kirsten A. 2010. *The Last Vikings: The Epic Story of the Great Norse Voyagers*. London: Tauris.
Segovia, Fernando F. 1995. Introduction: "And They Began to Speak in Other Tongues": Competing Modes of Discourse in Contemporary Biblical Criticism. Pages 1–32 in *Social Location and Biblical Interpretation in the United* States. Vol. 1 of *Reading from This Place*. Edited by Fernando F. Segovia and Mary Ann Tolbert. Minneapolis: Fortress.
———. 2000a. *Decolonizing Biblical Studies: A View from the Margins*. Maryknoll, N.Y.: Orbis.
———. 2000b. *Interpreting beyond Borders*. Sheffield: Sheffield Academic Press, 2000.
Seidman, Naomi. 2006. *Faithful Renderings: Jewish-Christian Difference and the Politics of Translation*. Chicago: University of Chicago Press.
Shandler, Jeffrey. 2006. *Adventures in Yiddishland: Postvernacular Language and Culture*. Berkeley and Los Angeles: University of California Press.
Shavit, Zohar. 1986. *Poetics of Children's Literature*. Athens: University of Georgia Press.
———. 2006. Translation of Children's Literature. Pages 25–40 in *The Translation of Children's Literature: A Reader*. Edited by Gillian Lathey. Topics in Translation 31. Clevedon: Multilingual Matters.
Simon, Sherry. 1996. *Gender in Translation: Cultural Identity and the Politics of Transmission*. London: Routledge.
Simpson, D. 1993. *Romanticism, Nationalism and the Revolt against Theory*. Chicago: University of Chicago Press.
Smith, G. Vance. 1881a. A Reviser on the New Revision. *The Nineteenth Century* 9:917–36.
———. 1881b. *Texts and Margins of the Revised New Testament Affecting Theological Doctrine Briefly Reviewed*. London: British and Foreign Unitarian Association.
Sonne, Birgitte. 1986. Toornaarsuk: An Historical Proteus. *Arctic Anthropology* 23:199–219.
Sørensen, Axel Kjær. 2006. *Denmark–Greenland in the Twentieth Century*. Meddelelser om Grønland. Man and Society 34. Copenhagen: Commission for Scientific Research in Greenland.
Soukop, Paul A., and Robert Hodgson, eds. 1999. *Fidelity and Translation: Communicating the Bible in New Media*. New York: American Bible Society.
Spivak, Gayatri Chakravorty. 1987. *In Other Worlds: Essays in Cultural Politics*. New York: Routledge.
———. 1990. *The Post-colonial Critic: Interviews, Strategies, Dialogues*. London: Routledge.
———. 1993. The Burden of English. Pages 134–57 in *Orientalism and the Postcolonial Predicament: Perspectives on South Asia*. Edited by Carol A. Breckenridge and Peter van der Veer. Philadelphia: University of Pennsylvania Press.
———. 1995. *Imaginary Maps: Three Stories by Mahasweta Devi*. New York: Routledge.

———. 2003. *Death of a Discipline*. New York: Columbia University Press.
———. 2005. Translating into English. Pages 93–110 in *Nation, Language, and the Ethics of Translation*. Edited by Sandra Berman and Michael Wood. Princeton: Princeton University Press.
Stampe, Laurids. 1946. Collegium de cursu Evangelii promovendo. Omkring dets Stiftelse og første Aar. *Dansk teologisk tidsskrift* 9:65–88.
Stern, David H. 1998. *The Complete Jewish Bible*. Clarksville, Md.: Jewish New Testament Publications.
Stine, Philip. 2004. *Let the Words Be Written: The Lasting Influence of Eugene A. Nida*. Leiden: Brill.
Stolt, Birgit. 2006. How Emil Becomes Michel: On the Translation of Children's Books. Pages 67–83 in *The Translation of Children's Literature: A Reader*. Edited by Gillian Lathey. Topics in Translation 31. Clevedon: Multilingual Matters.
Sugirtharajah, R. S. 1999. *Asian Biblical Hermeneutics and Postcolonialism: Contesting the Interpretations*. Maryknoll, N.Y.: Orbis.
———. 2001. *The Bible and the Third World: Precolonial, Colonial and Postcolonial Encounters*. Cambridge: Cambridge University Press.
———. 2002. *Postcolonial Criticism and Biblical Interpretation*. New York: Oxford University Press.
———. 2005. *The Bible and Empire: Postcolonial Explorations*. Cambridge: Cambridge University.
Tastamantitâk. 1893. Copenhagen: Rosenberg. Rev. eds. 1912, 1936.
Tastamantitoкaк. 1895–1900. 4 vols. Copenhagen.
Tatar, Magdalena. 2002. The Mongolian Pentateuch. Pages 145–54 in *Biblical Translation in Context*. Edited by Frederick W. Knobloch. Bethesda: University Press of Maryland.
Taylor, Charles. 1994. "The Politics of Recognition." Pages 25–73 in *Multiculturalism: Examining the Politics of Recognition*. Edited by Amy Gutman. Princeton: Princeton University Press.
Taylor, Kenneth N. 1992. *Family-Time Bible in Pictures*. Carol Stream, Ill.: Tyndale House.
Testamente nutak Kaladlin okauzeenut nuktersimarsok, nar'kiutingoænniglo sukuïarsimarsok. 1794. Repr. Copenhagen: 1827.
Testamentitâk, terssa: Nâlegauta annaursirsivta Jesusib Kristusib. 1822. Repr. London, 1851.
Testamentitoqaq. 1989. Copenhagen: Danske Bibelselskab.
Thalbitzer, William. 1905. Skrælingerne i Markland og Grønland, deres Sprog og Nationalitet. *Oversigt over Det Kgl. Danske Videnskabernes Selskabs Forhandlinger*. 185–209.
———. 1913. Four Skræling Words from Markland (Newfoundland) in the Saga of Erik the Red (Eirikr Rauði). Pages 87–95 in *International Congress of Americanists: Proceedings of the XVIII. Session, London, 1912*. London: Harrison.
———. 1932. *Fra grønlandsforskningens første dage*. Copenhagen: Bianco Luno.
Theissen, Gerd. 1987. *The Shadow of the Galilean: The Quest of the Historical Jesus in Narrative Form*. Translated by John Bowden. Philadelphia: Fortress.

Thiong'o, Ngugi wa. 1986. *Decolonising the Mind: The Politics of Language in African Literature*. London: James Curry.
Thisted, Kirsten. 2005. Oversætterens efterskrift. Pages 193–224 in *Taseralik*. Nuuk: Atuakkiorfik A/S.
Thomas, Christine M. 2003. *The Acts of Peter, Gospel Literature, and the Ancient Novel: Rewriting the Past*. Oxford: Oxford University Press.
Thuesen, Søren. 1988. *Fremad, opad. Kampen for en moderne grønlandsk identitet*. Copenhagen: Rhodos.
Todorov, Tzvetan. 1982. *The Conquest of America: The Question of the Other*. New York: Harper & Row.
Toury, Gideon. 1995. *Descriptive Translation Studies and Beyond*. Amsterdam: John Benjamins.
Trondhjem, Naja Blytmann. 2007. "Markering af tid i grønlandsk sprog med særlig fokus på fortid." PhD thesis. University of Copenhagen.
Trench, Richard C. 1859. *On the Authorised Version of the New Testament: In Connexion with Some Recent Proposals for Its Revision*. 2nd ed. London: Parker.
Tshehla, Maarman Sam. 2003. Translation and the Vernacular Bible in the Debate between My "Traditional" and Academic Worldviews. Pages 171–87 in *Orality, Literacy, and Colonialism in Southern Africa*. Semeia Studies 41. Edited by Jonathan A. Draper. Atlanta: Society of Biblical Literature.
Tuksiautit erinaglit Testamentitokane agleksimarsut. 1842 [The Book of Psalms in Greenlandic].
Ukpong, Justin S., et al. 2002. *Reading the Bible in the Global Village: Cape Town*. Global Perspectives on Biblical Scholarship 3. Atlanta: Society of Biblical Literature.
Venuti, Lawrence, ed. 2000. *The Translation Studies Reader*. 2nd ed. Repr. New York: Routledge.
———. 2008. *The Translator's Invisibility: A History of Translation*. 2nd ed. London: Routledge.
Vessey, Mark. 1986. The Great Conference: Augustine and His Fellow Readers. Pages 52–73 in *Augustine and the Bible*. Edited and translated by Pamela Bright. Notre Dame, Ind.: University of Notre Dame Press.
———. 2007. Theory, or the Dream of the Book (Mallarmé to Blanchot). Pages 241–73 in *The Early Christian Book*. Edited by William E. Klingshirn and Linda Safran. Washington, D.C.: The Catholic University of America Press.
Voort, Hein van der. 1996. Eskimo Pidgin in West Greenland. Pages 157–258 in *Language Contact in the Arctic*. Trends in Linguistics. Studies and Monographs 88. Edited by Ernst Håkon Jahr and Ingvild Broch. Berlin: de Gruyter.
Waisman, S. 2005. *Borges y la Traducción*. Buenos Aires: Adriana Hidalgo.
Waldman, J. T. 2005. *Megillat Esther*. Philadelphia: Jewish Publication Society.
Ward, W. 1912. *The Life of John Henry Cardinal Newman*. 2 vols. London: Longmans, Green.
Weber, Samuel. 2005. A Touch of Translation: On Walter Benjamin's "Task of the Translator." Pages 65–78 in *Nation, Language, and the Ethics of Translation*. Edited by Sandra Berman and Michael Wood. Princeton: Princeton University Press.

West, Gerald O., ed. 2007. *Reading Other-Wise: Socially Engaged Biblical Scholars Reading with Their Local Communities.* Semeia Studies 62. Atlanta: Society of Biblical Literature.
Westcott, Brooke F. 1901. *Lessons from Work.* London: Macmillan.
Westcott, Arthur. 1903. *The Life and Letters of Brooke Foss Westcott.* 2 vols. London: Macmillan.
Whelan, T. 2004. Joseph Angus and the Use of Autograph Letters in the Library at Holford House, Regent's Park College, London. *The Baptist Quarterly* 40, no. 8:455–76.
White, Carolinne. 1990. *The Correspondence (394–419) between Jerome and Augustine of Hippo.* Lewiston, N.Y.: Mellen.
Wilhjelm, Henrik. 1997. *De store opdragere: Grønlands seminarier i det 19. århundrede.* Det grønlandske Selskabs Skrifter 33. Copenhagen: Det grønlandske Selskab.
———. 2001. *»af tilbøielighed er jeg grønlandsk«: Om Samuel Kleinschmidts liv og værk.* Det grønlandske Selskabs Skrifter 34. Copenhagen: Det grønlandske Selskab.
Wolf, Niels Gjessing. 1824. *Testamentitokamit Davidim ivngerutéj* [The book of Psalms in Greenlandic]. Copenhagen: Schubart.
———. 1825. *Testamentitokamit Profetib Esaiasim aglegèj* [The book of Isaiah in Greenlandic]. Copenhagen: Schubart.
———. 1828. *Testamentitokamit Salomonib Ajokærsutêj Er' káïrseksæt* [The book of Proverbs in Greenlandic]. Copenhagen: Fabritius de Tengnagel.
Wosh, Peter J. 1994. *Spreading the Word: The Bible Business in Nineteenth-Century America.* Ithaca: Cornell University Press.
Yehoash [Solomon Blumgarten]. 1926. *Khumesh.* New York: Yehoash Farlag.
Young, Robert. 1995. *Colonial Desire: Hybridity in Theory, Culture and Race.* London: Routledge.

Contributors

George Aichele, Professor, Department of Philosophy and Religion, Adrian College (retired), Adrian, Michigan, U.S.A.

Roland Boer, Research Professor, School of Humanities and Social Science, Faculty of Education and Arts, University of New Castle, Newcastle, NSW, Australia

Virginia Burrus, Professor of Early Church History and Chair of the Graduate Division of Religion, Drew Theological School, Madison, New Jersey, U.S.A.

Alan Cadwallader, Senior Lecturer in Biblical Studies, Faculty of Theology and Philosophy, Australian Catholic University, Watson, ACT, Australia

K. Jason Coker, Adjunct Lecturer in Philosophy and Religion, Albertus Magnus College, New Haven, Connecticut, U.S.A.

Jaqueline S. du Toit, Professor, Postgraduate School, University of the Free State, Bloemfontein, South Africa

John Eipper, Professor of Spanish, Department of Modern Languages and Cultures, Adrian College, Adrian, Michigan, U.S.A.

Scott S. Elliott, Assistant Professor, Department of Philosophy and Religion, Adrian College, Adrian, Michigan, U.S.A.

Raj Nadella, Assistant Professor of New Testament, Columbia Theological Seminary, Decatur, Georgia, U.S.A.

Flemming A. J. Nielsen, Associate Professor, Department of Theology, Ilisimatusarfik (University of Greenland), Nuuk, Greenland

Christina Petterson, Center for Transdiciplinary Gender Studies, Gender as a Category of Knowledge, Humboldt Universität, Berlin, Germany

Naomi Seidman, Koret Professor of Jewish Culture and Director of the Richard S. Dinner Center for Jewish Studies, Graduate Theological Union, Berkeley, California, U.S.A.

Esteban Voth, Translation Coordinator for the Americas, United Bible Societies, San Diego, California, U.S.A.

Matt Waggoner, Assistant Professor in Philosophy and Religion, Albertus Magnus College, New Haven, Connecticut, U.S.A.

www.ingramcontent.com/pod-product-compliance
Lightning Source LLC
Chambersburg PA
CBHW021808220426
43662CB00006B/227